T0316882

The Takeover of Public Companies as a
Mode of Exercising EU Treaty Freedoms

Lex et Res Publica
Polish Legal and Political Studies
Edited by Anna Jaroń

Volume 6

Zur Qualitätssicherung und Peer Review der vorliegenden Publikation

Die Qualität der in dieser Reihe erscheinenden Arbeiten wird vor der Publikation durch den Herausgeber der Reihe geprüft.

Notes on the quality assurance and peer review of this publication

Prior to publication, the quality of the work published in this series is reviewed by the editors of the series.

Maciej Mataczyński (ed.)

The Takeover of Public Companies as a Mode of Exercising EU Treaty Freedoms

Bibliographic Information published by the Deutsche Nationalbibliothek
The Deutsche Nationalbibliothek lists this publication
in the Deutsche Nationalbibliografie; detailed bibliographic
data is available in the internet at http://dnb.d-nb.de.
Library of Congress Cataloging-in-Publication Data
Names: Mataczyński, Maciej, editor.
Title: The takeover of public companies as a mode of exercising EU treaty
freedoms / Maciej Mataczyński (ed.).
Description: Frankfurt am Main : Peter Lang GmbH, 2017. | Series: Lex et res
publica ; vol. 6
Identifiers: LCCN 2017028856 | ISBN 9783631670996
Subjects: LCSH: Consolidation and merger of corporations--Law and
legislation--European Union countries.
Classification: LCC KJE6467 .T35 2017 | DDC 346.24/06626--dc23
LC record available at https://lccn.loc.gov/2017028856

This publication was financially supported by financial grant from the Polish National
Centre of Science, on the basis of decision number DEC-201 3/09/B/HS5/00068.

Cover Design:
© Olaf Gloeckler, Atelier Platen, Friedberg

ISSN 2191-3250
ISBN 978-3-631-67099-6 (Print)
E-ISBN 978-3-653-06399-8 (E-Book)
E-ISBN 978-3-631-71037-1 (EPUB)
E-ISBN 978-3-631-71038-8 (MOBI)
DOI 10.3726/978-3-653-06399-8

© Peter Lang GmbH
International Academic Publishers
Frankfurt am Main 2017
All rights reserved.
PL Academic Research is an Imprint of Peter Lang GmbH.

Peter Lang – Frankfurt am Main · Bern · Bruxelles · New York ·
Oxford · Warszawa · Wien

This publication has been peer reviewed

www.peterlang.com

Table of contents

Introduction

The book we are so proud to present is the product of three years' work by an international research team financed by the National Centre of Science. Our studies focused on the relationships between the freedoms enshrined in the Treaty on the Functioning of the European Union, especially the free movement of capital and the freedom of establishment, and the law governing takeovers of public companies. Obviously, the research area defined in this way encompasses a multitude of issues, and the subsequent publication can, by definition, offer only a selection of them.

Adam Szyszka's article on *Economic aspects of mergers and acquisitions* offers a great starting point and a useful introduction to the topic. It was intended as a synthetic discussion of key economic issues inherent to mergers and acquisitions. The task that A. Szyszka, a professor at the Warsaw School of Economics, sets out for himself in that work, was to introduce the readers to the matters discussed in the book and equip them with an indispensable economic perspective. The two subsequent articles are intended to present the free movement of capital from a practical perspective, based on case law of the Court of Justice of the European Union (Sylwia Majkowska-Szulc), and the topic of the horizontal effect of treaty freedoms (Maciej Taborowski), which is of key importance in view of the relationships between freedoms and takeover law. The fourth article, written by me, summarises the friction between the development of EU law described in the previous two chapters and the national company law in force in member states. This text is intended to serve as a bridge between the EU and corporate parts, and is based on a paper presented by myself at the Sixth Max Planck PostDoc Conference on European Private Law, held at the *Max Planck Institut für ausländisches und internationales Privatrecht in Hamburg*, Germany on the 18th and 19th of April 2016.

The subsequent three texts offer a dogmatic legal analysis of key institutions of national legal systems. Tomasz Sójka, professor at Adam Mickiewicz University, scrutinizes the duties of corporate boards when faced with takeover attempts, and preventive anti-takeover defences from the perspective of Polish law. Meanwhile, Florian Möslein – a professor at the University of Marburg investigates general rules governing tender offers in German law. The author dedicated the second part of his text to a very valuable and methodologically-inspiring analysis of the structure and taxonomy of German legislation. Prof. Möslein's reasoning is embedded in the broader contemporary perspective of the United Kingdom's departure from the European Union (the so-called Brexit), and the possible impact of this event on the process of harmonising legislation – especially in the context of European takeover law – for which the English law has served as a benchmark.

The reference to this historical event underscores the fact that law is a social fact and a result of actions by specific political factions and interest groups. This is the issue scrutinized in the last article, co-authored by Mariusz Golecki, professor of legal theory at the University of Łódź, and myself. Our article discusses the so-called national champions – strategic state-controlled companies. We have attempted to apply the conceptual toolbox of law and economics to the issue, which is reflected in the title: *Between corporate and political governance – Institutional analysis of the forms of protectionism in the strategic sectors in EU Law.*

There's an interesting anecdote about the last article. It was inspired by a paper presented by both of us at a conference entitled *The Nature and Governance of the Corporation*, which was held by the World Interdisciplinary Network for Institutional Research (WINIR), and hosted by the Università della Svizzera italiana in Lugano (Switzerland) from the 22nd to 24th April 2015. When we were getting ready to speak, I received a call. It was a then secretary in the Ministry of Treasury requesting assistance in work on the draft act aimed at implementing control of investments in national champions. The subsequent three months were packed with intensive work on the Act on the Control of Certain Investments adopted on the 24th July 2015 (consolidated text: Polish Journal of Laws 2016, item 980). The Act – as I am fully aware of – is imperfect, but it aptly illustrates the thesis that law is a social fact that reflects current preferences of the majority in society. The Act passed through the Sejm almost unanimously. Obviously, I did not plan the call and invitation to cooperation or the legislative initiative of the former parliament when, in May 2013, I applied to the National Science Centre for financing of our research project. However, I am very pleased that due to this combination of facts, the research we carried out could be disseminated and applied in practice. Within the works financed with the grant, in November 2015 we published a commentary on the act in question. Meanwhile, the book you are holding in your hands is the key academic outcome of our research.

It was written by scholars of nearly the same age: four of the authors were born in 1975, and the remaining three in 1974, 1971 and 1978 respectively. Obviously, age was not among the criteria for selecting partners for this project, nonetheless the resultant work represents, at least in part, the voice of the generation of young professors in their forties.

Maciej Mataczyński
Warsaw, February 2017

Prof. Adam Szyszka

Collegium of World Economy, Warsaw School of Economics

Economic aspects of mergers and acquisitions[1]

Abstract: This chapter briefly outlines the topic of mergers and acquisitions in the economic and financial context. It provides a background for further discussion on the detailed legal solutions presented in subsequent papers. First, a multidimensional typology of mergers and acquisitions is presented. This is followed by a discussion on potential reasons for M&A transactions, including rational motivation that is in the best interest of shareholders, rational aims serving managerial interests, and finally, irrational and erroneous actions made due to the psychological biases of the decision-makers. We look at the problem of value creation and destruction in the M&A process, and at the capital market's short-term reaction to M&A announcements as well as the long-term returns to the shareholders of bidding firms. On the one hand, numerous reasonable grounds support the view that M&As can create value. On the other hand, the management's motivation and psychological biases can also result in a loss of value for shareholders.

Key words: typology of M&A, motivation for M&A, psychological biases, capital market reaction to M&A announcements, value creation/destruction

1. Introduction

In mergers and acquisitions, two companies merge together or one business takes over another by way of acquiring its shares. Such deals are core practices of inorganic growth, as opposed to the organic growth of a company (buy vs. build). While organic growth involves laborious development of an undertaking's own structure, inorganic growth consists in the takeover of outside assets, and, as a rule, is much faster. Nonetheless, from the business perspective, an increased scale of business operations does not necessarily translate into more value for shareholders, which should be the ultimate objective of M&A deals and a criterion for assessing their reasonability.

For decades, mergers and acquisitions have been studied as part of both legal and economic sciences. But the changing economic, geopolitical, legal, and socio-cultural environments leave numerous lacunae requiring investigation, and

---

1 This text is to certain extend based on another work of A. Szyszka, see. the A. Szyszka, *Behavioral Finance and Capital Markets, How Psychology Influences Investors and Corporations*, 2013, Palgrave Macmillan.

the current status of academic knowledge and business practice are subject to constant fluctuation[2].

The purpose of this chapter is to briefly outline the topic of mergers and acquisitions in the economic and financial context, and to provide a background for further discussion on the detailed legal issues presented in subsequent papers. Given the spatial constraints and legal orientation of this publication as a whole, the text does not present an in-depth analysis of the economic aspects of mergers and acquisitions.

2. Typology of mergers and acquisitions

2.1 Based on the form of payment

One way to classify M&A transactions is to examine a form of payment for the target company. Transactions can be either settled in cash (cash deals) or by exchanging shares of the target for shares issued for this purpose by the bidder (share/stock deals). Cash deals are an easier and more frequent option, and when selected, the key matter to be negotiated is the share price. Sellers can quote the future synergy effect and negotiate a price above the current market pricing (control premium). To ensure that the deal is profitable to the acquirer (bidder), the value of the control premium must be below the value of expected synergy effects. Obviously, the bidder alone bears the entire risk inherent to the likelihood of a synergy effect actually materializing.

A share deal requires a reconciliation between the value of the target and bidding companies on the basis of the so-called share exchange ratio. In share deals, the target company's valuation is typically higher than in transactions settled in cash. However, the seller's risk is not only limited to successful execution of the M&A process, but it involves all the risks related to the target's business operation.

Some transactions are settled through mixed means, wherein the shareholders of the target company are partially paid for their shares in cash, and partially in shares issued by the bidder. Although shares are the default security in such deals, bidders can issue bonds or convertible bonds to finance a merger or acquisition. In particular, the use of convertible bonds is an interesting option, as it allows the

---

2   For an in-depth, comprehensive review of current economic and financial issues concerning mergers and acquisitions, see *i.a.* T. H. Ismail, A. A. Abdou, R. Magdy, *Exploring Improvements of Post-Merger Corporate Performance: The Case of Egypt*, 'The IUP Journal of Business Strategy' Vol. VIII, No. 1/2011, pp. 7–24; D. DePamphilis, *Mergers, Acquisitions and Other Restructuring Activities*, Cambridge 2015; P. A. Gaughan, *Mergers, Acquisitions and Corporate Restructurings*, Hoboken 2015.

risk of failure to achieve the synergy effect to be split between the shareholders of both companies. On the one hand, shareholders of the target company relinquish control of their business and have no influence on the effectiveness of the integration process once the takeover is complete, but receive payment in the form of a bidder's obligation to repurchase the bonds for a specified amount. Meanwhile, the option to convert bonds into shares gives them an opportunity to participate in the potential value growth generated by the M&A process. As such, the use of convertible bonds to finance the acquisition can be a persuasive argument in encouraging sellers to sell at a slightly lower price than they would do in an all-shares deal.

2.2 Based on the source of financing

Mergers and acquisitions can be financed with a company's own capital (retained profit or capital on the issuance of own shares), or with debt. Transactions in which external capital prevails are referred to as leveraged buyouts (LBOs). In this type of deals, the assets of the target company are often used as collateral, securing debt incurred by the bidding company and repaid with cash flow generated by the subsequently merged businesses. One special type of leveraged buyout is a management buy-out (MBO). This transaction takes place when the management board of the target company decides to acquire the undertaking from its owners, usually by establishing a special purpose vehicle (SPV) to act as the bidder. Leveraged buyouts are typically characterised by high risk inherent to high levels of debt financing, but when successful, offer high returns on investment.

2.3 Based on the attitude of the target company's management

When analysed from the perspective of the attitude of the target company's management, takeovers can be classified as either friendly or hostile. Friendly mergers and acquisitions offer a much simpler and less expensive way of acquiring the target company. The management on both sides is willing to work together at the deal-making stage and communicate with the key stakeholders, whose positive attitude to the transaction is often pivotal. Apart from the target's shareholders, other stakeholders include trade unions, major suppliers and key accounts, financing institutions, state agencies and market regulators. Access to insider information in the target company is yet another crucial factor. A due diligence audit of the company, if conducted, reduces the information asymmetry and brings down the bidder's risk. Sometimes, the management of the bidding company is included in the process of jointly developing the operating plans for the merger or acquisition. In this case, the management board of the target typically retains its role after the merger or acquisition is complete. Although this situation can benefit the bidder, it also generates a potential conflict of interest between the management and the incumbent shareholders of the target company.

Hostile takeovers typically take place against the will of the target company's management and are carried out through the purchase of free-floating shares. Usually, the bidder makes a direct public tender offer. The management, or some of the shareholders of the target company, may then resort to defensive measures. (e.g. for example, by amending the company's articles of association, issuing shares with pre-emptive rights, purchasing own shares, selling key assets, and incurring long-term liabilities). All of these actions are designed to impede the takeover, boost the value of the deal or decrease the company's attractiveness to the bidder, and usually make a hostile takeover more complex and expensive. The control premium paid in hostile takeovers is higher than in friendly mergers or acquisitions. What is more, hostile takeovers carry additional risk from limited insight into the company's insider information, forcing the bidder to rely on public information and its own internal analyses when assessing the target company's potential and possible synergies.

Bidders may pursue hostile takeovers to seize the assets of the target company and use them more effectively. In consequence, active control on the public market and the risk of a hostile takeover are motivating factors for the incumbent management. As a rule, hostile takeovers affect companies with dispersed shareholding, where the potential agency costs are the highest.

Apart from the management, some of the shareholders might also show resistance to the deal, especially if they have managed to gain a privileged position (for instance, by serving on the supervisory board, or through transactions with affiliates). Often though, such shareholders' own interests in the target company, even if significant, may still not be sufficient to block the takeover.

2.4 Based on geographical criteria

Mergers and acquisitions can take place locally or across borders. Locally, the process might depend on the regulator's consent, especially when the deal would restrict competition on the relevant market. In the case of trans-border mergers, geopolitical and cultural factors also come into play, and both can have a significant impact on the success of the entire process.

2.5 Based on business activity

Analysed from the perspective of the relationship between the parties, M&A transactions can be classified as horizontal, vertical or conglomerate. In horizontal transactions, target and bidding companies compete with the same or substitute products or services, operating on substantially the same markets.

A horizontal deal boosts the scale of their operations, market concentration and market strength. In consequence, such deals are subject to particular scrutiny by regulators, for their possible impact on competition and the potential for quasi-monopolistic practices.

By contrast, in vertical transactions one company is the client of the other, both of them operating on two different levels of the supply chain. A vertical deal creates a concentration of value added in the production process. Many vertical transactions have a strategic dimension to them, for instance when the bidder wants to gain access to raw materials or components needed for production (takeover of a company on a lower level of the value chain), or relevant distribution channels for manufactured goods (takeover of a company from a higher level of the value chain).

Conglomerate transactions involve companies operating on largely unrelated markets. In conglomerate deals, the bidder seeks to expand into new business areas, already being explored by the target company. Such deals are used to build corporations that diversify their business risk by engaging in a variety of business sectors. Conglomerates can also allocate financial surpluses generated by some of their businesses to others in need of investment. A conglomerate can consist of companies at different stages of their life cycle; in this context, mergers and acquisitions allow for the transition of mature, declining businesses to new ones with more growth opportunity.

3. Reasons for mergers and acquisitions

Generally speaking, the aim of a merger or acquisition is the direct (merger) or indirect (acquisition) assumption of control of the target company's assets, as part of a specified operating or financial strategy. But in fact, such decisions are driven by a variety of reasons. Ideally, mergers and acquisitions should be based on reasonable premises and intended to generate increased value for shareholders. However, managerial motives may also come into play, and these tend to favour issues important to executives, often at the shareholders' expense. Finally, regardless of the overtly declared rationale and actual motivation, the decision-making processes involved in M&A deals reveal certain specific behavioural inclinations rooted in the decision-makers' psychology.

3.1 Technical-operating motives

3.1.1 Economies of scale and scope

The scale effect brings down unit costs by increasing production volume and spreading the overheads over a higher number of goods. The greater the proportion of overheads in total costs, the greater the potential benefits of the scale effect. Sometimes, such benefits are capped by a certain critical production threshold, which, once reached, triggers cost increases along the increased scale of operations. Usually, adverse outcomes of the scale effect are the result of simple production capacity reserves being exhausted, and the subsequent need for major capital investments. Other challenges include the administrative problems of running a larger business.

Benefits of scope are attained when the deal brings down marginal costs, for instance due to supply chain specificity or the use of common distribution channels. Meanwhile, in the service sector, benefits of scope might involve a broader offer, targeted at the same customer base.

3.1.2 Synergy effects

In the literature, synergy effects are broadly construed as being all sources of value that increase the total market capitalization of the companies after the deal[3]. The iconic formula illustrating synergy in M&As is that $2 + 2 = 5$. From this point of view, synergy effects are inclusive of all sources of value growth, such as the scale and scope effects described above.

However, synergy effects should not be confused with simple, technical operating benefits uniquely inherent to the increased scale of operations. A synergy effect, as such, results from the mutual adjustment of business processes and the improved use of resources in both the bidding and target companies. The examples include the reduction of total operating costs in both companies by eliminating doubled business processes, the increased effectiveness that comes with the exchange of experience and know-how, and the implementation of new management systems and improved organisation, especially when the resources owned by both companies complement each other[4].

---

3   See: M. Bradley, A. Desai, E. Kim, *Synergy Gains from Corporate Acquisitions and Their Division between the Stockholders of Target and Acquiring Firms*, 'Journal of Financial Economics', Vol. 21, No. 1/1988, pp. 3–40; F. Trautwein, *Merger Motives and Merger Prescriptions*, 'Strategic Management', Vol. 11, No. 4/1990, pp. 283–295; R. Brealey, S.C. Myers, F. Allen, *Principles of Corporate Finance*, New York 2011, pp. 792–821; P.A. Gaughan, *Mergers...*, pp. 136–148.

4   J. Farrel, C. Shapiro, *Horizontal Mergers: An Equilibrium Analysis*, 'The American Economic Review', Vol. 80, No. 1/1999, pp. 107–126.

3.1.3 Access to intellectual property and strategic resources

One special instance of benefits brought about by synergy is access to intellectual property (e.g. patents), or other rare assets (e.g. deposits of natural resources) held by the target company and instrumental to the business of the bidder. Decisions on takeovers based on the willingness to acquire know-how, patent rights or other special assets are usually strategic by nature. By executing an M&A transaction, the bidder can gain certain competitive advantages, or reduce its dependence on suppliers.

3.2 Market and marketing reasons

3.2.1 Market strength boost

Market strength can be defined as the capacity of an undertaking or a group of undertakings to raise a price above the level set on a perfect competitive market. The market strength of a single company is measured by its freedom to set a product's price. For example, a business producing and selling homogenous products on a highly competitive market would have no market strengths. In this theoretical situation, faced with fully homogeneous products, consumers would make their decisions based solely on price. To attract new customers, the undertaking would have to cut the price until it finally fell below its production cost. Conversely, a business monopoly represents the greatest market strength possible. In consequence, the impact on the possible market strength depends on a number of factors typical of the specific competitive context, including sector-specific concentration, product diversification and access barriers. Legislation and the attitude of institutions in charge of competition protection also play a role. Oftentimes, market regulators prevent companies from taking full advantage of their increased market strength, giving consent to a merger or acquisition deal dependent on ensuring an adequate level of market competition (e.g. through sale of a portion of assets following the transaction).

Many authors mention the willingness to reinforce one's market strength as being among the key drivers motivating horizontal deals. This view is supported by Scherer and Ross[5], Carlton and Perloff[6], as well as Hay and Morris[7]. They

---

5   F.M. Scherer, D. Ross, *Industrial Market Structure and Economic Performance*, Boston 1990.

6   W.D. Carlton, M.J. Perloff, *Modern Industrial Organization*, Glenview 1990, p. 878.

7   A.D. Hay, J.D. Morris, *Industrial Economics and Organization: Theory and Evidence*, Oxford 1991.

believe that horizontal consolidation increases market concentration, builds market strength, and consequently boosts the profitability of the consolidated undertaking. The market strength of merged companies can grow for a number of reasons – common distribution channels, sales boost from cross-selling, better brand recognition or use of a common client base.

3.2.2 Diversification of activity and access to new markets

The bidder's desire to diversify their operations and go beyond their current activity is one of the reasons behind horizontal transactions. A company can plan to launch operations in another sector to decrease its dependence on its current industry, especially if it is characterized by highly seasonal sales or cyclic demand. Diversification can also serve as the starting point of a strategic manoeuvre with the ultimate goal of leaving a declining sector with poor outlooks.

Typically, acquiring an undertaking means gaining access to new markets faster and more cheaply than laboriously building one's own position from scratch with organic investments. For obvious reasons, time and relevant competences are prerequisites for achieving a strong position in a new sector. In contrast, the acquisition of an active business operating in the desired sector comes with the immediate assumption of unique competences, recognisability (brand), market position and other elements that would otherwise require a lot of time and resources to build. In consequence, the bidder can relatively quickly begin to reap the benefits of the dynamic development of a new sector, compensating for the declining dynamics in their old, ailing industry.

3.3 Financial reasons

3.3.1 Improved financing structure

The willingness to improve the company's financing structure underpins a vast group of important reasons for mergers and acquisitions. These include better adjustment of current cash flows (for example, cash excess in one company and poor liquidity in the other), better accessibility of long-term financing, and the reduction in the average cost of equity.

Undertakings operating in mature sectors might have large cash reserves, but little opportunity to invest them profitably in their own market. Meanwhile, fast-developing companies from emerging sectors often fall victim to the financial gap, wherein the asset increase ratio is not matched by the undertaking's financial capacities. In this case, a merger or acquisition deal can be a good way to increase the efficiency of cash flow management in both companies.

What is more, mergers and acquisitions can be used to boost a business's ability to obtain credit, or reduce the weighted average cost of equity in the enterprise. One of its undertakings may not have depleted its capacity to incur debt, and in consequence can share its creditworthiness with another company. Additionally, the increased size of the undertaking following a merger can yield a larger asset pool that could be used as collateral, for better diversification of income and more effective cash flow management, reducing, in aggregate, lenders' risk. As a result, the share of debt in total equity can be increased, while the weighted average cost of equity can be reduced.

3.3.2 Tax effects

Mergers can also bring certain tax benefits, such as the option to charge a tax loss generated by one company against the taxable profit of the newly merged undertaking. This can apply both to current results (if, before the merger, one of the companies generated profit while the other generated loss), as well as results from previous years, as in most jurisdictions companies can settle tax losses over a period of 3–5 years.

3.3.3 Valuation of target and bidding companies

A bidding company might conclude that the target's current market price is potentially lower than its actual value. This in itself is a signal to go ahead with a deal for purely financial reasons, regardless of other benefits. To take this premise into account, one needs to assume the inefficiency of the capital market's valuation. In other words, one should accept the possibility that the market valuation might be incorrect.

One of the measures of incorrect valuation, or a market opportunity, is the so-called Tobin's Q ratio[8]. This corresponds to the relationship between the asset market price and the replacement value of the undertaking. If this value is less than one, the acquisition of the undertaking is potentially cheaper than making an investment in similar, new assets. Obviously, the replacement value must make economic sense to the acquirer – a low Tobin's Q ratio does not provide sufficient rationale for the acquisition of a company if its assets are of little use for the bidder, and would not be replaced by new investments in the typical course of business.

---

8   W. Brainard, J. Tobin, *Pitfalls in Financial Model Building*, 'American Economic Review' Vol. 58, No. 2/1968, pp. 99–122.

Apart from objective undervaluation, the undertaking might have a different subjective value for the acquirer, due to specific benefits that could be achieved only once a merger or acquisition goes through.

Furthermore, objective undervaluation of the target company is not the only possible financial driver supporting the transaction – it is sufficient for this value to be relatively lower in comparison to the bidder's valuation. This can occur when both undertakings are operating in the same sector, while the market ratios of their comparative valuation (EV/Sales, EV/EBITDA, P/E, MV/BV, etc.) show, for some reason, a much higher market valuation for the bidding company, ascribing higher value to each unit of sales or profit generated by that undertaking or its book value. Shleifer and Vishny demonstrate that it sometimes makes sense for the bidder to acquire a company that is objectively overvalued, as long as the bidder is even more overpriced. In such cases, an equity-based transaction would be preferred to a cash payment[9].

Based on his sample of takeovers completed in the 1950s, Gort found that on average, acquirers have higher price-to-earnings (P/E) ratios than their targets[10]. Andrade, Mitchell, and Stafford, analysing a sample covering the period from 1973 to 1998, found that two-thirds of bidders had higher Tobin's Q ratios than their targets[11]. In more recent studies, Rhodes-Kropf, Robinson, and Viswanathan[12]; Dong, Hirshleifer, Richardson, and Teoh[13]; and Ang and Cheng[14] all find that market-level mispricing proxies correlate positively with merger activity, and that acquirers tend to be more overpriced than targets. All three papers also indicate that equity offers are associated with a higher bidder and target valuations than cash offers. Additionally, Dong et al. show that the disparity between a bidder and target valuation is greater in equity deals than cash offers. They also find that offers for undervalued targets are more likely to be hostile, and have

9   A. Shleifer, R. Vishny, *Stock Market Driven Acquisition*, 'Journal of Financial Economics', Vol. 70, No. 3/2003, pp. 295–311.

10   M. Gort, *An Economic Disturbance Theory of Mergers*, 'The Quarterly Journal of Economics', Vol. 83, No. 4/1969, pp. 624–642.

11   G. Andrade, M. Mitchell, E. Stafford, *New Evidence and Perspectives on Mergers*, 'Journal of Economics Perspectives', Vol. 15, No. 2/2001, pp. 103–120.

12   M. Rhodes-Kropf, D.T. Robinson, S. Viswanathan, *Valuation Waves and Merger Activity: The Empirical Evidence*, 'Journal of Financial Economics', Vol. 77, No. 3/2005, pp. 561–603.

13   M. Dong, D. Hirshleifer, S. Richardson, S.H. Teoh, *Does Investor Misvaluation Drive the Takeover Market?*, 'Journal of Finance', Vol. 61, No. 2/2006, pp. 725–762.

14   J. Ang, Y. Cheng, *Direct Evidence on the Market-Driven Acquisition Theory*, 'The Journal of Financial Research', Vol. 29, 2006, pp. 199–216.

a lower probability of success[15]. More overpriced acquirers are prepared to pay higher takeover premiums, particularly if they bid equity. Similarly, the more undervalued the targets, the higher the premiums that are offered.

3.4 Managerial reasons

3.4.1 Pride and narcissism

Pursuant to the agency theory, the objectives of corporate management do not need to coincide with shareholders' interests[16]. A spectacular merger or acquisition deal might satisfy the management's personal goals or needs, especially the psychological need to boost one's own ego. Personal prestige, remuneration and power enjoyed by top management often go hand in hand with the size of a company they run.

Hayward and Hambrick documented that, after controlling for various known determinants of the acquisition premium, the value of premiums paid is highly correlated with four proxies of CEO hubris: the recent performance of the acquiring firm; recent media praise of the CEO; the compensation of the CEO relative to that of the next highest paid executive in the firm, and a composite factor of these three variables. They also showed that the relationship between managerial overconfidence and takeover premiums is stronger when corporate governance seems to be weaker, that is, when there is a high proportion of insider directors on the board and the CEO also serves as the chairman. They also found that in a sample of 106 large transactions between 1989 and 1992, on average acquirers destroyed shareholders' wealth, and that the greater the CEO hubris and acquisition premiums, the greater the shareholder losses[17].

Liu provides an extensive literature review of narcissism among leaders and corporate managers[18]. It turns out that negotiations in the process of mergers and acquisitions are an excellent environment for narcissism. Liu and Aktas, de Bodt, Bollaert, and Roll measure CEOs' narcissism by investigating linguistic

---

15 M. Dong, D. Hirshleifer, S. Richardson, S.H. Teoh, *Does Investor...*, pp. 725–762.

16 M. Jensen, R. Ruback, *The Market For Corporate Control: The Scientific Evidence*, 'Journal of Financial Economics', Vol. 11, Np. 1/1983, pp. 17–31.

17 M. Hayward, D. Hambrick, *Explaining the Premiums Paid for Large Acquisitions: Evidence of CEO Hubris*, 'Administrative Science Quarterly', Vol. 42, No. 1/1997, pp. 103–129.

18 Y. Liu, *CEO Narcissism in M&A Decision-Making and Its Impact on Firm Performance*, Doctorate Thesis, The University of Edinburgh, Edinburgh 2009.

aspects of their speeches[19]. Narcissistic CEOs are more likely to have initiated their transactions, and are more likely to be acquirers. Unfortunately, their high ego is maintained at the expense of shareholders. The narcissism of an acquiring firm's CEO has a significantly negative impact on the firm's announcement returns, as well as on long-term post-acquisition buy-and-hold returns. On the other hand, targets run by narcissists secure higher bid premiums, possibly because narcissistic managers demand extra compensation for the loss of ego associated with their loss of control. Securing higher returns to their shareholders might give them the recognition needed to feed their superior self-perception.

3.4.2 Changes to shareholder structure and more freedom to act

Mergers and acquisitions can be used as tools to solve conflicts between shareholders of the target, and, less often, the bidder company. In the former case, the takeover in itself may offer a solution to the conflict, as at least some of the conflicted shareholders will be bought out. In the latter case, when conflicting interests divide a bidder's shareholders, a merger changing the shareholder structure could provide a solution. However, it should be born in mind that whenever such transactions are executed in a situation of conflict, litigation may also be involved, effectively blocking the merger for long periods of time.

In many cases, mergers increase the top management's freedom to act. This comes as a consequence of the extended pool of resources they have at their disposal, coupled with a lower dependence on key shareholders. The dispersion of ownership and weaker shareholder control foster managerial independence, often leading to higher agency costs.

3.4.3 Overconfidence and excessive optimism

Even assuming that management should make M&A decisions with the shareholders' best interests in mind, this does not always have to be the case. In fact, management's perception of reality can be distorted by overconfidence combined with excessive optimism.

Roll suggests that successful acquirers are overconfident and optimistic in their valuation of deal synergies, and tend to fall victim to the winner's curse. An exuberant CEO bids too aggressively and is likely to overpay for the target, satisfying their pride and ego while destroying the wealth of the shareholders. Roll argues

---

19 Y. Liu, *CEO Narcissism…*, Edinburgh 2009; N. Aktas, E. De Bodt, H. Bollaert, R. Roll, *CEO Narcissism and the Takeover Process: From Private Initiation to Deal Completion*, 'AFA 2012 Chicago Meetings Paper', Chicago 2012.

that, on average, a takeover is associated with little or no change in combined value for the target and bidder firms[20].

Rovenpor's work is an early attempt to link managerial overconfidence with mergers. The author uses a kind of a linguistic proxy to measure overconfidence, relying on independent readers to rate the confidence levels of executives based on their most recent speeches. She finds that managers' confidence is positively correlated with the number of acquisitions they attempt, the number of transactions they complete, and the dollar value of these transactions[21].

Malmendier and Tate use two different proxies for overconfidence: one based on the executives' predisposition to voluntarily hold in-the-money stock options in their firm, and the second relying on managers' *press portrayals*. After controlling for various determinants of mergers, including size, cash flow, and Tobin's Q of the acquiring firm, they argue that the odds of making an acquisition are 65% higher if the CEO is classified as overconfident[22]. The effect is the greatest when a merger does not require external financing, which corresponds to the earlier findings associating overconfidence with investment sensitivity to internal cash flow. The market seems to recognize the problem of managerial overconfidence and the danger of falling prey to the winner's curse. On average, a negative reaction by the market to a merger announcement is significantly stronger when the CEO exhibits the signs of overconfidence, than when they don't.

Ben-David et al. investigated the calibration ability of CFOs and found that those who are overconfident about long-term return distributions tend to engage in more acquisitions[23]. And again, the market seems to notice the problem of managerial overconfidence. On average, its reaction to transaction announcements from groups of bidders with overconfident CEOs is more negative than for the median firms.

Using a similar methodology to stock options by Malmendier and Tate[24], and relying on merger data from the United Kingdom, Croci, Petmezas, and

---

20 R. Roll, *The Hubris Hypothesis of Corporate Takeovers*, 'The Journal of Business', Vol. 59, No. 2/1986, pp. 97–216.

21 J. Rovenpor, *The Relationship between Four Personal Characteristics of Chief Executive Officers and Company Merger and Acquisition Activity*, 'Journal of Business and Psychology', Vol. 8, No. 1/1993, pp. 27–55.

22 U. Malmendier, G. Tate, *Who Makes Acquisitions? CEO Overconfidence and the Market's Reaction*, 'Journal of Financial Economics', Vol. 89, 2008, pp. 20–43.

23 I. Ben-David, J. Graham, C. Harvey, *Managerial Overconfidence and Corporate Policies*, 'NBER Working Paper' No. 13711, 2007.

24 U. Malmendier, G. Tate, *Who Makes...*, pp. 20–43.

Vagenas-Nanos confirm that highly overconfident CEOs lead their firms into more value-destroying acquisitions than their less confident counterparts[25].

John, Liu, and Taffler explore the parallel role played by overconfident target firm CEOs in explaining the takeover premium and value destruction in such deals[26]. Using the same two proxy variables to measure CEO overconfidence as in Malmendier and Tate[27], they confirm that overconfident CEOs of acquiring firms pay more than non-overconfident ones. On the other hand, overconfident CEOs of target firms do not, on average, appear to be able to achieve a significantly higher bid premium. However, much more interestingly, the joint effect of acquirer and target firm CEO overconfidence is a major increase in the bid premium. John et al. also show that overconfidence on the part not only of the acquiring firm's CEO, but also of the target firm's CEO, has a significant impact on merger announcement returns[28]. The three-day market reaction is most negative when both the acquiring firm's and the target firm's CEOs are overconfident. This evidence might suggest that when an overconfident bidder meets an overconfident target, both sides are likely to overestimate the potential gains from the merger. Additionally, overconfident target management tends to bargain hard to secure the biggest possible portion of these 'virtual' synergy gains for their shareholders, because overconfidence and excessive optimism make the CEO subjectively perceive the market price of the stock to be too low. In other words, the overconfident target manager expects to be paid a higher premium that not only reflects their willingness to participate in potential, overestimated synergy gains, but also offers some compensation for the perceived undervaluation of the firm. The overconfident acquirer also overestimates the amount of synergy gains or capability of extracting value from the target firm, which the current management was not able to realize. Hence, they are ready to pay a lot to the target shareholders in order for the deal to succeed. And as the actual gains from the merger turn out to be much smaller or even non-existent, the transaction becomes harmful to the wealth of the bidder's shareholders.

---

25 E. Croci, D. Petmezas, E. Vagenas-Nanos, *Managerial Overconfidence in High and Low Valuation Markets and Gains to Acquisitions*, 'International Review of Financial Analysis', Vol. 19, 2010, pp. 368–378.

26 K. John, Y. Liu, R. Taffler, *It Takes Two to Tango: Overpayment and Value Destruction in M&A Deals*, 'BAFA 2011 Conference Presentation Paper', University of Sheffield, Sheffield 2011.

27 U. Malmendier, G. Tate, *Who Makes...*, pp. 20–43.

28 K. John, Y. Liu, R. Taffler, *It Takes Two...*, Sheffield 2011.

4. Distribution of value in M&A transactions

4.1 Premium for target company shareholders

In order to persuade a target company's shareholders to sell their controlling interest, the bidder typically offers a price above the market value, to create a premium for the sellers. The value of the premium depends on the bidder's potential benefits, current market situation, relative valuation of the bidder and target companies, transaction settlement method, the management's attitude, and other factors. In some transactions there is virtually no premium involved, while in others as much as several hundred percent can be achieved. Usually, the premium falls within a range of 20–50%. Small companies are taken over at a higher premium than companies with high market capitalisation and share deals typically involve higher premiums than transactions settled in cash. High premiums are also typical of hostile takeovers and are less likely to occur when the management and key shareholders of the target company cooperate together in the process.

Obviously, the higher the price offered to the target company's shareholders, the more likely they are to accept the bid. However, there is no direct linear peg to current market value, and decisions are strongly affected by historical peaks in the target's share price. The target's shareholders will anchor to historical peaks when they are considering responding to a public tender offer, or when voting for or against a merger. Baker, Pan, and Wurgler argue that deal participants in fact focus on recent price peaks[29]. They investigated over 7,000 transactions between 1984 and 2007 and saw that bid prices clearly tend to cluster around a 13-week high, 26-week high, 39-week high, 52-week high, and 104-week high. They noticed that 'peak' prices often serve not just as a subtle psychological anchor, but as one sufficiently heavy that there is no deviation from it at all. The probability of a deal being reached increases discontinuously when the offer even slightly exceeds the 52-week high. Conversely, bidding-firm shareholders react increasingly negatively as the offer price is pulled upward toward that historical peak. There is a negative relation between the bidder announcement return and the component of the offer price that is driven by the 52-week high. This suggests that the acquirer's shareholders interpret this portion of the offer price as unjustified overpayment.

The economic rationale for the entire transaction depends on the relation between the premium paid and the possible synergy effects or other benefits. If the

---

29 M. Baker, X. Pan, J. Wurgler, *The Effect of Reference Point Prices on Mergers and Acquisitions*, 'Journal of Financial Economics', Vol. 106, No. 1/2012, pp. 49–71.

bidder overpays, most of the benefits from the transaction will go to the target's shareholders.

In fact, empirical research in the United States and in Europe over the period of the last 30 years has shown that most of the value generated in M&A transactions goes to the shareholders of the target companies.

4.2 Returns to target company shareholders

4.2.1 Short-term market response

Although an M&A announcement typically gives a strong boost to the target company's share price, the market response with respect to the bidder does not always go one way. Older American research focusing on pre-1990 transactions reveals, on average, positive short-term returns on the bidder's shares following the announcement; however, the scale of the growth is incomparably lower than for the target companies[30]. Later research reveals either no response, or a negative response. For instance, Dong, Hirshleifer, Richardson and Teoh documented that the higher the premium paid for the acquired company, the higher the negative return on the bidding company's shares immediately following the announcement[31]. The conclusion is that the market seems to respond to the risk of the target company being overpriced.

4.2.2 Long-term returns

The long-term effect of acquisitions on bidding firms is sensitive to the method of payment and the sample period. It also runs into statistical problems of measuring abnormal returns in a long period. Early studies by Agrawal, Jaffe, and Mandelker[32], Loughran and Vijh[33], Rau and Vermaelen[34], and Agrawal and

---

30 See: H.P.L. Lang, R. Stulz, R. Walkling, *Managerial Performance, Tobin's Q, and the Gains from Successful Tender Offers*, 'Journal of Finance', Vol. 24, 1989, pp. 137–154; H. Servaes, *Tobin's Q and the Gains from Takeovers*, 'The Journal of Finance', Vol. 46, No. 1/1991, pp. 409–419.

31 M. Dong, D. Hirshleifer, S. Richardson, S.H. Teoh, *Does Investor...*, pp. 725–762.

32 A. Agrawal, J. Jaffe, G. Mandelker, *The Post-Merger Performance of Acquiring Firms: A Re-Examination of an Anomaly*, 'Journal of Finance', Vol. 47, No. 4/1992, pp. 1605–1621.

33 T. Loughran, A. Vijh, *Do Long-Term Shareholders Benefit from Corporate Acquisitions?*, 'Journal of Finance', Vol. 52, No. 5/1997, pp. 1765–1790.

34 P.R. Rau, T. Vermaelen, *Glamour, Value and the Post-Acquisition Performance of Acquiring Firms*, 'Journal of Financial Economics', Vol. 49, No. 2/1998, pp. 223–253.

Jaffe[35] looked at stock returns three or five years after an acquisition. They found negative abnormal returns following stock mergers, especially for low book-to-market glamour bidders, and positive abnormal stock returns following cash tender offers, based on sample periods prior to 1993. However, Mitchell and Stafford argue that this conclusion is sensitive to the treatment of cross-event return correlations[36]. To address the problem, Bouwman, Fuller, and Nain used the event-time buy-and-hold approach. They documented cash bidders outperforming in the 1980s, but underperforming in later periods, which suggests that cash bidders were also overpriced in the late 1990s[37]. Not surprisingly, there is convincing evidence of underperformance following stock mergers carried out in that period[38]. Friedman uses a large sample covering the period from 1962 to 2000 and documented poor post-merger performance of stock bidders, compared to outperformance following cash acquisitions[39].

5. Conclusion

Mergers and acquisitions are a complex research area in which many pivotal questions remain unanswered. There is a number of reasonable arguments that, on the one hand, support the view that mergers and acquisitions create economic value, but on the other hand the management's motivation and errors made in a transaction's cost-benefit analysis can bring about a loss of share value.

Empirical studies carried out in mature capital markets, mainly in the United States, show that most of the value generated in M&A transactions goes to the shareholders of the target company in the form of a relatively high takeover premium. On average, shareholders in bidding companies benefit less from such transactions.

A disappointing outcome for a bidder's shareholders can be attributed to excessive premiums paid for takeovers and the poor performance of the company

---

35 A. Agrawal, J. Jaffe, *The Post-Merger Performance Puzzle*, in: C. Cooper, A. Gregory (ed.), *Advances in Mergers and Acquisitions*, Vol. 1., New York 2000, pp. 7–41.

36 M. Mitchell, E. Stafford, *Managerial Decisions and Long-Term Stock Price Performance*, 'Journal of Business', Vol. 73, No. 3/2000, pp. 287–329.

37 C.H.S. Bouwman, K. Fuller, A.S. Nain, *Market Valuation and Acquisition Quality: Empirical Evidence*, 'Review of Financial Studies', Vol. 22, 2009, pp. 633–679.

38 See: C.H.S. Bouwman, K. Fuller, A.S. Nain, *Market Valuation...*, pp. 633–679; P. Savor, Q. Lu, *Do Stock Mergers Create Value for Acquirers?*, 'The Journal of Finance', Vol. 64, No. 3/2009, pp. 1061–1097.

39 J.N. Friedman, *Stock Market Driven Acquisitions: Theory and Evidence*, 'Working Paper. Harvard University', Cambridge 2006.

following the deal. This in turn often results from overestimation of the likely benefits and underestimation of the costs involved, as well as problems related to integration of the businesses. Managerial overconfidence and excessive optimism can contribute to overestimation of the benefits from mergers and acquisitions regardless of other factors, such as attainment of management's personal goals at shareholders' expense.

Yet despite concerns about poor value creation or even value destruction for the bidder, M&A transactions continue to be highly popular. Clearly, it is the management of the bidding company that is able to persuade shareholders to vote in favour of a deal, claiming that their specific case makes economic sense, and does not follow the market pattern.

Literature

Agrawal A., Jaffe J., Mandelker G., *The Post-Merger Performance of Acquiring Firms: A Re-Examination of an Anomaly*, 'Journal of Finance', Vol. 47, No. 4/1992;

Agrawal A., Jaffe J., *The Post-Merger Performance Puzzle*, in: Cooper C., Gregory A. (ed.), *Advances in Mergers and Acquisitions*, Vol. 1., New York 2000;

Aktas N., De Bodt E., Bollaert H., Roll R., *CEO Narcissism and the Takeover Process: From Private Initiation to Deal Completion*, 'AFA 2012 Chicago Meetings Paper', Chicago 2012;

Andrade G., Mitchell M., Stafford E., *New Evidence and Perspectives on Mergers*, 'Journal of Economics Perspectives', Vol. 15, No. 2/2001;

Ang J., Cheng Y., *Direct Evidence on the Market-Driven Acquisition Theory*, 'The Journal of Financial Research', Vol. 29, 2006;

Baker M., Pan X., Wurgler J., *The Effect of Reference Point Prices on Mergers and Acquisitions*, 'Journal of Financial Economics', Vol. 106, No. 1/2012;

Ben-David I., Graham J., Harvey C., *Managerial Overconfidence and Corporate Policies*, 'NBER Working Paper' No. 13711, 2007;

Bouwman C.H.S., Fuller K., Nain A.S., *Market Valuation and Acquisition Quality: Empirical Evidence*, 'Review of Financial Studies', Vol. 22, 2009;

Bradley M., Desai A., Kim E., *Synergy Gains from Corporate Acquisitions and Their Division between the Stockholders of Target and Acquiring Firms*, 'Journal of Financial Economics', Vol. 21, No. 1/1988;

Brainard W., Tobin J., *Pitfalls in Financial Model Building*, 'American Economic Review' Vol. 58, No. 2/1968;

Brealey R., Myers S.C., Allen F., *Principles of Corporate Finance*, New York 2011;

Carlton W.D., Perloff M.J., *Modern Industrial Organization*, Glenview 1990;

Croci E., Petmezas D., Vagenas–Nanos E., *Managerial Overconfidence in High and Low Valuation Markets and Gains to Acquisitions*, 'International Review of Financial Analysis', Vol. 19, 2010;

DePamphilis D., *Mergers, Acquisitions and Other Restructuring Activities*, Cambridge 2015;

Dong M., Hirshleifer D., Richardson S., Teoh S.H., *Does Investor Misvaluation Drive the Takeover Market?*, 'Journal of Finance', Vol. 61, No. 2/2006;

Farrel J., Shapiro C., *Horizontal Mergers: An Equilibrium Analysis*, 'The American Economic Review', Vol. 80, No. 1/1999;

Friedman J.N., *Stock Market Driven Acquisitions: Theory and Evidence*, 'Working Paper. Harvard University', Cambridge 2006;

Gaughan P.A., *Mergers, Acquisitions and Corporate Restructurings*, Hoboken 2015;

Gort M., *An Economic Disturbance Theory of Mergers*, 'The Quarterly Journal of Economics', Vol. 83, No. 4/1969;

Hay A.D., Morris J.D., *Industrial Economics and Organization: Theory and Evidence*, Oxford 1991;

Hayward M., Hambrick D., *Explaining the Premiums Paid for Large Acquisitions: Evidence of CEO Hubris*, 'Administrative Science Quarterly', Vol. 42, No. 1/1997;

Ismail T.H., Abdou A.A., Magdy R., *Exploring Improvements of Post-Merger Corporate Perfomance: The Case of Egypt*, 'The IUP Journal of Business Strategy' Vol. VIII, No. 1/2011;

Jensen M., Ruback R., *The Market For Corporate Control: The Scientific Evidence*, 'Journal of Financial Economics', Vol. 11, No. 1/1983;

John K., Liu Y., Taffler R., *It Takes Two to Tango: Overpayment and Value Destruction in M&A Deals*, 'BAFA 2011 Conference Presentation Paper', University of Sheffield, Sheffield 2011;

Lang H.P.L., Stulz R., Walkling R., *Managerial Performance, Tobin's Q, and the Gains from Successful Tender Offers*, 'Journal of Finance', Vol. 24, 1989;

Liu Y., *CEO Narcissism in M&A Decision-Making and Its Impact on Firm Performance*, Doctorate Thesis, The University of Edinburgh, Edinburgh 2009;

Loughran T., Vijh A., *Do Long-Term Shareholders Benefit from Corporate Acquisitions?*, 'Journal of Finance', Vol. 52, No. 5/1997;

Malmendier U., Tate G., *Who Makes Acquisitions? CEO Overconfidence and the Market's Reaction*, 'Journal of Financial Economics', Vol. 89, 2008;

Mitchell M., Stafford E., *Managerial Decisions and Long-Term Stock Price Performance*, 'Journal of Business', Vol. 73, No. 3/2000;

Rau P.R., Vermaelen T., *Glamour, Value and the Post-Acquisition Performance of Acquiring Firms*, 'Journal of Financial Economics', Vol. 49, No. 2/1998;

Rhodes-Kropf M., Robinson D.T., Viswanathan S., *Valuation Waves and Merger Activity: The Empirical Evidence*, 'Journal of Financial Economics', Vol. 77, No. 3/2005;

Roll R., *The Hubris Hypothesis of Corporate Takeovers*, 'The Journal of Business', Vol. 59, No. 2/1986;

Rovenpor J., *The Relationship between Four Personal Characteristics of Chief Executive Officers and Company Merger and Acquisition Activity*, 'Journal of Business and Psychology', Vol. 8, No. 1/1993;

Savor P., Lu Q., *Do Stock Mergers Create Value for Acquirers?*, 'The Journal of Finance', Vol. 64, No. 3/2009;

Scherer F.M., Ross D., *Industrial Market Structure and Economic Performance*, Boston 1990;

Servaes H., *Tobin's Q and the Gains from Takeovers*, 'The Journal of Finance', Vol. 46, No. 1/1991;

Shleifer A., Vishny R., *Stock Market Driven Acquisition*, 'Journal of Financial Economics', Vol. 70, No. 3/2003;

Trautwein F., *Merger Motives and Merger Prescriptions*, 'Strategic Management', Vol. 11, No. 4/1990.

Abbreviations

CEO – Chief Executive Officer;

EV/EBITDA – Enterprise Value/Earnings before Interest, Taxes, Depreciation and Amortization;

EV/Sales – Enterprise Value/Sales;

LBO – Leveraged Buyout;

M&A – Mergers and Acquisitions;

MBO – Management Buyout;

MV/BV – Market Value to Book Value;

P/E – Price to Earnings;

SPV – Special Purpose Vehicle.

Prof. Sylwia Majkowska-Szulc

University of Gdańsk, Faculty of Law and Administration

Restrictions and admissible exceptions to the free movement of capital in the European Union in Court of Justice case law

Abstract: This section focuses on analysis of the ECJ case law on restrictions and acceptable exceptions to the free movement of capital in the European Union, with special emphasis on the possible exceptions stipulated directly by the TFEU. An analysis of the current status of EU law on the free movement of capital in the context of the ECJ case law requires an in-depth examination of the scope of application of provisions governing the free movement of capital including its *ratione temporis, ratione loci, ratione personae* and *ratione materiae*. Firstly, the movement of capital has been liberalised gradually and its ratione *temporis* has made the principle applicable since the issue of the Directive 88/361. Secondly, any restrictions on the free movement of capital and payments between member states and between member states and third countries are prohibited. It means that the *ratione loci* of the free movement of capitals includes not only member states but also third countries, which makes the free movement of capitals the largest European economic freedom as far as the scope of territorial application is concerned. Finally, the established ECJ case law provides that, as a rule, restrictions on the movements of capital are inclusive of measures that may discourage non-residents from investing in a member state or discourage residents of that member state from investing in other states. Accordingly, *ratione personae* of the free movement of capitals includes non-residents investing in a member state or residents of that member state investing in other states provided that the notion of non-residents embraces EU residents as well as third countries residents and 'other states' covering both EU member states and third countries. Therefore, *ratione materiae* involves the prohibition of measures that may discourage from cross-border capital investment. However, by way of an exemption from the ban on restrictions on the movement of capital and payments, member states may apply relevant tax law provisions differentiating between taxpayers on the basis of their place of residence or the place of capital investment, member states have the right to all requisite measures to prevent infringements of national law and regulations, in particular in the field of taxation and the prudential supervision of financial institutions, or to lay down procedures for the declaration of capital movements for the purposes of administrative or statistical information, or to take measures which are justified on the grounds of public policy or public security. Overall, all exceptions mentioned above cannot include any means of arbitrary discrimination or a disguised restriction to the free movement of capital and payments.

Key words: restrictions on the free movement of capital, admissible exceptions to the free movement of capital, cross-border capital investment, declaration of capital movements, place of investment of capital

1. Introduction

As a rule, any restrictions on the free movement of capital and payments between member states and between member states and third countries are prohibited. This rule is directly effective, meaning that individuals may directly rely on it and no other provisions at the EU or member state level are needed to ensure its effectiveness. The obligation to abolish restrictions on the movement of capital between residents of member states was imposed on the member states by Art. 1 of Directive 88/361 on the implementation of Art. 67 of the Treaty[1]. The Directive came into force on 7 July 1988 and was to be transposed by 1 July 1990. This step resulted in the full liberalization of the movement of capital, while the Court of Justice found Art. 1 of the Directive to be directly effective[2]. Established Court of Justice case law provides that, as a rule, restrictions on the movements of capital are inclusive of measures that may discourage non-residents from investing in a member state or discourage residents of that member state from investing in other states[3]. Such measures are declared incompatible with the general principle of the free movement of capital expressed in Art. 63 TFEU.

However, by way of exception to the ban on restrictions on the movement of capital and payments, member states may apply relevant tax law provisions differentiating between taxpayers on the basis of their place of residence or the place of capital investment. Furthermore, member states have the right to all requisite measures to prevent infringements of national law and regulations, in

---

1 Directive 88/361 of the Council of 24 June 1998 on the implementation of Article 67 of the Treaty (Official Journal of European Economic Community L 178 of 8 June 1988, p. 5).

2 For the first time in the ECJ Judgment of 23 February 1995 in joined cases C-358/93 and C-416/93, *Criminal proceedings against Aldo Bordessa, Vicente Marí Mellado and Concepción Barbero Maestre*, paras. 32–35, ECLI:EU:C:1995:54. Furthermore: ECJ Judgment of 11 December 2003 in case C-364/01, *The heirs of H. Barbier v Inspecteur van de Belastingdienst Particulieren/Ondernemingen buitenland te Heerlen*, para 57, ECLI:EU:C:2003:665; ECJ Judgment of 8 December 2011 in case C-157/10, *Banco Bilbao Vizcaya Argentaria SA v Administración General del Estado*, para 24, ECLI:EU:C:2011:813.

3 ECJ Judgment of 25 January 2007 in case C-370/05, *Criminal procedure against Uwe Kay Festersen*, para 24, ECLI:EU:C:2007:5.

particular in the field of taxation and the prudential supervision of financial institutions, or to lay down procedures for the declaration of capital movements for the purposes of administrative or statistical information, or to take measures which are justified on the grounds of public policy or public security[4]. However, measures and procedures adopted by member states as such exceptions cannot include any means of arbitrary discrimination or a disguised restriction on the free movement of capital and payments[5]. This means that these exceptions, being a derogation of the fundamental principle of the free movement of capital, must be interpreted strictly[6], resulting in a narrow interpretation[7]. Nevertheless, this provision cannot be interpreted as implying that all tax legislation which draws a distinction between taxpayers on the basis of their place of residence or the State in which they invest their capital is automatically compatible with the TFEU[8]. The key difference lies in the fact that Art. 65(1)(a) TFEU allows for differences in treatment, while Art. 65(3) TFEU prohibits discrimination[9].

An analysis of the current status of EU law on the free movement of capital in the context of the ECJ case law cannot disregard the fact that movement of capital has been liberalised gradually. From the perspective of intertemporal rules for applying EU law governing the movement of capital, the date of decisive importance is the date of the occurrence of the facts being assessed. Even now, the ECJ examines cases the facts of which occurred before the full liberalisation of the movement of capital came into force. For example, in 2008 the ECJ examined a case in which it was assumed that the laws on the free movement of capital were not in conflict with national laws that attributed higher value to the assets of partnerships domiciled in other member states than the assets of the same partnerships in that state, because the national provisions challenged were compliant with the community law on the movement of capital in force when the facts of the case occurred, that is in the fiscal year 1988. In that case, *ratione*

---

4   Art. 65(1)(a) and 65(1)(b) TFEU.

5   Art. 65(3) TFEU.

6   ECJ Judgment of 10 February 2011 in joined cases C-436/08 and C-437/08, *Haribo Lakritzen Hans Riegel BetriebsgmbH and Österreichische Salinen AG v Finanzamt Linz*, para 56, ECLI:EU:C:2011:61.

7   ECJ Judgment of 10 April 2014 in case C-190/12, *Emerging Markets Series of DFA Investment Trust Company v Dyrektor Izby Skarbowej in Bydgoszcz*, para 55, ECLI:EU:C:2014:249.

8   ECJ Judgment *Haribo Lakritzen and Österreichische Salinen AG*, para 56; ECJ Judgment *Emerging Markets Series of DFA Investment Trust Company*, para 55.

9   ECJ Judgment *Haribo Lakritzen and Österreichische Salinen AG*, para 58.

temporis made the principle of the free movement of capital inapplicable[10]. Instead, the Court of Justice applied the provisions on the freedom of establishment and found that they do not allow for national fiscal legislation attributing higher value to non-quoted shares in a partnership domiciled in another member state than to shares in a partnership in that member state, on condition that the share awards the shareholder (a capital company in this case) the actual influence on the decisions made by the partnership in another member state and enables it to determine partnership's activity[11].

What is more, the foregoing example proves that the differentiation between the free movement of capital and the freedom of establishment is far from obvious. The only body competent to issue binding settlements in this respect is the Court of Justice. Pursuant to the established ECJ case law, the provisions of the TFEU concerning the freedom of establishment apply to national provisions which govern the situation when a national of another EU member state holds a stake in a company domiciled in a different member state big enough to influence the company's decisions and determine its activities. Pursuant to the Court of Justice, provisions exclusively concerning the relationships within a group of companies have a decisive influence on the freedom of establishment and as such should be examined from the perspective of Art. 49 TFEU. If the effects of such provisions were tantamount to the restriction of the free movement of services and the free movement of capital, such effects would be perceived as an unavoidable consequence of a potential restriction on the freedom of establishment and would not justify a separate examination of such provisions from the perspective of Art. 56 TFEU and 63 TFEU[12]. Despite the established case law, the inflow of cases concerning the differentiation between these two freedoms in the context of specific national provisions has not ceased. This is a consequence, among other things, of difficulties in defining the 'actual influence on the company's decisions' or the 'determination of its activity'.

In view of the foregoing, this section focuses on the analysis of the Court of Justice case law on restrictions and acceptable exceptions to the free movement of capital in the European Union, with special emphasis on the possible exceptions

---

10 Opinion of the Advocate General V. Trstenjak as presented on 10 January 2008 in case C-360/06, *Heinrich Bauer Verlag BeteiligungsGmbH v Finanzamt für Großunternehmen in Hamburg*, paras. 62–63, Judgments of 2008, I-07333.

11 ECJ Judgment of 2 October 2008 in case C-360/06, *Heinrich Bauer Verlag BeteiligungsGmbH v Finanzamt für Großunternehmen in Hamburg*, para 42, ECLI:EU:C:2008:531.

12 ECJ Judgment of 13 March 2007 in case C-524/04 *Test Claimants in the Thin Cap Group Litigation v Commissioners of Inland Revenue*, para 27, ECLI:EU:C:2007:161.

stipulated directly by the TFEU. However, this analysis is not inclusive of the restrictions of the freedom of establishment, based on the differentiation discussed above. What is more, this section does not cover the issue of possible financial penalties being imposed on natural persons, groups or entities other than states in order to prevent or combat terrorism[13] or the possibility of imposing penalties on third countries and natural persons or entities other than states on the basis of decisions taken within the framework of common foreign and security policies[14].

2. Restrictions on the free movement of capital justified by the different treatment of taxpayers due to a difference in place of residence or investment of capital

As an exception to the fundamental principle of the free movement of capital, the TFEU allows the member states to apply tax law provisions differentiating between taxpayers on the basis of their place of residence or the place of capital investment[15]. This provision must be interpreted narrowly, as an exception to the general principle of the free movement of capital. As a result, it does not mean that all tax legislation, which draws a distinction between taxpayers on the basis of their place of residence or the state in which they invest their capital, is automatically compatible with the TFEU. The exception in itself is restricted by Art. 65(3) TFEU pursuant to which national legislation referred to in Art. 65(1) TFEU cannot constitute a means of arbitrary discrimination or a disguised restriction on the free movement of capital and payments as defined in Art. 63. As emphasized by the ECJ, the different treatment allowed by Art. 65(1)(a) TFEU should be distinguished from the discrimination banned by Art. 65(3) TFEU. For example, national tax legislation may be declared compatible with the provisions of the TFEU on the free movement of capital, on condition that the difference in treatment which it prescribes, between portfolio dividends from resident companies and those from companies established in a non-member State party to the EEA Agreement, concerns situations which are not objectively comparable. Such legislation may also be justified by an overriding reason in the public interest[16].

In the context of a tax rule which aims to prevent the double taxation of distributed profits, the situation of a corporate shareholder receiving foreign-sourced dividends is comparable to that of a corporate shareholder receiving

---

13 Art. 75 TFEU.
14 Art. 215 TFEU.
15 Art. 65(1)(a) TFEU.
16 ECJ Judgment *Haribo Lakritzen and Österreichische Salinen AG*, paras. 56–58.

nationally-sourced dividends in so far as, in each case, the profits made are, in principle, liable to be subject to a series of tax charges. When it comes to the justification based on the public interest, it may be acceptable to make an exception concerning portfolio dividends from companies domiciled in a third country being a party to the EEA Agreement dependent on the existence of an agreement on mutual assistance with regard to administrative matters. This enables a member state to verify the effective level of taxation of the non-resident company distributing dividends. The national principle under discussion concerns the taxation of income received by non-Austrian residents in Austria with corporate income tax. In order to enforce such taxes, the Austrian authorities do not need any third state cooperation. However, making the exemption dependent on the existence of a comprehensive agreement on mutual assistance with regard to administrative matters and enforcement is incompatible with the TFEU, as the existence of an agreement on mutual assistance with regard to administrative matters is sufficient. The case being discussed concerned the taxation of income received by non-Austrian residents in Austria with corporate income tax. To enforce such taxes, the Austrian authorities do not need any third country cooperation. What is more, the Court rebutted the argument presented by the Austrian government that the assistance concerning enforcement is necessary when the taxpayer's seat is moved abroad, since such a transfer of the seat is too far-reaching a hypothesis to substantiate such dependence without any exceptions. For these reasons the Court of Justice found the Austrian provisions under examination incompatible with Art. 64 TFEU as far as they made the tax exemption dependent on the existence of a comprehensive agreement on mutual assistance with regard to administrative matters and enforcement between a member state and a third country, since in order to achieve the purpose of the examined provisions, the existence of an agreement on mutual assistance with regard to administrative matters is sufficient[17].

Meanwhile, the Court declared Dutch provisions to be an inadmissible exception to the prohibition of restrictions on the free movement of capital. The challenged provisions introduced the withholding of tax on dividends paid out by a resident company to taxpayers – residents and taxpaying-non-residents alike, with the reservation that for non-resident taxpayers who are natural persons and corporations, the withholding was a final tax if the final tax on the dividend payable in that state by non-resident taxpayers was higher than the tax applicable to resident taxpayers. When establishing the tax dues, the factors taken into account included the taxation of residents applicable to all shares held in resident

---

17 ECJ Judgment *Haribo Lakritzen and Österreichische Salinen AG*, paras. 71–75.

corporations throughout the calendar year, capital exempt from tax on the basis of national laws and costs directly connected with the collection of the dividends themselves. Such different fiscal treatment of residents and non-residents may be construed as an inadmissible restriction on the free movement of capital, as corporations which are residents in a specific member state may charge the tax on the dividend against corporate income tax, while non-resident shareholders do not have this option. In such a case, non-resident taxpayers may be discriminated against, and in consequence a restriction on the free movement of capital of that type cannot be considered justified. In the case in question, the potential existence of a restriction on the movement of capital could be neutralized by a bilateral agreement on the avoidance of double taxation between a member state where the corporate seat is located and a member state from which the dividend comes, but it would be feasible only on condition of waiving the difference in treatment with respect to the taxation of dividends between resident taxpayers and taxpayers resident in other member states[18].

A similar case appeared in the context of the Polish Corporate Income Tax Act[19]. The difference in treatment between a dividend paid to resident investment funds and non-resident investment funds involved the derogation of a tax exemption with respect to non-resident investment funds, which was considered an unjustified restriction on the free movement of capital[20]. Furthermore, the case is a typical example of the principle of the non-discriminatory treatment of entities from third countries. Pursuant to Polish law, the tax exemption did not apply to a dividend paid by companies domiciled in Poland to investment funds domiciled in a third state, while investment funds domiciled in Poland could enjoy the exemption. What is more, the Court of Justice reiterated that the diminution in tax revenue cannot be regarded as an overriding reason in the public interest which may be relied upon in order to justify a measure which is, in principle, contrary to a fundamental freedom[21].

The ECJ has declared tax legislation of a member state incompatible with the principle of the free movement of capital, in so far as it grants, with respect to the interim taxation covering capital gains income on the sales of shares obtained

---

18 ECJ Judgment of 17 September 2015 in joined cases C-10/14, C-14/14 and C-17/14, *J.B.G.T. Miljoen and X and Société Générale SA v Staatssecretaris van Financiën*, ECLI: EU:C:2015:608.

19 Act of 15 February 1992 on the Corporate Income Tax (consolidated text Journal of Laws of 2014, item 851, as amended).

20 ECJ Judgment *Emerging Markets Series of DFA Investment Trust Company.*

21 ECJ Judgment *Emerging Markets Series of DFA Investment Trust Company*, para 102.

by a resident private foundation, the right to deduct against tax donations made in the same tax year, charging tax on the beneficiaries of such donations in the member state where the foundation is taxed, while no such deduction is allowed by national tax legislation if the beneficiary lives in another member state and, on the basis of the agreement on the avoidance of double taxation, is exempted from tax charged, as a rule, on donations, in the member state where the foundation is taxed. The Court argued that the making of gifts by Austrian private foundations to resident beneficiaries is a situation objectively comparable to one where the same foundations make gifts to beneficiaries residing in another member state. In both cases, the gifts are made from the assets of the private foundation or from increases in those assets resulting from their investment[22]. To conclude, one should admit that it is not easy to identify a criterion according to which the situation of taxpayers from various member states would not be comparable.

The Court of Justice found it to be compliant with the principle of the free movement of capital when the rules of a member state, which, in the context of corporation tax and within the framework of provisions for the avoidance of double taxation, prohibit the deduction of amounts of tax due in other member states of the European Union on income subject to corporation tax and obtained in their territory where those amounts, though due, are not paid by virtue of an exemption, a credit or any other tax benefit, in so far as those rules are not discriminatory as compared with the treatment applied to interest obtained in that member state. The dispute pertained to the refusal to authorise the deduction, from the corporation tax due, for the 1991 tax year, on global income, of tax due in Belgium on interest obtained in that member state but not paid by virtue of an exemption[23].

3. Restrictions on the free movement of capital justified by requisite measures to prevent the infringement of national laws and regulations of member states

Member states have the right to all requisite measures to prevent infringements of national law and regulations, in particular in the field of taxation and the prudential supervision of financial institutions, or to lay down procedures for the declaration of capital movements for administrative or statistical purposes[24].

---

22 ECJ Judgment of 17 September 2015 in case C-589/13, *F.E. Familienprivatstiftung Eisenstadt*, operative part of the judgment and paras. 63 and 85, ECLI:EU:C:2015:612.

23 ECJ Judgment *Banco Bilbao Vizcaya Argentaria SA*.

24 Art. 65(1)(b) TFEU.

In the context of the member states' right to all requisite measures in the field of the prudential supervision of financial institutions, the Court of Justice examined a case concerning the Polish Pension Funds Act that, on the one hand, introduced a cap on investments made by open pension funds outside Poland at the level of 5% of the value of a given OPF, defining, on the other hand, the scope of foreign investments allowed as much narrower than the scope of investments possible in Poland. In this way, both qualitative and quantitative restrictions were imposed on OPF with respect to investments outside Poland, especially in other member states. In the Court's opinion, pension funds operating in accordance with the principle of capitalisation engage, notwithstanding their social objective and the compulsory affiliation to the second pillar for the retirement scheme to which they belong, in an economic activity. This is the case for open pension funds whose assets are invested and managed by separate companies, running their activity against payment of a fee, in the form of a joint-stock company. The prudential supervision of these funds and companies by the public authorities and the guarantee made by the state to cover any deficits in the funds is not such as to call into question the economic nature of the activities mentioned. Even if the public nature of those resources were to be accepted, as maintained by the Republic of Poland, notwithstanding the fact that they originate from pension contributions collected from the employers of the workers concerned, such a fact in itself would be insufficient, in any event, to exclude from the scope of Art. 56 TFEU any transactions concerning those resources, as is apparent from Annex I to Directive 88/361 which provides that the concept of 'capital movements' covers, inter alia, 'operations in respect of the assets or liabilities of member states or of other public administrations and agencies[25].

Furthermore, the Court found that while the national provisions at issue undoubtedly lay down the substantive content of the prudential rules applicable to the OPFs, they are not, by contrast, in any way whatsoever designed to prevent infringement of the laws and regulations in the field of the prudential supervision of financial institutions and do not fall within the scope of the exception introduced in Art. 65(1)(b) TFEU. With respect to the criterion of public interest the court found that the need to guarantee the stability and security of the assets administered by a pension fund constitutes an imperative reason of public interest, by which it is possible to justify restrictions on the free movement of capital. Such restrictions must, however, be appropriate to the objective pursued and must

---

25 ECJ Judgment of 21 December 2011 in case C-271/09, *European Commission v the Republic of Poland*, paras. 40–41, ECLI:EU:C:2011:855.

not go beyond what is necessary to attain that objective. The difficulties of open pension funds in evaluating the risks linked to foreign investments cannot justify quantitative restrictions to investments in securities issued in member states. The laws of the member states concerning the disclosure of information on financial products and the protection of investors and consumers have, to a large extent, been the subject of harmonisation at EU level. Likewise, such quantitative measures cannot be justified on the ground that it is easier for national monitoring authorities to implement them, even in the context of an emerging social security scheme or by claiming that some of these measures aim to protect the funds against the risk of additional or excessive costs, since such costs must, in any event, be taken into account by the investor when choosing his investments, irrespective of where they are made. In consequence, the Court found that by upholding the legislation which imposed qualitative and quantitative restrictions applicable to investments outside Poland on open pension funds, thereby restricting possible investments by the funds in other member states, Poland has infringed its obligations under the currently binding article of TFEU[26].

In the context of the member states' authority to establish procedures applicable to the declarations of the flow of capital for information, administration or statistical purposes, one should emphasize the role of secondary EU law, including Directive 91/308 on the prevention of the use of the financial system for the purpose of money laundering[27] and Regulation 1889/2005 on controls of cash entering or leaving the Community[28]. These regulations were intended to have preventative and deterrent effects as well, hence the obligation to submit a declaration when entering or leaving the European Union. The control has been limited to the flows of cash exceeding EUR 10,000, to ensure that state authorities focus on significant cash flows only. Member states and their authorities are to determine the penalties for the failure to submit the declaration[29]. The Court of Justice has

---

26 ECJ Judgment *Commission v Poland*, paras. 51–52, 56–58, 65–67, 69–71, 73 and the operative part of the judgment.

27 Council Directive 91/308/EEC of 10 June 1991 on the prevention of the use of the financial system for the purpose of money laundering (Official Journal of the European Economic Community L 166 of 28 June 1991).

28 Regulation (EC) No. 1889/2005 of the European Parliament and of the Council of 26 October 2005 on controls of cash entering or leaving the Community (Official Journal of the European Community L 309 of 25 November 2005).

29 Reasons 6 and 13 of the Regulation (EC) No. 1889/2005 of the European Parliament and of the Council of 26 October 2005 on controls of cash entering or leaving the Community.

had numerous opportunities to interpret these EU laws in connection with their implementation in member states.

As a rule, when secondary EU law harmonises a selected area of the TFEU, the Court of Justice starts with the assessment of the national law which is being challenged, in the context of the relevant secondary law. For instance, the above-mentioned regulation is intended to supplement Directive 91/308 by establishing harmonized rules for controlling cash brought to and from the EU[30]. In such cases, the Court of Justice starts from an assessment of national legislation in the context of the above-mentioned regulation, and an analysis in the context of Art. 65(3) TFEU will be carried out only if further doubts persist[31]. Pursuant to the regulation, penalties for failure to submit the declaration should be effective, proportional and should have a deterrent effect[32].

Pursuant to the established ECJ case law, whenever the law of the EU on penalties applicable in a specific area is not harmonized, the relevant member states select appropriate penalties. However, the states must exercise their competences in accordance with EU law and its general principles, including the principle of proportionality[33]. Administrative or punitive measures must not go beyond what is necessary for the objectives pursued and a penalty must not be so disproportionate to the gravity of the infringement that it becomes an obstacle to fundamental economic freedoms[34]. The severity of the sanctions should correspond to the severity of the punishable infringements, in particular by ensuring a genuinely repellent effect, and applying the principle of proportionality. Any breach of the obligation to declare must be penalised in a simple, effective and efficient way, and without the competent authorities necessarily having to take account of other circumstances, such as intention or recidivism. A progressive system that differentiates between the amount of the penalty depending on the amount of undeclared cash is

---

30 Art. 1(1) and reasons 1 and 3 of the Regulation (EC) No. 1889/2005 of the European Parliament and of the Council of 26 October 2005 on controls of cash entering or leaving the Community.

31 See e.g. ECJ Judgment of 16 July 2015 in case C-255/14, *Robert Michal Chmielewski v Nemzeti Adó- és Vámhivatal Dél-alföldi Regionális Vám- és Pénzügyőri Főigazgatósága*, paras. 15 and 34, ECLI:EU:C:2015:475.

32 Art. 9(1) of the Regulation (EC) No. 1889/2005 of the European Parliament and of the Council of 26 October 2005 on controls of cash entering or leaving the Community, pp. 9–12. Furthermore, the ECJ Judgment *Chmielewski*, para 20.

33 ECJ Judgment *Chmielewski*, paras. 21–23.

34 ECJ Judgment of 5 July 2007 in case C-430/05, *Ntionik Anonymi Etaireia Emporias H/Y, Logismikou kai Paroxis Ypiresion Michanografisis and Ioannis Michail Pikoulas v Epitropi Kefalaiagoras*, para 54, ECLI:EU:C:2007:410.

unproportionate= in its very nature. The capability to sequester, by administrative decision, cash which has not been declared can be an admissible measure insofar as it aims at allowing the competent authorities to carry out the necessary controls and checks relating to the provenance of that cash, its intended use and destination[35].

The ECJ found Hungarian provisions that imposed a fine equivalent to 60% of the amount of the undeclared cash, where that amount is more than EUR 50,000, for the breach of the obligation to declare, not to be proportionate, and as such incompliant with Regulation 1889/2005. Furthermore, the Court of Justice found it unnecessary to examine whether there exists a restriction within the meaning of Art. 65(3) TFEU, since it was obvious in view of the reasoning based on the interpretation of the regulation[36].

4. Restrictions on the free movement of capital justified by reasons of public policy or public security

The TFEU lists possible exemptions from the fundamental principle of the free movement of capital, including measures which are justified on grounds of public policy or public security[37]. Being exemptions from a general principle, these criteria must be interpreted narrowly in a way which prevents member states from defining their scope unilaterally without the control of the institutions of the European Union. It is admissible to rely on public policy and public security aspects only when there is an actual and sufficiently grave threat to basic social interests. Furthermore, such exceptions cannot have an actual sole economic purpose. Additionally, every person whose interest has been violated by the application of a restrictive measure based on such an exception must be guaranteed access to legal relief. Measures restricting the free movement of capital may be justified by public policy and public security only insofar as it is necessary from the perspective of the protection of the interests they are to secure and only in the scope in which such objectives cannot be achieved using less restrictive measures[38].

For instance, one of the basic elements of public security is the security of energy supply, as inherently connected to the efficient functioning of the internal market in electricity and the integration of the isolated electricity markets of

---

35 ECJ Judgment *Chmielewski*, paras. 30–31, 33.

36 ECJ Judgment *Chmielewski*, operative part and para 34.

37 Art. 65(1)(b) TFEU.

38 ECJ Judgment of 14 March 2000 in case C-54/99, *Association Eglise de scientologie de Paris and Scientology International Reserves Trust v The Prime Minister*, paras. 17–19, ECLI:EU:C:2000:124.

member states[39]. The Court of Justice has adjudicated on the issue of the privatization ban introduced in national law and governed by Art. 345 TFEU. The Court found that the reasons underlying the choice of the rules of property ownership adopted by the national legislation are constituted by factors which may be taken into consideration as circumstances capable of justifying restrictions on the free movement of capital. What is more, with respect to the prohibition of affiliation between enterprises operating in the field of production, supply and trade in electricity and gas, as well as the prohibition of activity which may adversely affect system operations, the Court found that the objectives of combating cross-subsidisation in a broad sense, including the exchange of strategic information, in order to achieve transparency within the electricity and gas markets, and to prevent distortions of competition which underpin the choice of the legislature in relation to the adopted rules governing the system of property ownership, may be taken into consideration as overriding reasons in the public interest to justify a restriction on the free movement of capital[40].

5. Differences in interpreting the concept of a restriction on the free movement of capital between member states and between member states and third party states

Free movement of capital and payments assumes not only the removal of barriers between member states, but also between member states and third countries. Insofar as it is easy to differentiate between a member state and a third country, one should add that overseas countries and territories[41] benefit from the liberalized free movement of capital in the capacity of third countries[42]. This issue had to be settled by the Court of Justice, since the potential granting of equal rights

---

39 Reason 25 to the directive of the European Parliament and the Council 2009/72/EC of 13 July 2009 concerning common rules for the internal market in electricity and repealing Directive 2003/54/EC (Text with EEA relevance) (Official Journal of the European Union L 211 of 14 August 2009).

40 ECJ Judgment of 22 October 2013 in joined cases C-105/12 to C-107/12, *Staat der Nederlanden v Essent NV, Essent Nederland BV, Eneco Holding NV and Delta NV*, para 68 and the operative part of the judgment, ECLI:EU:C:2013:677.

41 Overseas European countries and territories which maintain special relationships with Denmark, France, the Netherlands and the United Kingdom and listed in Annex II to TFEU; cf. Art. 198 TFEU.

42 ECJ Judgment of 5 May 2011 in case C-384/09, *Prunus SARL and Polonium SA v Directeur des services fiscaux*, items 31 and the operative part of the judgment, ECLI:EU:C:2011:276.

to overseas countries and territories determines whether general provisions of treaties are applicable to them or not. As a rule, overseas countries and territories are not governed by the general provisions of EU law without an explicit reference, and there is no such reference in the case of the free movement of capital[43], despite the fact that such a reference is present with respect to the freedom of establishment[44].

The Court of Justice has found that the concept of a restriction on the movement of capital should be interpreted in the same way in relationships between member states and third countries and in relationships between member states. However, at the same time the ECJ has admitted that the legal context is different depending on whether we are dealing with relations between member states and third countries. On the one hand, once the principle of the free movement of capital has been stretched under the TFEU to cover the movement of capital between third countries and member states, the member states have supported the introduction of this rule in the same article and in the same way with respect to the movement of capital within the European Union and in relationships with third countries. Therefore, a systemic interpretation speaks in favour of interpreting the concept of the free movement of capital in the same way regardless of whether the movement takes place between member states or between member states and third countries.

On the other hand, all the provisions of the TFEU on capital and payments suggest that, given the desire to take account of the circumstance that the objective and legal context differ depending on whether we are dealing with relationships between member states or member states and third countries, member states have found it necessary to include protective and derogation clauses applicable to the movement of capital to or from third countries. Sometimes member states argue that, if the concept of the restriction of capital movement was interpreted in the same way in relationships between member states and third countries as in relationships between member states, the result would be a unilateral opening of the EU market to third countries without the negotiations necessary to obtain the equivalent liberalization from such states. The Court of Justice does not consider this argument to be decisive due to the fact that the TFEU explicitly lists specific possibilities of restricting the free movement of capital in transactions with third countries[45]. As a consequence, with respect to third countries, the principle of

---

43 ECJ Judgment *Prunus and Polonium*, paras. 20, 29 and 31.
44 Art. 199(5) TFEU.
45 ECJ Judgment of 18 December 2007 in case C-101/05, *Skatteverket v A*, paras. 31, 32, 38 and 63, ECLI:EU:C:2007:804.

the free movement of capital has priority over the principle of reciprocity and the maintenance of member states' competitive advantage over third countries.

In this context it is interesting to determine whether a restriction on the movement of capital from or to third countries could be justified by a circumstance which would not classify as justifying a restriction on the movement of capital between member states. For instance, the laws of a member state may make granting a tax benefit dependent on meeting certain conditions. In such a case the fact of meeting conditions must be verifiable, which is possible only when information can be obtained from the competent authorities of another state. As a result, if the laws of a member state make a fiscal benefit dependent on meeting conditions that are verifiable only by way of obtaining information from competent authorities of a third country, as a rule it is legally justified for the member state to refuse such a benefit if, in particular due to a lack of obligation on the part of a third state arising out of a convention to provide information, it is impossible to obtain the requested information. Consequently, it is not impossible that a member state effectively proves that a restriction on the movement of capital from or to third countries is justified by a circumstance which would not classify as justifying a restriction on the movement of capital between member states[46].

The rules and procedures pursuant to which member states cooperate to exchange information that seem material for the purpose of applying and enforcing the national fiscal legislation of the member states with respect to each type of tax collected by or to the benefit of a member state by the local or administrative authorities of a member state, including taxes collected by or to local bodies, are governed by the directive 2011/16 on administrative cooperation in the field of taxation[47]. These harmonised cooperation rules are not applicable to cooperation between the competent authorities of a member state and a third state if no agreement on mutual assistance has been signed. In consequence, the Court of Justice case law on restrictions on the free movement of capital in the European Union cannot be applicable in its entirety to the movement of capital between member states and third countries, because these two types of movements occur in different legal contexts[48].

---

46 ECJ Judgment *Skatteverket*, paras. 36, 37, 60 and 63.
47 Art. 1 and 2 of the directive of the Council 2011/16/EU of 15 February 2011 on administrative cooperation in the field of taxation and repealing directive 77/799/EEC (Official Journal of the European Union L 64 of 11 March 2011).
48 ECJ Judgment *Haribo Lakritzen and Österreichische Salinen AG*, paras. 65–66.

6. Specific options to restrict the free movement of capital in the exchange between member states and third countries explicitly provided for in the TFEU

As already mentioned above, pursuant to the established ECJ case law, the concept of a restriction on the movement of capital should be interpreted in the same way for relationships between member states and third countries as for relationships between member states, but taking account of the potential differences which arise out of the purpose and legal context that differ depending on whether we are dealing with relations between member states and third countries. This thesis is supported by a number of arguments, including the fact that the TFEU explicitly provides for specific options to restrict the free movement of capital between member states and third countries. One of the restrictions available to member states is upholding restrictions which came into force before a prescribed deadline with respect to third countries and certain categories of the movement of capital[49]. Yet another option is the Council's right to take safeguarding measures with respect to third countries if, in exceptional circumstances, movements of capital to or from third countries cause, or threaten to cause, serious difficulties for the operation of the economic and monetary union. These measures may be introduced for a period not exceeding six months and only if they are strictly necessary[50].

The first of the foregoing situations involves upholding the restrictions which came into force before a prescribed deadline with respect to third countries and certain categories of the movement of capital. The general principle of the full liberalization of the free movement of capital does not infringe upon restrictions existing on 31 December 1993 with respect to third countries under either national or EU law with respect to the movement of capital to or from third countries when such restrictions apply to direct investments, including investments in real estate, or investments related to business activity, the provision of financial services or the admission of securities to capital markets. With respect to the restrictions existing in national law in Bulgaria, Estonia and Hungary, the relevant cut-off date is 31 December 1999[51]. This regulation establishes an exhaustive list of movements of capital which, by way of exception, do not have to be governed by the general principle of the free movement of capital. As with each exception to the general rule, this provision must be interpreted narrowly.

---

49 Art. 64(1) TFEU.
50 Art. 66 TFEU.
51 Art. 64(1) TFEU.

In order to classify a specific regulation of national law as meeting the criteria of the foregoing exception, it is necessary to establish whether the regulation was in force before the date specified in the TFEU and whether it concerns the movement of capital. To determine whether a specific national regulation concerns the movement of capital, it is possible to use the nomenclature annexed to Directive 88/36 for the implementation of Art. 67 of the Treaty[52] while bearing in mind that this catalogue is not exhaustive. If a specific national measure concerns the movement of capital, the second step is to determine whether such movements involve the provision of financial services. The criterion of decisive importance is the existence of a cause-effect relationship between the movement of capital and the provision of financial services, and not a criterion regarding entities to which the national law applies, or their relationship with a provider of rather than a client for such financial services. The foregoing is a consequence of the fact that the scope of application of Art. 64(1) TFEU has been defined by reference to the category of movement of capital that can be restricted. At the same time, this provision may also be applied to fiscal legislation, as proven by the established ECJ case law[53]. To conclude, a national measure may operate on the basis of the exception referred to in Art. 64(1) TFEU on condition that this measure is strictly related to the provision of financial services. In ECJ's view a relationship is sufficiently strict if there is a cause-effect relationship between the movement of capital and the provision of services.

National legislation that provides for lump sum taxation offering no option to tax an investor on the basis of actually earned income in a situation where an investment fund does not meet certain requirements stipulated by German law (the so-called black funds), may discourage investors other than residents and in consequence make investors less likely to use the services of such funds. In consequence, Art. 64 TFEU should be interpreted in such a way that the national laws referred to above, which introduce a lump sum taxation of income on the holders of units in a non-resident investment fund in a situation where the fund failed

---

52 Directive of the Council of 24 June 1998 on the implementation of Article 67 of the Treaty (Official Journal of the European Economic Community L 178 of 8 July 1988).

53 For example: ECJ Judgment of 12 December 2006 in case C-446/04, *Test Claimants in the FII Group Litigation v Commissioners of Inland Revenue*, paras. 174–196, ECLI:EU:C:2006:74; ECJ Judgment of 24 May 2007 in case C-157/05, *Winfried L. Holböck v Finanzamt Salzburg-Land*, paras. 37–45, ECLI:EU:C:2007:297; ECJ Judgment *Prunus and Polonium*, paras. 27–37.

to meet statutory requirements, constitute measures related to the movement of capital concerning the provision of financial services in the meaning of Art. 64[54].

The Court of Justice has found that the criteria for applying Art. 64(1) TFEU are met, and, in consequence, national laws are compliant with Art. 64 TFEU in a case where national legislation in force on 31 December 1993 exempted from a tax on the market value of immovable property located in the territory of a member state of the European Union the companies which have their registered office in the territory of that State and made entitlement to that exemption. This refers to companies whose registered office are in the territory of an OCT, conditional either on the existence of a convention on administrative assistance to combat tax evasion and avoidance concluded between that member state and that territory or on there being a requirement, under a treaty containing a clause prohibiting discrimination on grounds of nationality, that those legal persons are not to be taxed more heavily than companies established in the territory of that member state[55].

The second of the situations mentioned above pertains to the possibility of introducing safeguarding measures with respect to third countries, provided that such measures are strictly necessary. This option applies only to exceptional circumstances where the movement of capital to or from third countries causes or may cause significant difficulties in the functioning of the economic or currency union. Should that be the case, the Council, at the Commission's request and after having consulted the European Central Bank, may take safeguarding measures with respect to third countries for a period not exceeding six months. It is required that these measures be strictly necessary.

7. Procedure in the case of infringement of the free movement of capital by a member state

If a member state unreasonably restricts the free movement of capital, the general procedure concerning that member state's failure to fulfil an obligation applies[56]. Another important issue in this field involves the matters related to the special rights of public authorities in enterprises or in the private sector. These have been discussed in item 2. Furthermore, in certain cases the European Commission has instituted proceedings against specific member states, for example in connection with the restrictions of the free movement of capital in the field of fiscal matters.

---

54 ECJ Judgment of 21 May 2015 in case C-560/13, *Finanzamt Ulm v Ingeborg Wagner-Raith*, ECLI:EU:C:2015:347.
55 ECJ Judgment *Prunus and Polonium*, para 38 and the operative part of the judgment.
56 Art. 258–260 TFEU.

For instance, a member state fails to fulfil its obligations under TFEU when it taxes dividends paid out to companies domiciled in other member states less favourably than the dividends paid out to resident companies, exempting from tax up to 95% of the dividend paid out to resident companies and taxing dividends paid out to non-resident companies by withheld tax at the rate of 27%, of which only part is reimbursable on request. These differences in taxation have not been challenged by the existence of agreements on the avoidance of double taxation, since it is necessary to prove that the application of the agreement on the avoidance of double taxation has allowed the effects of the differing treatment arising from national provisions to be neutralized. The different treatment of dividends paid out to companies domiciled in other member states and dividends paid to resident companies disappears only when withholding tax collected on the basis of national legislation can be counted towards tax payable in another member state in an amount equal to the difference resulting from the different treatment of companies on the grounds of national legislation. Furthermore, the difference in treatment is not challenged by the argument that one needs to take account of the entire national fiscal system that aims at ensuring direct or indirect taxation of natural persons who are the beneficial recipients of dividends. The example presented, of different treatment, may, in the Court's opinion, discourage companies domiciled in other member states from investing in a specific member state and as such constitutes a restriction on the free movement of capital. In this case, the Commission sued the republic of Italy, which was found guilty by the Court of failure to fulfil its obligations under the treaty[57].

8. Conclusion

In conclusion, some evidence can be derived from the ECJ case law on restrictions and admissible exceptions to the free movement of capital in the European Union. Restrictions on the movements of capital include most of all the measures that may discourage non-residents from investing in a member state or discourage residents of that member state from investing in other states. Simultaneously, it must be noted that the obligation of member states to abolish restrictions on the movement of capital between residents of member states was imposed gradually and the full liberalization of the movement of capital occurred when the Directive 88/361 on the implementation of Art. 67 of the Treaty was to be transposed by 1 July 1990. On the one hand, exceptions to the ban on restrictions on

---

57 ECJ Judgment of 19 November 2009 in case C-540/07, *Commission of European Communities v the Republic of Italy*, ECLI:EU:C:2009:717.

the movement of capital and payments allow for differences in treatment when member states apply relevant tax law provisions differentiating between taxpayers on the basis of their place of residence or the place of capital investment. On the other hand, exceptions to the ban on restrictions on the movement of capital and payments prohibit discrimination, because measures and procedures adopted by member states cannot include any means of arbitrary discrimination or a disguised restriction on the free movement of capital and payments. As a consequence, all kinds of exceptions, constituting a derogation of the fundamental principle of the free movement of capital, must be interpreted strictly.

Moreover, some restrictions may result from the fact that the differentiation between the free movement of capital and the freedom of establishment is not obvious but crucial because the free movement of capital prohibits restrictions on the movement of capital between member states and between member states and third countries while the freedom of establishment prohibits restrictions exclusively between member states. Furthermore, member states have the right to all the requisite measures to prevent infringements of national law and regulations, in particular in the field of taxation and the prudential supervision of financial institutions, or to lay down procedures for the declaration of capital movements for administrative or statistical purposes. However, when secondary EU law harmonises a selected area of the TFEU, the Court of Justice starts with the assessment of the national law which is being challenged, in the context of the relevant secondary law. In addition, some specific restrictions on the free movement of capital may be justified. Firstly, the reasons of public policy or public security are admissible but only when there is an actual and sufficiently grave threat to basic interests. Secondly, the ECJ case law on restrictions on the free movement of capital in the EU cannot be applicable in its entirety to the movement of capital between member states and third countries, because these two types of movements occur in different legal contexts. By way of illustration, if the laws of a member state make a fiscal benefit dependent on meeting conditions that are verifiable only by way of obtaining information from competent authorities of a third country, as a rule it is legally justified for the member state to refuse such a benefit if, in particular due to a lack of obligation on the part of the third state arising out of a convention to provide information, it is impossible to obtain the requested information. Summing up, the established ECJ case law confirms differences in interpreting the concept of a restriction on the free movement of capital between member states and between member states and third party states.

Judgments

ECJ Judgment of 23 February 1995 in joined cases C-358/93 and C-416/93, *Criminal proceedings against Aldo Bordessa, Vicente Marí Mellado and Concepción Barbero Maestre*, ECLI:EU:C:1995:54;

ECJ Judgment of 14 March 2000 in case C-54/99, *Association Eglise de scientologie de Paris and Scientology International Reserves Trust v The Prime Minister*, ECLI:EU:C:2000:124;

ECJ Judgment of 11 December 2003 in case C-364/01, *The heirs of H. Barbier v Inspecteur van de Belastingdienst Particulieren/Ondernemingen buitenland te Heerlen*, ECLI:EU:C:2003:665;

ECJ Judgment of 12 December 2006 in case C-446/04, *Test Claimants in the FII Group Litigation v Commissioners of Inland Revenue*, ECLI:EU:C:2006:74;

ECJ Judgment of 25 January 2007 in case C-370/05, *Criminal procedure against Uwe Kay Festersen*, ECLI:EU:C:2007:5;

ECJ Judgment of 13 March 2007 in case C-524/04 *Test Claimants in the Thin Cap Group Litigation v Commissioners of Inland Revenue*, ECLI:EU:C:2007:161;

ECJ Judgment of 24 May 2007 in case C-157/05, *Winfried L. Holböck v Finanzamt Salzburg-Land*, ECLI:EU:C:2007:297;

ECJ Judgment of 5 July 2007 in case C-430/05, *Ntionik Anonymi Etaireia Emporias H/Y, Logismikou kai Paroxis Ypiresion Michanografisis and Ioannis Michail Pikoulas v Epitropi Kefalaiagoras*, ECLI:EU:C:2007:410;

ECJ Judgment of 18 December 2007 in case C-101/05, *Skatteverket v A*, ECLI:EU:C:2007:804;

ECJ Judgment of 2 October 2008 in case C-360/06, *Heinrich Bauer Verlag BeteiligungsGmbH v Finanzamt für Großunternehmen in Hamburg*, ECLI:EU:C:2008:531;

ECJ Judgment of 19 November 2009 in case C-540/07, *Commission of European Communities v the Republic of Italy*, ECLI:EU:C:2009:717;

ECJ Judgment of 10 February 2011 in joined cases C-436/08 and C-437/08, *Haribo Lakritzen Hans Riegel BetriebsgmbH and Österreichische Salinen AG v Finanzamt Linz*, ECLI:EU:C:2011:61;

ECJ Judgment of 5 May 2011 in case C-384/09, *Prunus SARL and Polonium SA v Directeur des services fiscaux*, ECLI:EU:C:2011:276;

ECJ Judgment of 8 December 2011 in case C-157/10, *Banco Bilbao Vizcaya Argentaria SA v Administración General del Estado*, ECLI:EU:C:2011:813;

ECJ Judgment of 21 December 2011 in case C-271/09, *European Commission v the Republic of Poland*, ECLI:EU:C:2011:855;

ECJ Judgment of 22 October 2013 in joined cases C-105/12 to C-107/12, *Staat der Nederlanden v Essent NV, Essent Nederland BV, Eneco Holding NV and Delta NV*, ECLI:EU:C:2013:677;

ECJ Judgment of 10 April 2014 in case C-190/12, *Emerging Markets Series of DFA Investment Trust Company v Dyrektor Izby Skarbowej in Bydgoszcz*, ECLI:EU:C:2014:249;

ECJ Judgment of 21 May 2015 in case C-560/13, *Finanzamt Ulm v Ingeborg Wagner-Raith*, ECLI:EU:C:2015:347;

ECJ Judgment of 16 July 2015 in case C-255/14, *Robert Michal Chmielewski v Nemzeti Adó- és Vámhivatal Dél-alföldi Regionális Vám- és Pénzügyőri Főigazgatósága*, ECLI:EU:C:2015:475;

ECJ Judgment of 17 September 2015 in joined cases C-10/14, C-14/14 and C-17/14, *J.B.G.T. Miljoen and X and Société Générale SA v Staatssecretaris van Financiën*, ECLI: EU:C:2015:608;

ECJ Judgment of 17 September 2015 in case C-589/13, *F.E. Familienprivatstiftung Eisenstadt*, ECLI:EU:C:2015:612.

Abbreviations

Court of Justice, ECJ – European Court of Justice, Court of Justice of the European Union;

EEA – European Economic Area;

EU – European Union;

OCT – Overseas Countries and Territories;

OPF – open pension funds;

TFEU – Treaty on the Functioning of the European Union (consolidated version Official Journal of the European Union C 326 of 26 October 2012, p. 47).

Dr Maciej Taborowski

Faculty of Law and Administration, Warsaw University

Horizontal direct effect of EU internal market freedoms – current status

Abstract: This article presents the current position of the ECJ with regard to horizontal direct effect of freedoms of the internal market. It states that the ECJ essentially rules out the possibility of such effect being exercised with regard to the freedom of movement of goods (Art. 34 and 35 TFEU) and that to date it has not taken a position regarding the possibility of such effect being exercised by the free movement of capital and of payments (Art. 63 TFEU). The ECJ admits horizontal direct effect with regard to the freedom of movement of services (Art. 56 TFEU) and of establishment (Art. 49 TFEU), though in cases in which private entities, which represented collective interests of individuals, appeared (both in relation to the prohibition of discrimination, and the prohibition of restrictions). With the exception of the controversial *Haug-Adrion* ruling (in the context of Art. 56 TFEU), the ECJ also has not to date ruled on horizontal direct effect of Art. 49 TFEU and 56 TFEU on the individual level (both in relation to the prohibition of discrimination, and the prohibition of restrictions). The argumentation disclosed by the ECJ justifying horizontal direct effect in the context of freedoms of movement of persons (general wording of the provisions, their mandatory character, the effectiveness of EU freedoms, their uniform application), as well as the fact that it was interchangeably used in the context of various freedoms and various scopes thereof also allows for application of this argumentation to these aspects which have not yet been covered by the ECJ case law.

Key words: horizontal direct effect, EU internal market freedoms, free movement of goods, free movement of workers, free movement of services, free movement of establishment, free movement of capital and payments

1. Preliminary remarks

The question of the extent to which individuals are bound by the provisions of primary EU law on the fundamental internal market freedoms has been present in the literature of the topic for many years[1]. Although the evolving case law

---

1   See i.a. J. Baquero Cruz, *Free Movement and Private Autonomy*, 'European Law Review' No. 1999, p. 603–620; S.C.G. van den Bogaert, *Horizontality: The Court Attacks?*, in: C. Barnard, J. Scott (eds.), *The Legal Foundations of the Single market: Unpacking the Premises*, Oxford 2002, p. 123–152; G. Davies, *Freedom of Contract and the Horizontal Effect of Free Movement Law*, in: D. Leczykiewicz, S. Weatherill (eds.), *The Involvement*

of the ECJ allows us to discover more clearly some further elements of this issue, many questions have not yet been answered. In recent years, an additional problem area referring to horizontal direct effect has arisen in the context of general EU law and protection of fundamental rights, including the EU Charter of Fundamental Rights[2]. The subject of the considerations included in this article will be a recapitulation of the current state of case law of the ECJ with regard to

---

of EU Law in Private Law Relationships, Oxford 2013, p. 53–69; R. Graber, *Die unmittelbare Drittwirkung der Grundfreiheiten. Eine Untersuchung anhand einer Auslegung des EG-Vertrages, der Rechtsprechung des Gerichtshofes und der Folgen einer angenommenen unmittelbaren Drittwirkung*, Munich 2002; A.S. Hartkamp, *"Horizontal Effects" (or "Effects in Relationships between Individuals") of EU Law*, in: A.S. Hartkamp, C.H. Sieburgh, L.A.D. Keus, J.S. Kortmann (eds.), *The Influence of EU law on Private Law*, Volume 81-I, Deventer 2014, p. 57–71; M. Jaensch, *Die unmittelbare Drittwirkung der Grundfreiheiten. Untersuchung der Verpflichtung Verpflichtung von Privatpersonen durch Art. 30, 48, 52, 59, 73b EGV*, Baden-Baden 1997; M.T. Karayigit, *The horizontal effect of the free movement provisions*, 'Maastricht Journal' No. 2001, p. 303–335; R.W.E. van Leuken, *Direct Horizontal Effect of the Fundamental Freedoms*, in: A.S. Hartkamp, C.H. Sieburgh, L.A.D. Keus, J.S. Kortmann (eds.), *The Influence of EU law on Private Law*, Volume 81-I, Deventer 2014, p. 73–93; R.W.E. van Leuken, *Rechtsverhoudingen tussen particulieren en de verdragsrechtelijke verkeersverijheden. Directe horizontale werking van de vrijverkeerbepalingen in het VWEU*, Deventer 2015; R.W.E. van Leuken, *The Internal Market Principle and Private Law*, in: A.S. Hartkamp, C.H. Sieburgh, L.A.D. Keus, J.S. Kortmann (eds.), *The Influence of EU Law on Private Law*, Volume 81-I, Deventer 2014, p. 315–322; S. Löwisch, *Die horizontale Direktwirkung der Europäischen Grundfreiheiten. Zur Frage der unmittelbaren Verpflichtung Privater durch die Grundfreiheiten des EG-Vertrages*, Baden-Baden 2009; P.Ch. Müller-Graff, *Die horizontale Direktwirkung der Grundfreiheiten*, 'Europarecht' No. 1/2014, p. 3; J. Snell, *Private Parties and the Free Movement of Goods and Services*, in: M. Andenas, W.H. Roth (eds.), *Services and Free Movement in EU Law*, Oxford 2003, p. 211–243; S.A. de Vries, R. van Mastrigt, *The Horizontal Direct Effect of the Four Freedoms: From a Hodgepodge of Cases to a Seamless Web of Judicial Protection in the EU Single Market?*, in: U. Bernitz, X. Groussot, F. Schulyok (eds.), *General Principles of EU Law and European Private Law*, Alphen aan den Rijn 2013, p. 249–280.

2 See i.a. J. Krzeminska-Vamvaka, *Horizontal effect of fundamental rights and freedoms—much ado about nothing? German, Polish and EU theories compared after Viking Line*, 'Jean Monnet Working Paper' No. 11/2009; D. Leczykiewicz, *Horizontal application of the Charter of Fundamental rights*, 'European Law Review' No. 2013, p. 479–497; C.H. Sieburgh, *General principles and the Charter in private law relationships. Constructive and critical input from private law*, in: U. Bernitz, X. Groussot, F. Schulyok (eds.), *General Principles of EU Law and European Private Law*, Alphen aan den Rijn 2013, p. 233–247;

horizontal direct effect of EU internal market freedoms, i.e. the free movement of goods (art. 34–35 TFEU), workers (art. 45 TFEU), services (56 TFEU), establishment (art. 56 TFEU) and capital (art. 63 TFEU). In order to determine the exact subject of the considerations, it is necessary to make certain preliminary remarks.

Firstly, over time various concepts have arisen from the principle of direct effect with regard to the provisions of EU law, which is of importance both for vertical relations (between individuals and the state) and horizontal relations (between individuals), being the subject of this article. The divergence of these concepts determines directly the subject of considerations in the context of horizontal direct effect of the provisions on the EU internal market.

From the point of view of the doctrine of EU law, direct effect may be understood as the possibility of invoking a provision of EU law before a national court (the so-called objective or broad direct effect). Direct effect may also be understood narrowly (subjectively) as concerning only a situation in which a provision of EU law grants a right to individuals (enforceable before a national court) or imposes certain obligations on individuals[3] (though this may not be possible for other reasons in a specific situation, in particular in the context of directives in horizontal relations). The broad concept contains, as it were, the narrow concept (direct effect in a subjective sense). In addition, it makes it possible to include in the issue of direct effect the norms which are not sufficiently precise to enable one to argue rights from them, but which are at the same time sufficiently concrete to cause before a national court an inspection of the legality of national legal acts from the point of view of EU law. It is said in that case that EU law acts as a shield since they allow one to 'defend oneself' against national law which does not conform to EU law. In other words, the broad definition covers situations in which not only does the effect of substitution occur, i.e. when a national court directly assumes an provision, granting an individual a right (imposing an obligation), as the legal basis for handing down a decision (it is said in that case that EU law acts as a sword), but also when there occurs an excluding effect without the substitution effect, i.e. when the national court eliminates from the legal state of the case provisions which breach EU law. As S. Prechal accurately summed up these issues: 'Direct effect is the obligation of a court or another authority to apply the relevant provision of Community law, either as a norm which governs the case or as a standard for legal review'[4]. Both these elements are covered by the concept of broad direct effect.

---

3   See P. Craig, G. de Búrca, *EU Law. Text, Cases, and Materials*, Oxford 2015, p. 186.
4   S. Prechal, *Directives in EC law*, 2nd edition, Oxford 2005, p. 241.

Secondly, one should note certain conceptual differences in the approach to the issue of horizontal direct effect from the point of view of the study of public law and private law. Attention to this is drawn by Ch. Timmermans[5], who states that the terminology used by the public law doctrine covers two forms of direct effect – legal review (shield) and substitution (sword). On the other hand, obligations related to a duty of interpretation of national law in conformity with EU law were covered by the concept of indirect effect of EU law[6]. In the terminology of private law, only the substitution effect (sword) is classified as direct effect, whereas the issue of legal review and the interpretation consistent with EU law are classified as indirect effect of EU law[7]. From the point of view of private law, only direct effect in the narrow sense can have an impact on the substance of a private law relation, i.e. may directly result in the creation, change or cessation of that relation. However, such effect is not created by the interpretation of national law in the light of EU provisions or indeed a verification of national law from the point of view of EU law – in these cases it is still national law, whilst remaining under the influence of EU law, which directly regulates the creation, change or cessation of a legal relation. The legal basis for taking a decision for the authority applying the law will also in that case be directly found in national law.

2. Starting point for further considerations

A starting point for further considerations in this article will be a narrowly understood concept of direct effect, i.e. the one which relates only to rights granted to individuals and, potentially, also obligations imposed on individuals. More specifically, with regard to the issue of horizontal direct effect, we will reflect on the extent to which the provisions establishing the fundamental EU freedoms may impose obligations on individuals (that is, to what extent individual entities are bound by the provisions of EU freedoms of the internal market), which directly impact their legal situation, i.e. create, change or put an end to legal relations with other individuals. Thus, the considerations will not concern the vertical direct effect, though in the light of case law of the ECJ there is no doubt that the provisions

---

5　See Ch. Timmermans, *Horizontal Effect/Indirect Effect or Direct/Indirect Horizontal Effect: What's in a Name?*, 'European Review of Private Law' No. 3–4/2016, p. 673.

6　*Ibidem*, p. 676–677.

7　*Ibidem*, p. 677.

concerning all internal market freedoms (Art. 34, 45, 56, 63 TFEU) have direct effect, in the narrow sense, on vertical relations[8].

It must be emphasized that if we were to adopt the broad concept of direct effect in horizontal relations as a starting point, then most likely we would have to accept that all the said freedoms have a horizontal direct effect in that sense. They all may serve as a shield for provisions of national law in disputes which have a horizontal character, even if they do not grant individuals rights which have their correlation in obligations imposed on another individual. By way of an example, I would cite the free movement of goods and Art. 34 TFEU (prohibition on establishing quantitative restrictions and restrictions having equivalent effect[9]). There exists in this regard a dominant position that Art. 34 TFEU grants rights to individuals only in a vertical relation, but not the horizontal one[10]. Nonetheless, also in a horizontal dispute, one of the parties may invoke Art. 34 TFEU in order to exclude application of a provision of national law – being contrary to it – in case pending before a national court. This occurred, *inter alia*, in a horizontal dispute in which on the basis of a court judgment the possibility of using the logo of a company was blocked on the basis of national legal provisions on combating unfair competition[11], which also made the distribution of goods marked with this logo impossible. The ECJ emphasized that an individual may, in his/her defence, point to the conflict between Art. 34 TFEU and the national law (on combating unfair competition), making it possible to block the import of goods. In this case, Art. 34 TFEU thus served as a criterion of review of the legality of national law. The individual did not argue any rights from Art. 34 TFEU vis-à-vis the other individual. This is why, in the broad concept, we could say that Art. 34 TFEU has direct effect in horizontal relations.

For the sake of honest argumentation, it should be stated that invoking provisions on the EU internal market in order to exclude application in a case of national law which breaches these provisions (i.e. direct effect in the broad sense) may also have an impact on the rights and duties of individuals. It may also place the individual in a worse legal situation than he/she was in before. What is more, this mechanism may indeed decide about the existence, validity or change of a

---

8   See N.N. Shuibhne, *The Coherence of EU Free Movement Law. Constitutional Responsibility and the Court of Justice*, Oxford 2013, p. 100.

9   See point 4 below.

10 See *i.a.* ECJ Judgment of 6 June 2002 in case C-159/00 *Sapod Audic v. Eco-Emballages SA.*, ECLI:EU:C:2002:343, para 74.

11 See ECJ Judgment of 6 November 1984 in case 177/83 *Th. Kohl KG v. Ringelhan & Rennett SA and Ringelhan Einrichtungs GmbH*, ECLI:EU:C:1984:334.

legal relation, but merely via national law the non-applicability of which is established as a result of an inspection of the national law from the point of view of the internal market freedoms. For example, in the *Las*[12] case, inspection of the norm of national law from the point of view of the free movement of workers caused that the employment contract was not subject to the sanction of invalidity. According to national law, an employment contract which was not drawn up in Dutch should be deemed invalid. Verification of this regulation of national law from the point of view of Art. 45 TFEU caused the contract to give rise to the legal effects appropriate to it since this language requirement was deemed to be contrary to EU law[13]. This results from the fact that the mechanisms of the direct effect in the narrow sense and in the broad sense may give rise to similar legal effects. The difference will lie in the source of the creation, change or ending of the legal relation – in the national law partly with EU law (broad effect) or exclusively EU law (narrow effect).

Finally, we do not include in the issues of direct effect (and still less horizontal) TFEU provisions which initially seem to concern individuals, but upon closer examination refer however to omissions of Member States in relations to actions of individuals (they thus impose obligations directly on Member States, and not on individuals), which themselves, however, are not covered by the personal scope of application of a given EU law provision. Referring to examples concerning the free movement of goods, there is a mention here of such cases as, *inter alia*, *Commission v. France*[14], *Schmidberger*[15], in which, even though the actions of individuals caused a breach of Art. 34 TFEU (mass protests combined with destruction of goods, demonstration on a motorway blocking transport of goods), still the charges against the Member State concerned its omissions vis-à-vis these individuals.

Thus, to sum up, the starting point for further considerations will be, as already mentioned above, merely a narrow, subjective concept of direct effect in horizontal relations. In these cases, it is thus a matter that not only we are dealing with a horizontal dispute or the impact of the verification of the legality of national law on the legal situation of individuals, but that the norm of EU law directly decides

---

12 Case ECJ Jugdment of 16 April 2013 in case C-202/11 *Anton Las v PSA Antwerp NV*, ECLI:EU:C:2013:239.
13 Ch. Timmermans, *Horizontal Effect...*, p. 679.
14 ECJ Judgment of 9 December 1997 in case C-265/95 *Commission of the European Communities v French Republic*, ECLI:EU:C:1997:595.
15 ECJ Judgment of 12 June 2003 in case C-112/00 *Eugen Schmidberger, Internationale Transporte und Planzüge v Republik Österreich*, ECLI:EU:C:2003:333, paras. 53–57.

about the creation, change or ceasing of a legal relation between individuals. Therefore, it must be a norm which substantively grants individuals rights which have their equivalent in the obligation imposed on another individual. Apart from the provisions on the freedoms of the internal market, Art. 101 TFEU is, for example, such a provision which establishes a prohibition on the conclusion of specific agreements and grants rights to individuals. This provision may be invoked by individuals, *inter alia*, as a source of invalidity of an agreement concluded between individuals, a source of compensation liability of an individual for their breach of the prohibition, or finally as a legal basis of the undue enrichment of one individual at the expense of the other individual[16].

3. Free movement of workers (Art. 45 TFEU), establishment (Art. 49 TFEU) and services (Art. 56 TFEU)

A joint discussion of Art. 45, 49 and 56 TFEU is justified in such a sense that in the judgments of the ECJ these freedoms are, from the point of view of horizontal direct effect, often examined jointly, while the arguments cited in them are to a certain extent interchangeable. A key role in this case law is played by entities which have, to put it broadly, an impact on the collective interests of individuals by way of their representation or regulation. There are relatively few judgments in which, in the discussed context, the entities of this type do not appear. The foregoing division is accompanied by the scope of the prohibition confirmed by the ECJ as part of a specific freedom, i.e. the issue of whether horizontal direct effect concerns only the prohibition of discrimination following from a given freedom, or a prohibition on creating non-discriminating restrictions. The above aspects taken into account determine a true picture of horizontal direct effect of freedoms under Art. 45, 49 and 56 TFEU. Below, we have first presented the view of the current state of case law with regard to horizontal direct effect of Art. 45, 49 and 56 TFEU, and then summed up on the argumentation of the ECJ aimed at justifying horizontal direct effect of these freedoms.

3.1. Horizontal relations with the participation of entities representing the collective interests of individuals

Art. 45, 49 and 56 TFEU bring about a horizontal direct effect vis-à-vis entities which represent the collective interests of individuals or which may accept provisions (regulations) which serve the collective regulation of work, service activity

---

16 See R.W.E. van Leuken, *Rechtsverhoudingen…*, p. 46.

or the conduct of business activity. This concerns both prohibitions of discrimination following from these freedoms, and prohibitions on creating restrictions of a non-discriminatory nature.

3.1.1. Prohibition on discrimination

The resolution which made the way for horizontal effect of the prohibition of discrimination with regard to Art. 45 and 56 TFEU was the ruling in the *Walrave* case[17]. This concerned a pacemaker (driving on a motorbike before a cyclist) in a cycling race, who questioned the rule introduced by the *Union Cycliste Internationale* (UCI), an international federation of cyclists, pursuant to which a cyclist and his/her pacemaker in championships had to be of the same nationality. Walrave thus demanded before a national court an abrogation of the citizenship clause in the UCI regulations, stating that it infringes, *inter alia*, on the prohibition of discrimination currently expressed, *inter alia*, in the context of freedom of movement of workers (Art. 45 TFEU) and freedom of provision of services (Art. 56 TFEU). The basic issue to be resolved was whether the private organization setting down the regulations concerning cycling competitions is obligated to respect these freedoms. In this regard, the ECJ gave a positive answer. It stated that the prohibition of such discrimination did not only apply to the action of public authorities but extended likewise to rules of any other nature aimed at regulating gainful employment and the provision of services in a collective manner[18]. Thus, Art. 45 and 56 TFEU must be taken into account by a national court when evaluating the validity or effects of the citizenship clause included in the regulations of a sports federation[19]. The ECJ has made a similar decision in the context of Art. 45 and 56 TFEU with regard to the Italian Football Federation. Under its regulation, only football players affiliated with the Federation, which involved a citizenship requirement, could take part in professional or semi-professional games within the territory of Italy[20]. This regulation has been deemed to be contrary to the prohibition of discrimination enshrined in Art. 45 and 56 TFEU.

---

17 ECJ Judgment of 12 December 1974 in case 36/74 *B.N.O. Walrave and L.J.N. Koch v Association Union cycliste internationale, Koninklijke Nederlandsche Wielren Unie and Federación Española Ciclismo*, ECLI:EU:C:1974:140, para 16.

18 *Ibidem*, para 17.

19 *Ibidem*, para 25.

20 ECJ Judgment of 14 July 1976 in case 13/76 *Gaetano Donà v Mario Mantero*, ECLI:EU:C:1976:115.

The ECJ has also confirmed horizontal direct effect of the prohibition of discrimination in the context of entities representing the collective interests of individuals with regard to the freedom of establishment (Art. 49 TFUE) in the *van Ameyde* ruling[21]. This case concerned a dispute between a loss-adjusters' undertaking and the *Ufficio Centrale Italiano di Assistenza Assicurativa Automobilisti in Circolazione Internazionale* (UCI) which associated all or most of the insurers against civil liability in respect of motor vehicles who operate in Italy. The UCI took steps, the object of which was to confine the handling of the examination of accidents on the territory of Italy to only those entities being members of UCI. This created the need for the company van Ameyde to cease its activity, which company, up to that date, had – at the mandate of foreign insurance companies – examined damage resulting from accidents in Italy involving vehicles which were insured by these insurance companies. Though ultimately the ECJ did not ascertain a breach of the prohibition of discrimination, it confirmed once again that it was sufficient that the discrimination followed from rules of whatever kind which seek to govern collectively the operation of the business in question and that it was irrelevant whether the discrimination originated in measures of a public authority or, on the contrary, in measures attributable to the National Insurers' Bureau, which was not deemed by the ECJ to be part of a public authority[22].

3.1.2. Prohibition on creating non-discriminatory restrictions

Since the ruling of the ECJ in the *Bosman* case it has become clear that, in the context of freedom of movement of workers, the prohibition on creating restrictions of a non-discriminatory nature referred to in Art. 45 TFEU also has horizontal direct effect. In this case, the dispute concerned a football player and the transfer rules imposed by the European football federation (*Union des Associations Européennes de Football* – UEFA) with regard to the transfer fee, among other things, which the club acquiring the player (employee) had to pay to the club which sold the player (regardless of the fact that the contractual relation between the existing club and the player had expired). Such a restriction did not have a discriminatory character and was independent of the player's citizenship or the nationality of the club. As it is known, the UEFA is not a public entity, but a Swiss law private-legal association. The ECJ stated that this type of entity was obligated to comply with

---

21 ECJ Judgment of 9 June 1977 in case 90/76 *Ufficio Henry van Ameyde v S.r.l. Ufficio centrale italiano di assistenza assicurativa automobilisti in circolazione internazionale (UCI)*, ECLI:EU:C:1977:101.

22 *Ibidem*, para 28.

the prohibition ensuing from Art. 45 TFEU and that prohibition might have a direct impact on the contractual rights and duties of the parties. The ECJ also emphasized that the abolition, as between Member States, of obstacles to the freedom of movement for persons and to the freedom of provision of services would be compromised if the abolition of State barriers were neutralized by obstacles resulting from the exercise of their legal autonomy by associations or organizations not governed by public law[23]. What is interesting, the ECJ also pointed out that, in principle, individual entities may – in a horizontal relation – cite exceptions to the freedoms which could restrict the established infringement, such as public policy, public security or public health[24]. This means that these exceptions may also justify restrictions created by individual entities which, acting in their own interests, will – by the way – be carrying out also certain public objectives. The statements contained in the *Bosman* ruling were then confirmed in other rulings concerning organizations carrying out collective interests of individuals, such as the Belgian judo union (in the context of Art. 45, 49 and 56 TFEU)[25], a federation organizing basketball games[26], or an organization made up of lawyers[27].

With regard to services and establishment, what one should consider important are the *Viking Line* ruling[28] (Art. 49 TFEU) and the *Laval* ruling[29] (Art. 56 TFEU)[30]. In the *Viking Line* ruling, the ECJ stated that collective actions carried

---

23　*Ibidem*, para 83.

24　*Ibidem*, paras 85–86.

25　ECJ Judgment of 11 April 2000 in joined cases C-51/96 and C-191/97 *Christelle Deliège v Ligue francophone de judo et disciplines associées ASBL, Ligue belge de judo ASBL, Union européenne de judo and François Pacquée*, ECLI:EU:C:2000:199.

26　ECJ Judgment of 13 April 2000 in case C-176/96 *Jyri Lehtonen and Castors Canada Dry Namur-Braine ASBL v Fédération royale belge des sociétés de basket-ball ASBL (FRBSB)*, ECLI:EU:C:2000:201, para 35.

27　ECJ Judgment of 19 February 2002 in case C-309/99, *J. C. J. Wouters, J. W. Savelbergh and Price Waterhouse Belastingadviseurs BV v Algemene Raad van de Nederlandse Orde van Advocaten*, ECLI:EU:C:2002:98, para 120.

28　ECJ Judgment of 11 December 2007 in case C-438/05 *International Transport Workers' Federation and Finnish Seamen's Union v Viking Line ABP and OÜ Viking Line Eesti*, CLI:EU:C:2007:772, para 33.

29　ECJ Judgment of 18 December 2007 in case C-341/05 *Laval un Partneri Ltd v. Svenska Byggnadsarbetareförbundet and Others*, CLI:EU:C:2007:809, para 98.

30　See N.N. Shuibhne, *Settling dust? Reflections on the Judgments in Viking and Laval'*, 'European Business Law Review' No. 2010, p. 681; N. Reich, *Free Movement v. Social Rights in an Enlarged Union – the Laval and Viking Cases before the ECJ*, 'Germal Law Journal' No. 2008, p. 125.

out by trade unions or associations of trade unions not being a public law entity, and whose goal is that of inducing entrepreneurs to conclude a collective agreement, the content of which may dissuade that entrepreneur from availing of the freedom to conduct a business activity, were covered by the scope of application of the provisions of the original law concerning the freedom of enterprise, and might constitute a non-discriminatory restriction within the meaning of Art. 49 TFEU. G. Davies underlines that by stating that the case law on the horizontal application of the freedom of movement of persons and the freedom to provide services does not only apply to associations or to organizations exercising a regulatory task or having *quasi*-legislative powers[31], the ECJ suggested in the *Viking Line* judgment that horizontal effect should encompass any private actions restricting free movement[32].

In the *Laval* case, on the other hand, a protest of a trade union was deemed to be a restriction within the meaning of Art. 56 TFEU, as it attempted to force a service-provider, having its seat in another Member State to engage in negotiations with it in the matter of wage rates which should be paid out to posted employees, as well as to accede to a collective agreement the provisions of which set down, with regard to certain discussed issues, more favorable terms and conditions than the terms and conditions following from the pertinent statutory provisions.

3.2. Individual contractual relations between individuals

The undisputed and full scope of horizontal direct effect in relation to contractual relations between ordinary individuals (individual contractual relations), i.e. those who do not represent collective interests, has been argued to date by the ECJ only in the context of the free movement of workers (Art. 45 TFEU). In the *Angonese* ruling[33], the ECJ accepted that a prohibition of discrimination for the reason of nationality contained in Art. 45 TFEU applies to a private Italian bank (in the Bolzano region). In this case, a dispute arose with regard to taking part in a competition for a vacant position in the bank, which was made dependent on the possession of a certificate proving the ability to use two languages, issued

---

31   See ECJ Judment of 11 December 2007 in case C-438/05 *International Transport Workers' Federation and Finnish Seamen's Union v Viking Line ABP and OÜ Viking Line Eesti*, CLI:EU:C:2007:772, paras. 64–65.

32   See G. Davies, *Freedom of Contract and the Horizontal Effect of Free Movement Law*, in: D. Leczykiewicz, S. Weatherill (eds.), *The Involvement of EU Law in Private Law Relationships*, Oxford 2013, p. 61–62.

33   ECJ Judgment of 6 June 2000 in case C-281/98 *Roman Angonese v. Cassa di Risparmio di Bolzano SpA*, ECLI:EU:C:2000:296.

by the authorities of the province of Bolzano and only there it could be obtained. Though Mr. Angonese did not hold this certificate, he spoke the two languages and had diplomas to confirm this. Nonetheless, he was denied permission to take part in the competition. In this case, the ECJ, citing, *inter alia*, the general wording of the prohibition of discrimination from Art. 45 TFEU, and the effectiveness of prohibitions following from freedoms[34], stated that the prohibition of discrimination on grounds of nationality laid down in Art. 45 TFEU must be regarded as applying to private persons as well. The ECJ referred here to its ruling in the *Defrenne* case[35], stating that Art. 45 TFEU has an imperative character (similar to Art. 157 TFEU) and thus that the prohibition of discrimination applied equally to all agreements intended to regulate paid labour collectively, as well as to contracts between individuals. The position of the ECJ concerning horizontal direct effect expressed in the *Angonese* ruling with regard to the prohibition of discrimination in the context of Art. 45 TFEU was subsequently confirmed in other rulings concerning an employment relationship and other private entities, such as the Max Planck Institute for Radio Astronomy[36] or the Daimler AG – Werk Wörth[37].

However, there are no rulings in which the ECJ states that in individual relations between individuals the prohibition on creating restrictions of a non-discriminatory nature follows from Art. 45 TFEU, as occurred in the *Bosman* case. Nor has the ECJ had an occasion to date to rule on horizontal direct effect of Art. 49 TFEU (freedom of establishment) on an individual level (both with regard to the prohibition of discrimination and the prohibition of restrictions).

With regard to the freedom of provision of services, on the other hand, a ruling was issued in the *Haug-Adrion* case[38], which, however, gives rise to certain doubts as to whether it should be classified in the category of individual relations. In that case a dispute arose between an insured person and an insurance company, where the latter refused to accept a discount for an accident-free period in Germany (15 years) in a situation in which the owner of the vehicle placed customs registration plates on a newly acquired vehicle in Germany in order to be able

---

34 Ibidem, paras. 30–36.

35 ECJ Judgment of 8 April 1976 in case 43/75 *Gabrielle Defrenne v Société anonyme belge de navigation aérienne Sabena*, ECLI:EU:C:1976:56, para 31.

36 ECJ Judgment of 14 July 2008 in case C-94/07 *Andrea Raccanelli v Max-Planck-Gesellschaft zur Förderung der Wissenschaften e V.*, ECLI:EU:C:2008:425.

37 ECJ Judgment of 28 June 2012 in case C-172/11 *Georges Erny v Daimler AG - Werk Wörth*, ECLI:EU:C:2012:399.

38 ECJ Judgment of 13 December 1984 in case C-251/83, *Eberhard Haug-Adrion v Frankfurter Versicherungs-AG*, ECLI:EU:C:1984:397.

to move it to Belgium. The absence of the discount resulted in this case from the contractual provisions included in the general conditions of insurance offered by the insurance company. While it is true that the ECJ did not state in this case that an infringement of the prohibition of discrimination occurred, nonetheless it carried out an examination of the regulations contained in the general terms and conditions of the contract, which may mean that, in principle, the ECJ permits, in a direct individual relation, a horizontal direct effect of the prohibition of discrimination contained in Art. 56 TFEU. The ECJ also stated directly that Art. 56 TFEU intends to eliminate all measures which, in the fields of the freedom to provide services, treat a national of another Member State more severely or place him in a situation less advantageous, from a legal or factual point of view, than the Member State's own nationals in the same circumstances[39].

It should be pointed out, however, that a different position regarding the relation which existed in the *Haug-Adrion* case was taken, *inter alia,* by J. Snell[40]. This author states that in this case it was not a matter of an individual decision of an independent insurance company, but of the general terms and conditions of contracts, which had their basis in a government regulation. Thus, these regulations were authorized, as it were, by the government, and moreover most likely also commonly used vis-à-vis customers by other insurance companies on the market (thus, in reality they had the character of collective regulations)[41]. Apart from this, in the opinion of J. Snell, the ruling was that of a chamber composed of three judges who, faced with the absence of the prospect of declaring the existence of an infringement of the prohibition of discrimination, did not concentrate on the character of the provisions with regard to which they issued a decision. This author is of the opinion that had the ECJ wished in the *Haug-Adrion* case to confirm such an important issue as horizontal direct effect of the prohibition of discrimination following from Art. 56 TFEU in an individual relation, then without a doubt it would have ruled on it as in Full Court. Taking the above doubts into consideration, one should expect that there will only be further rulings of the ECJ concerning this type of relation that would make it possible to unequivocally define the issue of whether Art. 56 TFEU is indeed aimed at eliminating all the discriminatory measures also in individual horizontal relations.

---

39 *Ibidem*, para 14.
40 See R.J. Snell, *Goods and Services in EC Law: A Study of the Relationship Between the Freedoms*, Oxford 2002, p. 142–143.
41 See also G. Davies, *Freedom of Contract...*, p. 65–67, who states that the ECJ ruling was about national rules which regulated the way insurance contracts were to be formed.

3.3. Argumentation used by the ECJ

Creating horizontal direct effect in the context of Art. 45, 49 and 56 TFEU, the ECJ used in the reasoning of the rulings arguments which were similar to each other.

Firstly, in the context of the prohibition of discrimination the ECJ pointed out that the provisions concerning freedom to provide services, freedom of movement for workers, and of establishment are worded in a quite general way – they are not addressed directly only to Member States. Thus, their wording does not exclude the possibility of imposing obligations on individual entities[42].

Secondly, with regard to the prohibition of discrimination a statement appeared in the *Walrave* ruling that the prohibition of discrimination expressed in Art. 45 and 56 TFEU has an imperative (mandatory) character, which means that it should be applicable to all legal relationships[43].

Thirdly, as the reason justifying horizontal direct effect the ECJ gives the need to ensure proper effectiveness of the internal market freedoms. This argument appears in the context of both the prohibition of discrimination and the prohibition of restrictions. The ECJ accepts that the goal of the EU consisting in the abolition, as between Member States, of obstacles to freedom of movement of persons and freedom to provide services would be compromised if the abolition of State barriers could be neutralized by obstacles resulting from the exercise, by associations or organizations not governed by public law, of their legal autonomy[44]. Thus, what is of importance is not the source of the existing restrictions, but merely the effect these restrictions have on the internal market of the EU[45]. Moreover, the ECJ emphasizes that since working conditions in the various Member States are governed sometimes by means of provisions laid down by law or regulation and sometimes by agreements and other acts concluded or adopted by private persons, the limitation of the prohibitions in question to acts of a public authority would risk creating inequality in their application[46]. Thus, the reason for the need to adopt horizontal direct effect is also the need for a uniform application of the provisions regulating internal market freedoms.

Fourthly, additional arguments appear in the context of Art. 45 TFEU and of the freedom of movement for workers. Already in the *Walrave* ruling the ECJ

---

42 See e.g. ECJ Judgments: *Walrave*, para 20; *Angonese*, paras. 30–36.
43 See ECJ Judgment *Walrave*, para 28.
44 See ECJ Judgments: *Viking Line*, para 57; *Walrave*, para 18; *Bosman*, para 83; *Deliège*, para 47; *Angonese*, para 32.
45 See R.W.E. van Leuken, *Rechtsverhoudingen tussen particulieren…*, p. 105.
46 See ECJ Judgment *Walrave*, para 18.

points to the supportive character of the provisions of secondary legislation (at the time, Regulation 1612/68[47]), which provide that the prohibition on discrimination shall apply to agreements and any other collective regulations concerning employment[48]. Moreover, the ECJ cites its ruling in the *Defrenne* case, issued in the context of Art. 157 TFEU[49], which the ECJ believes to have a mandatory character. According to the ECJ, Art. 45 TFEU, which lays down a fundamental freedom, just as Art. 157 TFEU, is mandatory and designed to ensure that there is no discrimination on the labour market.

Taking into consideration the arguments indicated above, it may be stated that in various contexts they are cited by the ECJ interchangeably. What is particularly noteworthy is that the ECJ points to similar arguments, stating that horizontal direct effect with regard to the prohibition of discrimination (*Walrave*) and the prohibition on restrictions (*Bosman*). Furthermore, similar arguments appear in the context of entities representing the collective interests of individuals (*Walrave*), as well as individual contractual relations (*Angonese*). An interaction of arguments also occurs between various freedoms. And so, in the *Viking Line* ruling, the ECJ invokes arguments derived from the *Angonese* ruling (i.e. additionally in a ruling concerning collective relations it invokes a ruling concerning an individual relation). Such a significant use of the argumentation in reasoning means that, in principle, it may be also used in relation to the areas not yet covered by the ECJ rulings, for example, in relation to the establishment of a prohibition of restrictions in the context of individual contractual relations or making precise the functioning of the prohibition of discrimination in horizontal relations in the context of Art. 49 and 56 TFEU. Such a general argumentation which the ECJ used in the context of Art. 45, 49 and 56 TFEU also makes it possible to introduce, for policy reasons, certain different solutions to the imprecise areas in relation to those elements of horizontal effect already discovered in the rulings of the ECJ.

4. Free movement of goods (Art. 34–35 TFEU)

In our considerations we have ignored (as having at present negligible practical importance in ECJ rulings) the prohibition on the establishment of customs duty and charges equivalent to customs duty which, by their very nature, in principle

---

47 Regulation (EEC) No 1612/68 of the Council of 15 October 1968 on freedom of movement for workers within the Community (Official Journal of the European Economic Community L 257 of 19 October 1968, p. 2–12).

48 ECJ Judgment *Walrave*, para 22.

49 ECJ Judgment *Sabena*, paras. 31 and 39.

will be introduced only by States or their extensions, and not by individual entities (even if these latter may sometimes collect those charges on behalf of the State)[50]. We will concentrate rather on Art. 34 and 35 TFEU[51] which create a prohibition on the establishment of quantitative restrictions and restrictions having equivalent effect[52]. The wording of these Treaty provisions seems at first glance to not rule out in advance their horizontal direct effect[53] as there is a mention in them of a prohibition applicable 'between' Member States, and not of prohibitions created exclusively by Member States[54]. Nonetheless, we do not find any further guidelines concerning this in the content of the provisions themselves.

As regards case law, a certain fragment contained in the *Dansk Supermarked*[55] ruling initially created the impression (a wrong impression, as it turned out) that Art. 34 TFEU could impose obligations on individual entities or indeed directly influence contractual obligations of individuals. This matter concerned a dispute between two Danish companies, of which one (Imerco) attempted – with the aid of a court prohibition (injunction) – to prevent the other (Dansk Supermarked) from selling a type of goods (china service decorated with pictures of Danish royal castles) on the territory of Denmark, manufactured and imported from Great Britain. Under the agreement, Imerco permitted the British producer to sell the product in Albion on condition of complying with the prohibition on its sale on the territory of Denmark. However, Dansk Supermarked purchased the product on the British market and engaged in sales in Denmark. In the context of this dispute, the ECJ stated that 'it is impossible in any circumstances for agreements between individuals to derogate from the mandatory provisions of the Treaty on the free movement of goods' and that '[..] an agreement involving a prohibition on the importation into a Member State of goods lawfully marketed in another Member State may not be relied upon or taken into consideration in order to classify the marketing of such goods as an improper or unfair commercial

---

50 C. Barnard, *The Substantive Law of the EU. The Four Freedoms*, Oxford 2013, p. 48.

51 Art. 34 TFEU: Quantitative restrictions on imports and all measures having equivalent effect shall be prohibited between Member States; Art 35 TFEU: Quantitative restrictions on exports, and all measures having equivalent effect, shall be prohibited between Member States.

52 See S. Schmahl, F. Jung, *Horizontale Drittwirkung der Warenverkehrsfreiheit?*, 'Neue Zeitschrift für Verwaltungsrecht' No. 2013, p. 607–612.

53 P.Ch. Müller-Graff, *Die horizontale…*, p. 8.

54 For a different point of view see J. Snell, *Goods and Services…*, p. 129–130.

55 ECJ Judgment of 22 January 1981 in case C-58/80 *Dansk Supermarked A/S v A/S Imerco*, ECLI:EU:C:1981:17.

practice.'[56]. This fragment of the *Dansk Supermarked* ruling could suggest that individual entities, when concluding an agreement, must expect certain obligations (restrictions), having a direct impact on the possible validity (effectiveness) of the contractual provisions, and thus that this provision exercises a horizontal direct effect[57]. Nonetheless, upon closer examination, it turned out that between the main parties in the dispute before a national court there was no contractual relation (such relation existed between Imerco and the British producer of the product), while the liability of Dansk Supermarked was of a tort nature. This company was to be liable under an act of unfair competition and it was those provisions which potentially would allow Imerco to obtain a temporary court injunction, which could breach Art. 34 TFEU by way of the establishment of a prohibition on the sale of goods acquired in another EU Member State. If one were to interpret the *Dansk Supermarked* ruling in this way, then it would not be the contractual clause prohibiting the sale of the product on the territory of Denmark which would collide directly with Art. 34 TFEU, but the provision of national law which allowed the enforcement of such a clause.

Later case law of the ECJ showed that this latter interpretation of the *Dansk Supermarked* ruling was correct, and that art. 34 TFEU may impact on the contractual relations between individuals only indirectly. In the *van de Haar* ruling the ECJ stated that the prohibitions contained in Art. 34 TFEU belong 'to the rules which seek to [..] eliminate measures taken by Member States which might in any way impede such free movement'[58]. It follows from *Vlaamse Reisbureaus* that Art. 34 TFEU concerns 'only public measures and not the conduct of undertakings', stating further that, as a result, from the point of view of this provision one may examine only national regulations, and not agreements between individual

---

56 *Ibidem*, para 17.
57 Some authors interpreted the ECJ Judgment *Dansk Supermarked* that way, see e.g. P. Pescatore, *"The Doctrine of "Direct Effect": An Infant Disease of Community Law"*, 'European Law Review' No. 1983, p. 163; D. Schaefer, *Die unmittelbare Wirkung des Verbots de nichttarifären Handelshemmnisse (Article 30 EWGV) in den Rechtsbeziehungen zwischen Privaten. Probleme der horizontalen unmittelbaren Wirkung des Gemeinschaftsrechts, gezeigt am Beispiel des Article 30 EWGV*, Frankfurt am Main 1987, p. 102–104; See also J. Snell, *Goods and Services...*, p. 129–130.
58 See ECJ Judgment of 5 April 1984 in joined cases 177/82 and 178/82 *Criminal proceedings against Jan van de Haar and Kaveka de Meern BV Van der Haar*, ECLI:EU:C:1984:144, para. 11–12.

entities[59]. Finally, in *Sapod Audic*[60], the ECJ stated that an obligation which arises out of a private contract between the parties to the main proceedings 'cannot be regarded as a barrier to trade for the purposes of Article 30 of the Treaty since it was not imposed by a Member State but agreed between individuals', citing in this context the wording from the *Dassonville* ruling[61]. The profile itself of this wording showed that the ECJ refers in the context of Art. 34 TFEU to 'all trading rules enacted by Member States'[62]. Also, the wording which arose at a later time following from the *Keck* ruling relating to a certain selling arrangement the ECJ refers essentially to 'requirements laid down by the State'[63]. It is no different in rulings relating to 'measures which hinder access of products originating in other Member States to the market of a Member State'[64].

In light of the above arguments one may perhaps unequivocally state that the ECJ holds the view that Art. 34 TFEU does not have a direct effect on horizontal relations, and thus cannot directly constitute a source of rights and obligations of individuals in these relations. As already mentioned above, individual entities may, however, play a key role in the context of Art. 34 TFEU[65]. Firstly, as a reason for the infringement of this prohibition by way of an omission on the part of the Member State, to appropriately prevent an interruption in the trade of goods[66]. Secondly, natural persons who act on behalf of a Member State, such as public officials, may cause a Member State to be accused of an infringement of Art. 34 TFEU[67].

---

59 ECJ Judgment of 1 October 1987 in case 311/85 *Vereniging van Vlaamse Reisbureaus v. ASBL Sociale Dienst van de Plaatselijke en Gewestelijke Overheidsdiensten*, ECLI:EU:C:1987:418, para 30.

60 ECJ Judgment of 6 June 2002 in case C-159/00 *Sapod Audic v. Eco-Emballages SA.*, ECLI:EU:C:2002:343, para 74.

61 ECJ Judgment of 11 July 1974 in case 8/74 *Procureur du Roi v Benoît and Gustave Dassonville*, ECLI:EU:C:1974:82, para 5, and ECJ Judgment of 10 February 2009 in case C-110/05 *Commission of the European Communities v Italian Republic*, ECLI:EU:C:2009:66, para 37.

62 ECJ Judgment of 2 December 2010 in case C-108/09 *Ker-Optika bt v ÀNTSZ Dél-dunántúli Regionális Intézete*, ECLI:EU:C:2010:725, para 47.

63 See ECJ Judgment of 24 November 1993 in joined cases C-267/91 and C-268/91 *Criminal proceedings against Bernard Keck and Daniel Mithouard*, ECLI:EU:C:1993:905, paras. 16 and 17.

64 ECJ Judgment C-110/05 *Commission v Italy*, para 33.

65 Cf. N.N. Shuibhne, *The Coherence...*, p. 104.

66 See e.g. ECJ Judgment C-265/95 *Commission v France* and ECJ Judgment *Schmidberger*.

67 Case ECJ Judgment of 17 April 2007 in case C-470/03 *A.G.M.-COS.MET Srl v Suomen valtio and Tarmo Lehtinen*, ECLI:EU:C:2007:213.

This latter case falls within a broader trend in the case law in which a Member State, with the aid of a broad extension of the State, may be attributed an activity of certain non-State entities[68]. Thirdly, individuals may initiate before national authorities an inspection of the compliance of national regulations with Art. 34 TFEU. In that case, an individual, acting as it were in his/her own interests, enables, e.g. national courts, at the same time to verify the compliance of national law with EU law (as part of a broad direct effect of Art. 34 TFEU)[69].

A controversy, similar to the *Dansk Supermarked* ruling mentioned at the beginning of this point, has recently been caused by the ruling in the *Fra.bo* case[70]. This case concerned a private law body (*Deutsche Vereinigung des Gas- und Wasserfaches eV* – DVGW) which was engaged in standardization and certification activities, where the national legislation considered the products certified by that body to be compliant with national law and that has the effect of restricting the marketing of products which are not certified by that body. The ECJ stated that it was clear in this case that a private body, by virtue of its authority to certify the products, in reality holds the power to regulate the entry into the German market of products such as the copper fittings at issue in the main proceedings. Therefore, it stated that Art. 34 TFEU applies to the activity of such an entity, in particular in view of the fact that 'the national legislation considers the products certified by that body to be compliant with national law and that has the effect of restricting the marketing of products which are not certified by that body'[71]. Thus, on the one hand, in the *Fra.bo* case we are dealing with a private entity which is not financed (or otherwise influenced) by the State and upon which the State does not exercise any powers with regard to the membership and activity. On the other hand, however, this entity was equipped – as the only one in a Member State and

---

68 See e.g. ECJ Judgment of 24 November 1982 in case 249/81 *Commission of the European Communities v Ireland*, ECLI:EU:C:1982:402; ECJ Judgment of 13 December 1983 in case 222/82 *Apple and Pear Development Council v K.J. Lewis Ltd and others (Buy Irish)*, ECLI:EU:C:1983:370; ECJ Judgment of 18 May 1989 in joined cases 266 and 267/87 *The Queen v Royal Pharmaceutical Society of Great Britain, ex parte Association of Pharmaceutical Importers and others*, ECLI:EU:C:1989:2055.

69 See e.g. ECJ Judgment of 21 June 2012 in case C-5/11 *Criminal proceedings against Titus Alexander Jochen Donner*, ECLI:EU:C:2012:370, para 31.

70 See ECJ Judgment of 12 July 2012 in case C-171/11 *Fra.bo SpA v Deutsche Vereinigung des Gas- und Wasserfaches eV (DVGW) – Technisch-Wissenschaftlicher Verein*, ECLI:EU:C:2012:453. See also H. van Harten, T. Nauta, *Towards horizontal direct effect for the free movement of goods? Comment on Fra.bo*, 'European Law Review' No. 2013, p. 677.

71 ECJ Judgment *Fra.bo*, para 32.

pursuant to the legislation – with powers to certify products which for this reason are deemed to be in compliance with national law. Other procedures in this regard involve material difficulties and costs, and additionally are used rarely or not at all (*inter alia*, also in view of the lack of executive regulations in this respect). Moreover, in practice German consumers do not buy products without such a certificate. These factors have the effect that the barrier to entry to the German market, caused by the rights to certify products, is significant.

With regard to the classification of the *Fra.bo* ruling, as in the case of the *Dansk Supermarked* judgment, two trends have emerged in the doctrine. The first one accepts that we are dealing with a new approach of the ECJ to Art. 34 TFEU as a regulation having a direct effect in the horizontal sense[72]. Such a solution is indeed suggested by Advocate General Trstenjak[73], in her opinion, where she advocates assigning the case law concerning the free movement of persons to Art. 34 TFEU. The authors of the second trend suggested that the *Fra.bo* ruling did not constitute a change of direction in the case law of the ECJ and that in this case a direct effect in horizontal relations was not created in the context of Art. 34 TFEU.[74]

It is my conviction that the *Fra.bo* ruling should not be treated directly as a confirmation that Art. 34 TFEU may have a direct effect on a horizontal relation. I would classify this ruling rather as a further step on the path set down by the case law of the ECJ concerning the broad concept of an entity of the State. In particular, this ruling constitutes a further step in the context of such rulings as *Royal Pharmaceutical Society*[75], in which organizations regulating access to a specific profession control access to the market. The further step refers to the case of *Fra.bo* where we are dealing with a purely private entity, nonetheless - by virtue of the legislation of a Member State - having the task of inspecting access of goods to a market, which are similar to the tasks carried out by the State. However, some type of delegation of this right by the State has occurred and this is why one cannot look at the *Fra.bo* ruling in the context of a pure horizontal direct effect of Art. 34 TFEU. This is because a change of this situation in which

---

72 See e.g. M. Kloepfer, H. Greve, *Zur Drittwirkung der Warenverkehrsfreiheit – Die horizontale Wirkung der Warenverkehrsfreiheit am Beispiel der technischen Regelsetzung*, 'Deutsches Verwaltungsblatt' No. 2013, p. 1148; For further references see See R.W.E. van Leuken, *Rechtsverhoudingen tussen particulieren…*, p. 125.

73 Opinion of Advocate General Trstenjak in case C-171/11 *Fra.bo*.

74 See e.g. C. Barnard, *The Substantive…*, p. 77 and R. van Gestel, H.W. Micklitz, *European integration through standardization: How judicial review is breaking down the club house of private standardization bodies*, 'Common Market Law Review' No. 2013, p. 159.

75 ECJ Judgment in joined cases 266 and 267/87 *Royal Pharmaceutical Society*.

access to the market is restricted lies in a change in the national regulations, and not in a change in the contractual relations between individual entities. Undoubtedly, however, as stated by N.N. Shuibhne[76], one can see here a similarity also to certain rulings on the free movement of persons, including the *Walrave* ruling[77], which relates to some kind of a collective regulation. Nonetheless, in the *Fra.bo* ruling the vertical trend still comes across strongly, as the ECJ clearly states that a Member State assigned to the DVGW 'a right to restrict the marketing of products'[78] in a Member State[79].

5. Freedom of movement of capital and payments (Art. 63 TFEU)

In the context of Art. 63 TFEU, pursuant to which all restrictions on the movement of capital between Member States and between Member States and third countries shall be prohibited, in principle there is no case law of the ECJ which would relate directly to horizontal direct effect of this freedom. One of the reasons for this situation is undoubtedly the fact that even the vertical direct effect of the freedom of movement of capital had not been established by the ECJ until 1995[80].

In order to illustrate the problem of horizontal direct effect of Art. 63 TFEU, one may ask a question of whether a private investor could, for example, in the context of acquisition of shares in an entirely private company from another EU Member State (operating without the participation, supervision or intervention of a Member State), invoke Art. 63 TFEU in order to exclude certain restrictions contained, for example in the statutes of that company admitted by national law of the companies of a given Member State? Up to the present time, the case law of the ECJ has shared a possible element of discouraging investors from acquiring shares with some form of interference of a Member State, e.g. by way of supervising the operations of the company via instruments established on the basis of national

---

76 See N.N. Shuibhne, *The Coherence…*, p. 106–107.

77 ECJ Judgment *Walrave*.

78 ECJ Judgment *Fra.bo*, para 31.

79 See also the proposals in C. Krenn, *A Missing Piece in the Horizontal Effect 'Jigsaw'*: *Horizontal Direct Effect and the Free Movement of Goods*, 'Common Market Law Review' No. 2012, p. 177.

80 ECJ Judgment of 14 December 1995 in joined cases C-163/94, C-165/94 and C-250/94, *Criminal proceedings against Lucas Emilio Sanz de Lera, Raimundo Díaz Jiménez and Figen Kapanoglu*, ECLI:EU:C:1995:451, para 43.

law[81]. The general axis of this case law is that the ECJ does not allow a Member State to influence the operations of a company if this influence illegitimately and disproportionately gives an advantage to the State over normal shareholders[82]. In certain cases the arguments used by Member States, based on the assumption that the contested measure has been taken by the State not in its capacity as a public authority but in its capacity as a private operator, have been raised in order to exclude application in the case of Art. 63 TFEU. In principle, Member States, arguing in this way, assumed that they would exclude application of Art. 63 TFEU in view of the ascertainment of a horizontal relation. However, to date, the ECJ has rebutted this type of argument, seeking and finding a link between the investment restrictions and the State activity[83]. This is what happened, for example, to the case of *Commission v. United Kingdom*[84], in which the State had a special share in the privatized enterprise British Airport Authority (BAA), a company being the owner of airports within Great Britain. This share entitled the British government to grant prior consent to decisions of the company in certain, strategic matters, such as liquidation of an airport. Moreover, the statutes of the company BAA i.a. did not permit any entity to purchase more than 15% of the shares in this enterprise. The ECJ stated that in the case it was not a matter solely of the application of private company-law mechanisms, as stated by Great Britain, because the investment restrictions at issue did not arise as the result of the normal operation of company law. This was because the company statutes, with regard to which the restriction on the possibility of investing was to be approved by the Secretary of State pursuant to the national law. In those circumstances, the Member State acted in this instance in its capacity as a public authority, and not as a normal private law entity on the basis of normal company law.

---

81 See C. Gerner-Beuerle, *Shareholders between the Market and the State. The VW Law and other Interventions in the Market Economy*, 'Common Market Law Review' No. 2012, p. 97.

82 See W.G. Ringe, *Company Law and Free Movement of Capital*, 'Cambridge Law Journal', No. 69(2)/2010, p. 382.

83 ECJ Judgment of 26 September 2000 in case C-478/98 *Commission of the European Communities v Kingdom of Belgium*, ECLI:EU:C:2000:497, paras. 20–25. See also R.W.E. van Leuken, *Rechtsverhoudingen tussen particulieren…*, p. 129.

84 ECJ Judgment of 13 May 2003 in case C-98/01 *Commission of the European Communities v United Kingdom of Great Britain and Northern Ireland*, CLI:EU:C:2003:273, paras. 24 and 48.

In recent years the above problem has been seen very well in the ruling the *Volkswagen I* case[85]. The essence of the proceedings was a German act on the privatization of equity in the *Volkswagenwerk* limited company ('the VW Law'). The Commission stated that the provisions of the VW Law which, by way of a departure from the general provisions on joint stock companies, restrict the voting right of all shareholders to 20% of the share capital of Volkswagen; secondly, require a majority exceeding 80% of the represented capital for a decision of the general meeting, the adoption of which on the basis of general provisions requires a majority of 75% of the capital; thirdly, by way of a departure from the general provisions, enable the Federal State and the Lower Saxony state to appoint two representatives each to the supervisory board of that company, may discourage direct investments, and thus constitute a restriction of freedom of movement of capital within the meaning of Art. 63 TFEU. Moreover, it followed from the case files that the Lower Saxony state still retained a share of 20% in the company. Thus, the ECJ stated that the foregoing solutions allow a public entity to have a material influence on the company, which constitutes an infringement of Art. 63 TFEU. What is more, this material influence did not follow from normal national regulations (or the company statutes based on normal national regulations), but rather introduced, to the advantage of the public investor, a departure giving – at the expense of other investors – benefits exceeding its actual capital commitment.

Nonetheless, in its defence the German government pointed out that the VW Law is based on an understanding reached in 1959 between persons and groups which in the 1950's made claims to the limited liability company *Volkswagenwerk*. Under this understanding, employees and trade unions, in exchange for waiving claims to ownership rights to the enterprise, obtained protection guarantees against the majority shareholder which could gain independent control over the company. The source of the regulating VW Law was thus the shareholder agreement and statutes of the company Volkswagen. The VW Law is thus an expression of the will of the shareholders and all other persons and groups who invoke rights of a private nature to that enterprise. From the point of view of the free movement of capital, this law must therefore be treated as an understanding between shareholders. Therefore, Germany argued that if the restriction on the movement of capital came from shareholders (has thus a horizontal character), then Art. 63 TFEU should not be applied to such an understanding. However, the ECJ stated that the fact that this understanding became the subject of national law is

85 ECJ Judgment of 23 October 2007 in case C-112/05 *Commission of the European Communities v Federal Republic of Germany*, ECLI:EU:C:2007:623.

sufficient for – from the point of view of the freedom of movement of capital – it to be deemed to be a national regulation. This is because the exercise of legislative powers by the national authorities so empowered is to the highest degree a demonstration of the powers of the State. The *Volkswagen I* case does not confirm, therefore, to any degree a potential horizontal direct effect of Art. 63 TFEU since the ECJ deemed that the source of the restrictions on the freedom of movement of capital is national law, and not directly the company statutes or the shareholder agreement which, however, contained those same restrictions. It was the national law which was also the subject of examination by the ECJ, and not the statutes themselves, which was ultimately confirmed by the *Volkswagen II* case[86]. In order for it to be accepted that the ruling in the *Volkswagen I* case had been correctly carried out, it was sufficient that Germany changed the VW Law, and not the provisions of the statutes.

Undoubtedly, however, the restrictions in the rights of shareholders of the companies may also follow from actions of private entities (agreements, company statutes, etc.), be it through the granting of a veto right to a specific shareholder, the possibility of appointing the majority of the members of the management board or supervisory board of the company, or a restriction of the voting right of shareholders having a larger number of shares, etc. In other words, under the national law of individual Member States, specific rights may be created which give the privileged shareholder the possibility of having an impact on the company, which possibility does not follow from its level of capital commitment. Such special rights, even if they are not in the hands of public entities, may of course in certain situations discourage foreign investors from investing. To date, however, the ECJ has not resolved whether this type of measures may be classified as an infringement of Art. 63 TFEU, be it in the context of prohibition of discrimination or the prohibition on creating restrictions.

In this regard a question therefore arises: to what extent will the arguments used by the ECJ to establish a horizontal direct effect (e.g. in the context of freedoms of persons) be applicable to the freedom of movement of capital. In this context, various concepts are put forward in the doctrine. Some doctrine representatives believe that the arguments used to date by the ECJ, in particular the argument based on the need to ensure freedoms of due effectiveness, have lent themselves to analogical application in the context of Art. 63 TFEU[87]. As stated by

---

86 ECJ Judgment of 23 October 2013 in case C-95/12 *European Commission v Federal Republic of Germany*, ECLI:EU:C:2013:676.

87 See i.a. R.W.E. van Leuken, *Direct horizontal effect…*, p. 104 and H. Schepel, *Constitutionalising the Market, Marketising the Constitution, and to Tell the Difference: On*

the Advocate General, V. Trstenjak, it would be difficult to understand a situation in which, with the fulfillment of specific conditions, there would exist a possibility of direct application of the free movement for workers, freedom of enterprise, and freedom to provide services in relation to collective regulations not having a public law character, whereas such direct application would be categorically excluded with regard to the free movement of capital[88]. In the opinion of W.G. Ringe, Art. 63 TFEU should have a direct effect when, if on the basis of the effects of a given measure, it were to turn out that it would have a deterring (discouraging) impact on potential investors from other EU Member States[89]. In contrast, D. Wyatt believes that Art. 63 TFEU should be read as having a solely vertical effect[90]. He believes also that excluding horizontal direct effect of that article would prevent private operators in Member States from being vulnerable to actions at the suit of third country market operators in circumstances where it is unlikely that such third country operators would be similarly vulnerable. Referring to the *Mangold* ruling[91] and the general rule of equal treatment in EU law, this author proposes to restrict the effects of Art. 63 TFEU in horizontal relations to the prohibition of discrimination as regards citizenship. On the other hand, e.g. C. Barnard believes that the establishment of horizontal direct effect is unlikely[92]. Finally, there are authors who believe that in light of currently applicable EU law, Art. 63 TFEU does not apply to restrictions on the freedom of movement of capital introduced by private entities (it does not bring about horizontal effect)[93]. Taking into account the general character of the arguments used by the ECJ to date in relation to horizontal direct effect of freedoms of persons (see point 3.3. above), the ECJ has in this respect left itself with all paths open.

---

the Horizontal Application of the Free Movement Provisions in EU Law, 'European Law Journal' No. 18/2012, p. 179–180.

88 Opinion of Advocate General Trstenjak in case C-171/11 *Fra.bo,* para 44.

89 See W.G. Ringe, *Company Law…,* p. 308.

90 D. Wyatt, *Horizontal Effect of Fundamental Freedoms and the Right to Equality after Viking and Mangold, and the Implications for Community Competence,* 'Croatian Yearbook of European Law and Policy' No. 4/2008, p. 38.

91 ECJ Judgment of 22 November 2005 in case C-144/04 *Werner Mangold v Rüdiger Helm,* ECLI:EU:C:2005:709.

92 C. Barnard, *The Substantive Law…,* p. 526.

93 E.g. M. Mataczyński, in: A. Wróbel, D. Miąsik, N. Półtorak (eds.), *Traktat o Funkcjonowaniu Unii Europejskiej. Komentarz,* Warsaw 2012, commentary to Art. 63 TFEU, p. 995.

6. Final remarks

This article presents the current position of the ECJ with regard to horizontal direct effect of freedoms of the internal market. It was stated that the ECJ essentially rules out the possibility of such effect being exercised with regard to freedom of movement of goods (Art. 34 and 35 TFEU) and that to date it has not taken a position regarding the possibility of such effect being exercised by the freedom of movement of capital and of payments (Art. 63 TFEU). The ECJ admits horizontal direct effect with regard to the freedom of movement of services (Art. 56 TFEU) and of establishment (Art. 49 TFEU), though in cases in which private entities which represented collective interests of individuals appeared (both in relation to the prohibition of discrimination, and the prohibition of restrictions). With the exception of the controversial *Haug-Adrion* ruling (in the context of Art. 56 TFEU), the ECJ also has not to date ruled on horizontal direct effect of Art. 49 TFEU and 56 TFEU on the individual level (both in relation to the prohibition of discrimination, and the prohibition of restrictions).

The ECJ disclosed the broadest scope of horizontal direct effect in relation to the freedom of movement for workers (Art. 45 TFEU) – both as regards entities representing the collective interests of individuals, and as regards individual contractual relations. However, there are no rulings in which the ECJ stated that in individual relations between individuals Art. 45 TFEU provides for a prohibition of restrictions of a non-discriminatory character. What is visible here is the most significant development of horizontal direct effect in individual contractual relations concerning the employment relationship. G. Davies deems this situation to be justified by the fact that the decision in the *Angonese* case was clearly within the spirit and goal of EU secondary legislation – to prevent nationality discrimination in employment – they fell just outside the letter of that law because of the specific facts involved. That case may be thus understood as plausibly as the attempts to ensure consistency between secondary and primary law[94].

It follows from the case law of the ECJ that from the point of view of horizontal direct effect it treats the freedom of movement of goods differently from the freedom of persons. To date the ECJ has not explained this distinction directly in its case law. S. Weatherill points here to the lack of coherence in the argumentation of the ECJ and the lack of a coherent approach to all EU freedoms[95]. This distinction is perhaps justified by the fact that contractual relations between individuals

---

94 G. Davies, *Freedom of Contract…*, p. 66.

95 S. Weatherill, *The Elusive Character of Private Autonomy in EU Law*, in: *The Involvement of EU Law in Private Law Relationships*, Oxford 2013, p. 13.

with respect to the commodity market are subject to the provisions of competition law (Art. 101 and 102 TFEU). However, as accurately stated by G. Davies, this is not a very satisfying or complete argument—it is rather casual on the important and difficult issue of whether competition and free movement could or should sometimes address the same actions—but it does reject, as a matter of principle, the application of free movement to private contractual preferences[96].

What also follows from the above remarks is that not all the aspects of horizontal direct effect of freedoms of the EU internal market have been covered by the ECJ case law to date. The argumentation disclosed by the ECJ justifying horizontal direct effect in the context of freedoms of movement for persons (general wording of the provisions, their mandatory character, the effectiveness of EU freedoms, their uniform application), as well as the fact that it was interchangeably used in the context of various freedoms and various scopes thereof also allows for application of this argumentation to these aspects which have not been covered by the ECJ case law yet. Undoubtedly, however, in this respect there exist various alternatives in the literature. For example, in J. Snell's view, application of the provisions on freedoms of the internal market with respect to private entities may lead to an ineffective and unnecessary intervention in the economy[97] and thus is not advisable[98]. On the other hand, G. Davies[99] understands the established ECJ case law in the sense that apart from the area of employment of workers, a restriction on movement exists only where a party intervenes in the contracts of others. This is why a departure from this path for the purpose of restrictions on the contractual freedom of individuals in a direct manner (i.e. above all on the individual level of horizontal direct effect) would be a departure from the existing line of case law of the ECJ. This author, in reference to the *Mangold*-type[100] form of reasoning, suggests also allowing, to a certain degree, horizontal action of the prohibition of discrimination on grounds of nationality depending on the character of a contracting party or a contract. He points out that an employer as well as entities offering goods and services to the general public have a particular social role to play, in view of which it would be justified to impose on them the need to comply with the prohibition of discrimination in view of nationality. On

---

96   G. Davies, *Freedom of Contract…*, p. 67.

97   See H. Schepel, *The Enforcement of EC Law in Contractual Relations: Case Studies in How Not to 'Constitutionalize' Private Law*, 'European Review of Private Law' Issue 5 No. 12/2004, p. 663.

98   A similar view presents H. Schepel, *The Enforcement…*, p. 663.

99   G. Davies, *Freedom of Contract…*, p. 53–54.

100 ECJ Judgment *Mangold v Helm*.

the other hand, D. Wyatt[101] proposes a rule, in the context of horizontal direct effect, that normal market behavior on the part of one market operator should not in principle lead to a restriction on the fundamental freedom of another. But discriminatory conduct by market operators, or another conduct which falls outside the range of normal market behavior, would seem capable of falling within horizontal effect of a fundamental freedom, at any rate where it restricts access of other market operators, or consumers, to the market, or places, market operators or consumers at a disadvantage because they have exercised a fundamental freedom. In this regard this author attaches much weight to market participants' sales choices (but not purchase choices) which discriminate on grounds of nationality, or by reference to the residence of potential purchasers. Moreover, he proposes that horizontal effect be exercised by the prohibition of discrimination in view of nationality in all the freedoms, unless the discriminatory choice is caused by normal market behavior.

The above indicated proposals point to a certain problem in finding a balance between the benefits and the negative effects of introducing horizontal direct effect of the freedoms of the internal market in areas not yet covered by the ECJ case law. The basic question in this context is whether the actions of individuals which do not have a specific scale of impact on the internal market, and thus on other individuals, or individuals who do not require special protection (e.g. workers), should be covered by the prohibitions of EU freedoms, and if so, to what extent. In vertical relations, to date the ECJ has not applied the *de minimis* threshold in the context of freedoms of the internal market nor has it realized this in full scope (prohibition of discrimination and non-discrimination restrictions). However, in the context of horizontal relations the ECJ will have to set a standard which will allow it, on the one hand, to ensure reasonable and necessary supervision of the internal market, but, on the other hand, will take account of the contractual autonomy of individuals. The ECJ case law to date has realized this standard in the context of horizontal direct effect, above all concentrating on the entities which have an impact on the collective interests of individuals (they thus have a specific scale of impact on the internal market and other individuals) and by permitting horizontal effect of the prohibition of discrimination in view of nationality (at present expressly only in the context of Art. 45 TFEU) which, as an elementary principle, permeates the entire EU law. Perhaps this is a direction which the ECJ will continue also in future rulings with respect to as yet unresolved aspects of horizontal direct effect of the freedoms of the EU internal market.

---

101   D. Wyatt, *Horizontal Effect…*, p. 1 *passim.*

Literature

Baquero Cruz J., *Free Movement and Private Autonomy*, 'European Law Review' No. 1999;

Barnard C., *The Substantive Law of the EU. The Four Freedoms*, Oxford 2013;

Craig P., de Búrca G., *EU Law. Text, Cases, and Materials*, Oxford 2015;

Davies G., *Freedom of Contract and the Horizontal Effect of Free Movement Law*, in: Leczykiewicz D., Weatherill S. (eds.), *The Involvement of EU Law in Private Law Relationships*, Oxford 2013;

Davies G., *Freedom of Contract and the Horizontal Effect of Free Movement Law*, in: Leczykiewicz D., Weatherill S. (eds.), *The Involvement of EU Law in Private Law Relationships*, Oxford 2013;

de Vries S.A., van Mastrigt R., *The Horizontal Direct Effect of the Four Freedoms: From a Hodgepodge of Cases to a Seamless Web of Judicial Protection in the EU Single Market?*, in: Bernitz U., Groussot X., Schulyok F. (eds.), *General Principles of EU Law and European Private Law*, Alphen aan den Rijn 2013;

Gerner-Beuerle C., *Shareholders between the Market and the State. The VW Law and other Interventions in the Market Economy*, 'Common Market Law Review' No. 2012;

Graber R., *Die unmittelbare Drittwirkung der Grundfreiheiten. Eine Untersuchung anhand einer Auslegung des EG-Vertrages, der Rechtsprechung des Gerichtshofes und der Folgen einer angenommenen unmittelbaren Drittwirkung*, Munich 2002;

Hartkamp A.S., *"Horizontal Effects" (or "Effects in Relationships between Individuals") of EU Law*, in: Hartkamp A.S., Sieburgh C.H., Keus L.A.D., Kortmann J.S. (eds.), *The Influence of EU law on Private Law*, Volume 81-I, Deventer 2014;

Jaensch M., *Die unmittelbare Drittwirkung der Grundfreiheiten. Untersuchung der Verpflichtung von Privatpersonen durch Art. 30, 48, 52, 59, 73b EGV*, Baden-Baden 1997;

Karayigit M.T., *The horizontal effect of the free movement provisions*, 'Maastricht Journal' No. 2001;

Kloepfer M., Greve H., *Zur Drittwirkung der Warenverkehrsfreiheit – Die horizontale Wirkung der Warenverkehrsfreiheit am Beispiel der technischen Regelsetzung*, 'Deutsches Verwaltungsblatt' No. 2013;

Krenn C., *A Missing Piece in the Horizontal Effect 'Jigsaw': Horizontal Direct Effect and the Free Movement of Goods*, 'Common Market Law Review' No. 2012;

Krzeminska-Vamvaka J., *Horizontal effect of fundamental rights and freedoms— much ado about nothing? German, Polish and EU theories compared after Viking Line*, 'Jean Monnet Working Paper' No. 11/2009;

Leczykiewicz D., *Horizontal application of the Charter of Fundamental rights*, 'European Law Review' No. 2013;

Löwisch S., *Die horizontale Direktwirkung der Europäischen Grundfreiheiten. Zur Frage der unmittelbaren Verpflichtung Privater durch die Grundfreiheiten des EG-Vertrages*, Baden-Baden 2009;

Müller-Graff P.Ch., *Die horizontale Direktwirkung der Grundfreiheiten*, 'Europarecht' No. 1/2014;

Pescatore P., *"The Doctrine of "Direct Effect": An Infant Disease of Community Law"*, 'European Law Review' No. 1983;

Prechal S., *Directives in EC law*, 2nd edition, Oxford 2005;

Reich N., *Free Movement v. Social Rights in an Enlarged Union – the Laval and Viking Cases before the ECJ*, 'Germal Law Journal' No. 2008;

Ringe W.G., *Company Law and Free Movement of Capital*, 'Cambridge Law Journal', No. 69(2)/2010;

Schaefer D., *Die unmittelbare Wirkung des Verbots de nichttarifären Handelshemmnisse (Article 30 EWGV) in den Rechtsbeziehungen zwischen Privaten. Probleme der horizontalen unmittelbaren Wirkung des Gemeinschaftsrechts, gezeigt am Beispiel des Article 30 EWGV*, Frankfurt am Main 1987;

Schepel H., *The Enforcement of EC Law in Contractual Relations: Case Studies in How Not to 'Constitutionalize' Private Law*, 'European Review of Private Law' Issue 5 No. 12/2004;

Schepel H.W., *Constitutionalising the Market, Marketising the Constitution, and to Tell the Difference: On the Horizontal Application of the Free Movement Provisions in EU Law*, 'European Law Journal' No. 18/2012;

Schmahl S., Jung F., *Horizontale Drittwirkung der Warenverkehrsfreiheit?*, 'Neue Zeitschrift für Verwaltungsrecht' No. 2013;

Shuibhne N.N., *Settling dust? Reflections on the Judgments in Viking and Laval*, 'European Business Law Review' No. 2010;

Shuibhne N.N., *The Coherence of EU Free Movement Law. Constitutional Responsibility and the Court of Justice*, Oxford 2013;

Sieburgh C.H., *General principles and the Charter in private law relationships. Constructive and critical input from private law*, in: Bernitz U., Groussot X., Schulyok F. (eds.), *General Principles of EU Law and European Private Law*, Alphen aan den Rijn 2013;

Snell J., *Private Parties and the Free Movement of Goods and Services*, in: Andenas M., Roth W.H. (eds.), *Services and Free Movement in EU Law*, Oxford 2003;

Snell R.J., *Goods and Services in EC Law: A Study of the Relationship Between the Freedoms*, Oxford 2002;

Timmermans Ch., *Horizontal Effect/Indirect Effect or Direct/Indirect Horizontal Effect: What's in a Name?*, 'European Review of Private Law' No. 3–4/2016;

van den Bogaert C.S.G., *Horizontality: The Court Attacks?*, in: Barnard C., Scott J. (eds.), *The Legal Foundations of the Single market: Unpacking the Premises*, Oxford 2002;

van Gestel R., Micklitz H.W., *European integration through standardization: How judicial review is breaking down the club house of private standardization bodies*, 'Common Market Law Review' No. 2013;

van Harten H., Nauta T., *Towards horizontal direct effect for the free movement of goods? Comment on Fra.bo*, 'European Law Review' No. 2013;

van Leuken R.W.E., *Direct Horizontal Effect of the Fundamental Freedoms*, in: Hartkamp A.S., Sieburgh C.H., Keus L.A.D., Kortmann J.S. (eds.), *The Influence of EU law on Private Law*, Volume 81-I, Deventer 2014;

van Leuken R.W.E., *Rechtsverhoudingen tussen particulieren en de verdragsrechtelijke verkeersverijheden. Directe horizontale werking van de vrijverkeerbepalingen in het VWEU*, Deventer 2015;

van Leuken R.W.E., *The Internal Market Principle and Private Law*, in: Hartkamp A.S., Sieburgh C.H., Keus L.A.D., Kortmann J.S. (eds.), *The Influence of EU law on Private Law*, Volume 81-I, Deventer 2014;

Weatherill S., *The Elusive Character of Private Autonomy in EU Law*, in: *The Involvement of EU Law in Private Law Relationships*, Oxford 2013;

Wróbel A., Miąsik D., Półtorak N. (eds.), *Traktat o Funkcjonowaniu Unii Europejskiej. Komentarz*, Warsaw 2012;

Wyatt D., *Horizontal Effect of Fundamental Freedoms and the Right to Equality after Viking and Mangold, and the Implications for Community Competence*, 'Croatian Yearbook of European Law and Policy' No. 4/2008.

Judgments

ECJ Judgment of 11 July 1974 in case 8/74 *Procureur du Roi v Benoît and Gustave Dassonville*, ECLI:EU:C:1974:82;

ECJ Judgment of 12 December 1974 in case 36/74 *B.N.O. Walrave and L.J.N. Koch v Association Union cycliste internationale, Koninklijke Nederlandsche Wielren Unie and Federación Española Ciclismo*, ECLI:EU:C:1974:140;

ECJ Judgment of 8 April 1976 in case 43/75 *Gabrielle Defrenne v Société anonyme belge de navigation aérienne Sabena*, ECLI:EU:C:1976:56;

ECJ Judgment of 14 July 1976 in case 13/76 *Gaetano Donà v Mario Mantero*, ECLI:EU:C:1976:115;

ECJ Judgment of 9 June 1977 in case 90/76 *Ufficio Henry van Ameyde v S.r.l. Ufficio centrale italiano di assistenza assicurativa automobilisti in circolazione internazionale (UCI)*, ECLI:EU:C:1977:101;

ECJ Judgment of 22 January 1981 in case C-58/80 *Dansk Supermarked A/S v A/S Imerco*, ECLI:EU:C:1981:17;

ECJ Judgment of 24 November 1982 in case 249/81 *Commission of the European Communities v Ireland*, ECLI:EU:C:1982:402;

ECJ Judgment of 13 December 1983 in case 222/82 *Apple and Pear Development Council v K.J. Lewis Ltd and others (Buy Irish)*, ECLI:EU:C:1983:370;

ECJ Judgment of 5 April 1984 in joined cases 177/82 and 178/82 *Criminal proceedings against Jan van de Haar and Kaveka de Meern BV Van der Haar*, ECLI:EU:C:1984:144; ECJ Judgment of 1 October 1987 in case 311/85 *Vereniging van Vlaamse Reisbureaus v. ASBL Sociale Dienst van de Plaatselijke en Gewestelijke Overheidsdiensten*, ECLI:EU:C:1987:418;

ECJ Judgment of 6 November 1984 in case 177/83 *Th. Kohl KG v. Ringelhan & Rennett SA and Ringelhan Einrichtungs GmbH*, ECLI:EU:C:1984:334;

ECJ Judgment of 13 December 1984 in case C-251/83, *Eberhard Haug-Adrion v Frankfurter Versicherungs-AG*, ECLI:EU:C:1984:397;

ECJ Judgment of 18 May 1989 in joined cases 266 and 267/87 *The Queen v Royal Pharmaceutical Society of Great Britain, ex parte Association of Pharmaceutical Importers and others*, ECLI:EU:C:1989:2055;

ECJ Judgment of 24 November 1993 in joined cases C-267/91 and C-268/91 *Criminal proceedings against Bernard Keck and Daniel Mithouard*, ECLI:EU:C:1993:905;

ECJ Judgment of 14 December 1995 in joined cases C-163/94, C-165/94 and C-250/94, *Criminal proceedings against Lucas Emilio Sanz de Lera, Raimundo Díaz Jiménez and Figen Kapanoglu*, ECLI:EU:C:1995:451;

ECJ Judgment of 9 December 1997 in case C-265/95 *Commission of the European Communities v French Republic*, ECLI:EU:C:1997:595;

ECJ Judgment of 11 April 2000 in joined cases C-51/96 and C-191/97 *Christelle Deliège v Ligue francophone de judo et disciplines associées ASBL, Ligue belge de judo ASBL, Union européenne de judo (C-51/96) and François Pacquée (C-191/97)*, ECLI:EU:C:2000:199;

ECJ Judgment of 13 April 2000 in case C-176/96 *Jyri Lehtonen and Castors Canada Dry Namur-Braine ASBL v Fédération royale belge des sociétés de basket-ball ASBL (FRBSB)*, ECLI:EU:C:2000:201;

ECJ Judgment of 6 June 2000 in case C-281/98 *Roman Angonese v. Cassa di Risparmio di Bolzano SpA*, ECLI:EU:C:2000:296;

ECJ Judgment of 26 September 2000 in case C-478/98 *Commission of the European Communities v Kingdom of Belgium*, ECLI:EU:C:2000:497;

ECJ Judgment of 19 February 2002 in case C-309/99, *J. C. J. Wouters, J. W. Savelbergh and Price Waterhouse Belastingadviseurs BV v Algemene Raad van de Nederlandse Orde van Advocaten*, ECLI:EU:C:2002:98;

ECJ Judgment of 6 June 2002 in case C-159/00 *Sapod Audic v. Eco-Emballages SA.*, ECLI:EU:C:2002:343;

ECJ Judgment of 6 June 2002 in case C-159/00 *Sapod Audic v. Eco-Emballages SA.*, ECLI:EU:C:2002:343;

ECJ Judgment of 13 May 2003 in case C-98/01 *Commission of the European Communities v United Kingdom of Great Britain and Northern Ireland*, CLI:EU:C:2003:273;

ECJ Judgment of 12 June 2003 in case C-112/00 *Eugen Schmidberger, Internationale Transporte und Planzüge v Republik Österreich*, ECLI:EU:C:2003:333;

ECJ Judgment of 22 November 2005 in case C-144/04 *Werner Mangold v Rüdiger Helm*, ECLI:EU:C:2005:709;

ECJ Judgment of 17 April 2007 in case C-470/03 *A.G.M.-COS.MET Srl v Suomen valtio and Tarmo Lehtinen*, ECLI:EU:C:2007:213;

ECJ Judgment of 23 October 2007 in case C-112/05 *Commission of the European Communities v Federal Republic of Germany*, ECLI:EU:C:2007:623;

ECJ Judgment of 11 December 2007 in case C-438/05 *International Transport Workers' Federation and Finnish Seamen's Union v Viking Line ABP and OÜ Viking Line Eesti*, CLI:EU:C:2007:772;

ECJ Judgment of 18 December 2007 in case C-341/05 *Laval un Partneri Ltd v. Svenska Byggnadsarbetareförbundet and Others*, CLI:EU:C:2007:809;

ECJ Judgment of 14 July 2008 in case C-94/07 *Andrea Raccanelli v Max-Planck-Gesellschaft zur Förderung der Wissenschaften eV.*, ECLI:EU:C:2008:425;

ECJ Judgment of 10 February 2009 in case C-110/05 *Commission of the European Communities v Italian Republic*, ECLI:EU:C:2009:66;

ECJ Judgment of 2 December 2010 in case C-108/09 *Ker-Optika bt v ÀNTSZ Dél-dunántúli Regionális Intézete*, ECLI:EU:C:2010:725;

ECJ Judgment of 21 June 2012 in case C-5/11 *Criminal proceedings against Titus Alexander Jochen Donner*, ECLI:EU:C:2012:370;

ECJ Judgment of 28 June 2012 in case C-172/11 *Georges Erny v Daimler AG - Werk Wörth*, ECLI:EU:C:2012:399;

ECJ Judgment of 12 July 2012 in case C-171/11 *Fra.bo SpA v Deutsche Vereinigung des Gas- und Wasserfaches eV (DVGW) – Technisch-Wissenschaftlicher Verein*, ECLI:EU:C:2012:453;

ECJ Judgement of 16 April 2013 in case C-202/11 *Anton Las v PSA Antwerp NV*, ECLI:EU:C:2013:239;

ECJ Judgment of 23 October 2013 in case C-95/12 *European Commission v Federal Republic of Germany*, ECLI:EU:C:2013:676.

Abbreviations

ECJ – European Court of Justice, Court of Justice of the European Union;

EU – European Union;

TFEU – Treaty on the Functioning of the European Union (consolidated version Official Journal of the European Union C 326 of 26 October 2012, p. 47).

Prof. Maciej Mataczyński

Adam Mickiewicz University in Poznań

Intuitive and counterintuitive reasons for the refusal to recognize horizontal effect of free movement of capital

Abstract: Pursuant to the ECJ case law, 'restrictions' in the meaning of Article 63(1) TFEU are national measures that are likely to prevent or limit the acquisition of shares in the undertakings concerned or to deter investors of other member states from investing in their capital. However, so far the proceedings pending before the European Commission in the context of Article 258 TFEU and subsequent judgments of the Tribunal have pertained only to national law of the member states (and, in exceptional cases, to articles of association adopted by the state being the sole or the dominant shareholder) granting benefits to such states. Although for more than a decade researchers have been wondering whether the lack of judgments regarding entities other than states is a mere consequence of the fact that no such cases have been submitted by the Commission, and despite the hypotheses which extend the concept of the freedom of capital movements to cover all company law provisions that may deter a person from investing in shares, with all its consequences, as of today there are no normative grounds to conclude that such an interpretation would be correct. This article lists and elaborates arguments leading to refusal to grant horizontal effect to the free movement of capital.

Key words: Treaty on functioning of European Union, freedoms, company law, horizontal effect

1. Preliminaries

The preceding articles elaborated on the importance that the ECJ ascribes to Art. 63 TFEU and the admissibility of reliance on treaty norms that enshrine specific freedoms in the context of horizontal relationships. The crucial issue for the analysis of the impact of Treaty freedoms on the takeover of public companies is whether such freedoms can modify national law, and corporate law in particular, in EU member states. What is more, if such modifications do occur, we need to delineate their extent and scrutinize their effects with respect to public law. For the purpose of this article, I leave aside the entire area regarding the impact of the freedom of capital movement (and the freedom of establishment) on privileges in companies enjoyed by the state. These issues have already been discussed in detail both in international[1] and Polish literature[2]. What is more, a research project that resulted in this publication also involved the development of a commentary dedicated entirely to this topic[3]. Basic theses elaborated by the ECJ in the early 2000s continue to be valid also today. The development in the ECJ case law has focused on specific practical matters relating to the application of the general rule, rather than modifications to the rule as such. In consequence, I will dedicate the space below to the arguments that speak against recognizing horizontal effect of the freedom of capital movement (and the freedom of establishment). I have already presented this thesis in my previous work[4] and, although a decade has passed since it was published, I believe that the legal framework has not changed, though a number of minor arguments that have been raised in the discussion so far deserve more elaboration.

2. The scope of freedom of movement of capital

Article 63 TFEU provides that 'all restrictions on the movement of capital between Member States and between Member States and third countries shall be prohibited'. The term 'movement of capital' has not been defined in the Treaty. In view of the ECJ case law, this term should be interpreted using the nomenclature in Annex No. 1 to the directive 88/361[5]. This directive is no longer in force, yet in the judgement referred to above, as in many decisions issued afterwards, the ECJ has confirmed that the specification of this term laid down in the directive remains valid and may be used for the purpose of interpretation of Article 63 TFEU[6]. Pursuant to the glossary provided in Annex No. 1 to the directive 88/361, capital movements include, among other things, direct investments and operations in securities normally dealt in on the capital market – the so-called portfolio

---

1   See W.G. Ringe, *Company Law and Free Movement of Capital*, 'Cambridge Law Journal' Vol. 69, No. 2/2010, p. 382.
2   M. Mataczyński, *Swoboda przepływu kapitału a złota akcja Skarbu Państwa*, Warsaw 2007.
3   M. Mataczyński (ed.), *Komentarz do ustawy z 24 lipca 2015 r. o ochronie niektórych inwestycji*, Warsaw 2016.
4   M. Mataczyński, *Swoboda…*, pp. 135 et seq.
5   Council directive of 24 June 1988 for the implementation of Article 67 of the Treaty (Official Journal of the European Communities L 178 of 8 July 1988, p. 5).
6   ECJ Judgement of 12 June 2003 in case C-222/97, *Trummer and Mayer*, ECLI:EU:C:1999:143, para 21.

investments[7]. Unlike in the case of the freedom of establishment, the movement of capital does not depend on running permanent activity abroad – the intent to acquire shares in a company in another state is sufficient[8]. Since capital markets are open to investors from other states, it is justified to assume that the sole fact that shares in a company are offered publicly results in the inclusion of all related provisions into the scope of application of the discussed freedom[9].

The scopes of the application of the freedom of capital movement and the freedom of establishment coincide[10]. In view of the latest ECJ case law, the scope of application of the freedom of establishment includes national law applicable to a case where a national of an EU member state holds a stake in the capital of a company established in a another member state big enough to exert influence on the company's decisions and determine its activities[11]. On the other hand, the freedom of movement of capital concerns the provisions applicable to shareholders holding a stake in a company insufficient to exercise full control[12], but with the purpose of establishing or maintaining lasting and direct links between the persons providing the capital and the undertakings to which that capital is made available in order to carry out an economic activity[13]. In the first case, the conditions for the application of both freedoms being discussed are met jointly, since the provisions also fall within the scope of the freedom of capital movement.

---

7   M. Mataczyński, in: A. Wróbel, D. Miąsik, N. Półtorak (eds.), *Traktat o Funkcjonowaniu Unii Europejskiej. Komentarz*, Vol. 1, Warsaw 2012, pp. 986–990.

8   W.G. Ringe, *Company Law...*, p. 381.

9   S. Grundmann, *Golden Shares – State Control in Privatised Companies: Comparative Law, European Law and Policy Aspects*, 'EUREDIA – European Banking and Financial Law Journal' No. 4/2001–2002, p. 657. See also M. Mataczyński, *Swoboda przepływu...*, p. 74.

10 M. Mataczyński, in: A. Wróbel, D. Miąsik, N. Półtorak (eds.), *Traktat...* Vol. 1, p. 983.

11 ECJ Judgement of 26 March 2009 in case C-326/07, *European Commission v Italy*, ECLI:EU:U:2009:193, para 34. See also M. Mataczyński, in: A. Wróbel, D. Miąsik, N. Półtorak (eds.), *Traktat...* Vol. 1, p. 983.

12 The determination of the control threshold in a company depends on the facts of a specific case – for instance, the dilution of shareholding, statutory restrictions in exercising the right to vote, etc. EU law offers no clear-cut solution in this respect. It is only Article 5 of the directive of the European Parliament and the Council of 21 April 2004 (2004/25/EC) on takeover bids (Official Journal of the European Community L 142 of 30 April 2004, p. 12), i.e. the so-called Takeover Directive, that introduces the obligation to announce a call in order to take over control of a company. When implementing the directive, most member states set this threshold in the range between 30 and 33% of the total number of votes.

13 ECJ Judgment C-326/07, *European Commission v Italy*, para 35.

However, in such a case the ECJ – as explicitly stated in its judgements – will give priority to the freedom of establishment[14]. However, the ECJ is not consistent in this respect[15]. As aptly emphasized in legal literature, transactions aimed at taking control of a company are special forms of direct investments[16]. The borderline between a takeover of control and active participation in company management is not always pronounced. Portfolio investments, defined by the ECJ as the acquisition of shares on the capital market with the sole purpose of making a financial investment without any intention to influence the management and control of the undertaking[17], constitute a separate category. In case law and literature, such investments are deemed to be covered by the scope of the freedom of capital movement[18].

3. The concept of a restriction of freedom

Pursuant to the ECJ case law, 'restrictions' in the meaning of Article 63(1) TFEU are national measures that are likely to prevent or limit the acquisition of shares in the undertakings concerned or to deter investors of other member states from investing in their capital[19]. However, so far the proceedings pending before the European Commission in the context of Article 258 TFEU and subsequent judgements of the Tribunal have pertained only to the national law of the member states (and, in exceptional cases, to articles of association adopted by the state being the sole or the dominant shareholder[20]) granting benefits to such states. Although for more than a decade Polish[21] and European[22] researchers have been

---

14 ECJ Judgment C-326/07, *European Commission v Italy*, para 39.

15 ECJ Judgment of 18 May 2006 in case C-122/05, *European Commission v Italy*, ECLI:EU:C:2006:336, referred to provisions aimed at preventing takeovers of a company. It is and was examined as a classic example of a case concerning restrictions to the free movement of capital.

16 W.G. Ringe, *Company Law...*, p. 382.

17 ECJ Judgment of 28 September 2006 in joint cases C-282/04 and 283–04, *European Commission v The Netherlands*, ECLI:EU:C:2006:608, para 19.

18 W.G. Ringe, *Company Law...*, p. 382.

19 ECJ Judgment *European Commission v The Netherlands*, para 20.

20 ECJ Judgment *European Commission v The Netherlands*, para 22.

21 M. Mataczyński, *Czy swoboda przepływu kapitału wywiera horyzontalny skutek? Przyczynek do dyskusji nad wpływem tej swobody na prawo spółek*, in: J. Kruczalak-Jankowska (ed.) *Wpływ europeizacji prawa na instytucje prawa handlowego*, Warsaw 2013, pp. 109–120.

22 For a review of literature see W.G. Ringe, *Company Law...*, p. 382.

wondering whether the lack of judgements regarding entities other than states is a mere consequence of the fact that no such cases have been submitted by the Commission, and despite the hypotheses which extend the concept of the freedom of capital movement to cover all company law provisions that may deter a person from investing in shares, with all its consequences[23], as of today there have been no normative grounds to conclude that such an interpretation would be correct.

4. Why refuse HE of FC? State sovereignty. Democratic legitimacy. Proper division of competence between EU and Member States. Who is the actual addressee of Treaty freedoms? 'Historical', original interpretation of the Treaty: 'What would Mrs. Spaak and de Gasperi think'?

In this section I would like to discuss a category of reasons that, concisely speaking, refer to a legislator's intent, including the specific approach of member states which assume obligations under international agreements, with all subsequent amendments, as their signatories. The European Union is an international organization whose scope of competence is based on the so-called attributed powers principle. In other words, the European Union can act only within the scope in which it has been authorized to do so by member states. From the perspective of public international law, these states are the original subjects of international law, while international organizations enjoy secondary/derivative subjectivity. It means that these organisations are created by member states that define the scope of their operations. As the German Constitutional Court put it in one of its judgements, member states remain the Masters of the Treaties ('*Herren des Vertrages*'). The foregoing rules find their reflection in the provisions of the treaties. Pursuant to Article 5.1 TEU 'the limits of Union competences are governed by the principle of conferral'. Meanwhile, Article 5.2 TEU provides that 'under the principle of conferral, the Union shall act only within the limits of the competences conferred upon it by the Member States in the Treaties to attain the objectives set out therein. Competences not conferred upon the Union in the Treaties remain

---

23   '(…) the rules of general company law that have been enacted by legislation and do not necessarily secure any prerogatives for the State and do not benefit the State in any other way, but merely shape the legal relations between private persons can potentially be subject to the free movement of capital. This conclusion can be reached from a consistent extrapolation of the Court's interpretation of the fundamental freedoms'. W.G. Ringe, *Company Law...*, p. 403.

with the Member States'. The scope of competence conferred on the Union has been defined in the TFEU.

Pursuant to Article 4(2)(a) TFEU, the competence with respect to the internal market is shared between the European Union and the Member States. Pursuant to Article 26(2) TFEU, the internal market comprises an area without internal frontiers in which the free movement of goods, persons, services and capital is ensured in accordance with the provisions of the Treaties.

Article 2(2) TFEU provides that when the Treaties confer on the Union a competence shared with the Member States in a specific area, the Union and the Member States may legislate and adopt legally binding acts in that area. The Member States exercise their competence to the extent that the Union has not exercised its competence. The Member States again exercise their competence to the extent that the Union has decided to cease exercising its competence.

Importantly, it would be a distortion of the Treaty drafters' intent if the Union vested the competence to interfere with private law relationships in the area of the internal market in the ECJ, as the internal market is supposed to be free from authoritative interference by the states. The foregoing should not be interpreted as my support for originalism, that is the observance of the strict historic interpretation of an act of law giving preference to the intent of the original legislator, in the political-sociological sense (specific people involved in the legislative process at that time and social groups represented by them). Obviously, more than half a century of the ECJ case law has fundamentally transformed the original text and its understanding, even if the wording of certain provisions has remained intact. It does not mean, however, that today an interpreter enjoys complete freedom, including the freedom to disregard the linguistic wording of the text and its systemic coherence. When it comes to the latter, the internal market regime, as a rule, was supposed to prevent the introduction of restrictions on business dealings by member states (such as customs, quantitative restrictions and measures having equivalent effect to quantitative restrictions in the trade in goods, rationing of the access to the labour market, self-employment, services and establishment, rationing of capital transactions). Meanwhile, the restrictions on business dealings that stem from the operation of private entities, undertakings, were to be waived by the competition protection regime, exemplified by a ban on collusive price fixing or dominant position abuse. In this model, the provisions on freedoms, as a rule, were not meant to be applicable to undertakings as such.

As M. Taborowski aptly points out, the issue of horizontal effectiveness of freedoms has evolved from two interpretative currents[24]. The first, more influential, though chronologically posterior one, here referred to as the *Bosman*[25] case current, built on the concept of direct effectiveness of the Treaty freedoms that has already existed in the case law, with the *Marshall*[26] case being its most prominent manifestation. Its core premise is a broad understanding of the term 'Member State'. In consequence, the internal market freedoms are applicable to the activity of states, and they apply to private entities only exceptionally when, due to the scale of their operations or their actual impact (e.g. UEFA rules that lay down the transfer mechanism applicable to all professional football players in Europe), a private entity operates as if it were a state. It can be concluded that this interpretative current is generally consistent with the systemic classification of provisions into Title Ia and Title VII in the third part of the Treaty. However, the word 'generally' is of key importance here, because, despite its consistency, the current opens the door to extending the applicability of regulations on freedoms to private entities. In this case, the role of the conflict of laws rule is performed by the quantitative criterion, defined as the scale of impact that results in a quasi-state type of operations. However, this criterion cannot be measured by objective units. EU member states differ in size. Rules or other internal legislation adopted by a German postal services provider *ex definitione* have a broader scope of impact than Cypriot legislation. Obviously, statutes by large European public companies, as W.G. Ringe[27], is right to note, influence significant areas of business operations, including human behaviour, often in a manner that significantly goes beyond a single state. Does it mean, though, that from the legal perspective they should be treated as states? We should bear in mind that the only certainty that we arrive at in this way is a significant empowerment of the arbitrary authority of the ECJ, which, as the only one, will be competent to decide which rules are of quasi-state nature, and which are not. Obviously, the ECJ, just as any skilful playwright, always reserves the right

---

24 M. Taborowski, *Horizontal direct effect of EU internal market freedoms – current status*, in: M. Mataczyński (ed.), *Takeover of public company as a mode of exercising EU Treaty freedoms*, Warsaw 2017.

25 ECJ Judgment of 15 December 1995 in case C-415/93, *Union royale belge des sociétés de football association ASBL v Jean-Marc Bosman, Royal club liégeois SA v Jean-Marc Bosman and others and Union des associations européennes de football (UEFA) v Jean-Marc Bosman*, ECLI:EU:C:1995:463.

26 ECJ Judgment of 26 February 1986 in case C-152/84, *M. H. Marshall v Southampton and South-West Hampshire Area Health Authority (Teaching)*, ECLI:EU:C:1986:84.

27 W.G. Ringe, *Company Law…*, p. 382.

to surprise its audience and decide that also a single announcement of an open vacancy in a provincial Italian bank enjoys such a status[28].

The second current, which – as I have mentioned above – is antecedent to the *Bosman* one, derives from the *Defrenne*[29] case and concerns a substantially different aspect of direct effectiveness of the Treaty norms in horizontal relationships (i.e. relationships between private entities). In other words, it pertains to the binding force of obligations imposed by a Treaty rule with respect to private entities. In the *Defrenne* case, this – basically technical – issue of the hierarchy of the sources of law coincided with an axiological challenge to enforce the actual implementation of the ban on discrimination (in general) and a ban on discrimination due to gender – or, precisely speaking, the ban on the discrimination of women in employment relationships – in the European Community at that time. As a result, in that case we deal with a triple *partie faible*: a person discriminated against – as a woman and as an employee. It is difficult to separate the reasoning concerning the technical issue (direct effectiveness of Treaty norms in horizontal relationships) from the duty to further the right cause. As other rulings, and in particular as the judgement in the *Kücükdeveci* case has shown, the ECJ endeavours in this respect are not always successful[30]. However, at this point we should clarify that from the perspective of the Polish Constitution the issue of direct effectiveness of the Treaty norms in horizontal relationships is entirely uncontroversial. Pursuant to Article 91(2) of the Constitution, 'an international agreement ratified upon prior consent granted by statue shall have precedence over statutes if such an agreement cannot be reconciled with the provisions of such statutes'[31]. In consequence, a Treaty rule can create obligations in private law relationships since on the grounds of the Constitution it is not only equal to a statute but prevails over it. In this respect, the Polish systemic regulation is not exceptional, but rather reflects a widespread

---

28 ECJ Judgment of 6 June 2000 in case C-281/98, *Roman Angonese v. Cassa di Risparmio di Bolzano SpA*, ECLI:EU:C:2000:296.

29 ECJ Judgment of 8 April 1976 in case C-43/75, *Gabrielle Defrenne v Société anonyme belge de navigation aérienne Sabena*, ECLI:EU:C:1976:56.

30 ECJ Judgment of 19 January 2010 in case C-555/07 *Seda Kücükdeveci v. Swedex GmbH & Co KG* ECLI:EU:C:2010:21. I am referring to a particularly bold interpretation of the TFEU and deducing a direct effect of the prohibition of discrimination due to age as an (unwritten) general rule of the EU law. For a critical discussion of this judgement see M. de Mol, *Kücükdeveci: Mangold Revisited – Horizontal Direct Effect of a General Principle of EU Law*, 'European Constututional Law Review' No. 6/2010, pp. 293–308.

31 For a review of literature see A. Capik, A. Łazowski, in: M. Safjan, L. Bosek (eds.), *Konstytucja. Komentarz*, Vol. II, commentary to Art. 91, Warsaw 2016, pp. 163–168.

European standard. To sum up this portion of the discussion, let us state that the first of the two analysed legal currents inadvertently results in arbitrariness, while the other one – due to systemic regulations – is no longer valid.

Yet another reason against the recognition of horizontal effect of the freedom of capital movement is the importance of legal certainty, and its impact on private law relationships in particular. The recognition of horizontal effect would involve a dramatic increase in instability with respect to the binding power and interpretation of basic corporate law institutions. The effectiveness of any of them (such as a squeeze-out, for instance) could be questioned, since it may be argued that their existence discourages minority shareholders from investing in their shares.

I must admit that I have not investigated the issue of the certainty or predictability of law as a value in the European Union. I have no doubt that the rule of the state of law on which the Union is based, as explicitly declared in Article 2 TEU, comprises a detailed directive to shape the legal system in such a way so that the target groups to which specific rules are addressed are not taken by surprise and that no uncertainty is introduced by way of unstable case law. Related problems include the potential scale of modifications (all the institutions of corporate law and capital market law pertaining to public companies?) and the vagueness of the model ('deterring investors from investing'). Disregarding the axiological or normative layer, such an activity would be counterproductive in the age of regulatory competition, and would potentially entice decision makers to move their companies to jurisdictions perceived as more stable, including Switzerland, Norway or the United States (and soon also the United Kingdom). One of the objectives of the European legislator is to make the European Union attractive to investors by way of improving the regulatory environment. Making the effectiveness of shareholders' vested rights dependent on their compliance with horizontal effect of the freedom of establishment or the freedom of capital movement is bound to spur a knee-jerk reaction among entrepreneurs who will vote 'with their feet' by moving the seats of their companies to other states.

On top of this, one should consider the protection of previously acquired rights. As a rule, the interpretation of the EU law by the ECJ has *ex tunc* effect and provides explanation with regard to the correct understanding of a norm as from its effective date, and not from the date of the relevant ruling[32]. Only in exceptional

---

32 ECJ Judgment of 27 March 1980 in case C-61/79, *Amministrazione delle finanze dello Stato v Denkavit italiana Srl*, ECLI:EU:C:1980:100, para 16: 'The interpretation which, in the exercise of the jurisdiction conferred upon it by Article 177 (now 234), the Court of Justice gives to a rule of Community law clarifies and defines where necessary the meaning and scope of that rule as it must be or ought to have been understood and

situations can the ECJ restrict the temporal effectiveness of its judgement[33]. In consequence, the unclear, but potentially very vast application scope of this freedom would also extend to legal relationships established before this direction in the ECJ case law developed. This in turn could result in depriving parties of their rights (e.g. voting preference) acquired before. Let us recall a similar problem that appeared at the turn of the 20th and 21st century in the course of legislative works on the Takeover Directive[34]. The directive introduced a number of rules, including the so-called breakthrough rule[35]. It involves repealing all preference with respect to voting and other measures that prevent a shareholder who has acquired more than 75% shares in the company from taking over full control of that company. Some member states, including Sweden, have pointed out that the breakthrough rule, if introduced in that form, could violate the right to ownership protection enshrined in those states' constitutions[36]. Obviously, in this case ownership is interpreted broadly, from the constitutional law perspective[37]. In this case the protected rights would be the subjective rights of Swedish public company shareholders to exercise a specific number of votes under a share, to exercise the veto right, etc. In the opinion of the Swedish government, these rights could be assigned a specific material value, and depriving shareholders of them by way of secondary legislation could give raise to claims brought by such shareholders. Finally, the discussion ended with reducing the breakthrough rule to one of the options that can, but do not have to be adopted by member states (or specific companies)[38].

---

applied from the time of its coming into force. It follows that the rule as thus interpreted may, and must, be applied by the courts even to legal relationships arising and established before the judgment ruling on the request for interpretation, provided that in other respects the conditions enabling an action relating to the application of that rule to be brought before the courts having jurisdiction, are satisfied'.

33 ECJ Judgment *Sabena*; ECJ Judgment of 20 September 2001 in case C-184/99, *Rudy Grzelczyk v Centre public d'aide sociale d'Ottignies-Louvain-la-Neuve*, ECLI:EU:C:2001:458, para 53.

34 Finally, the works culminated with the adoption of the Takeover Directive.

35 Currently governed by Article 11 of the Takeover Directive.

36 M. Mataczyński, *Swoboda...*, p. 259.

37 For a review of literature see K. Zaradkiewicz, in: M. Safjan, L. Bosek (eds.), *Konstytucja...*, Vol. II, commentary to Art. 64, pp. 1457–1463.

38 According to Art. 12 of the Takeover Directive (Optional arrangements) 'Member States may reserve the right not to require companies as referred to in Article 1(1) which have their registered offices within their territories to apply Article 9(2) and (3) and/or Article 11'.

We should bear in mind that this situation pertained to legislative work on secondary legislation, with all the guarantees specific to this process, starting with the democratic legitimacy of the European Parliament, to broad social consultations instituted already at the stage of European Commission's proposal for EU legislation, to the involvement of the mass media, and finally to the possibility to review the adopted law from the perspective of the compliance of secondary legislation with acts having hierarchical precedence under Article 263 TFEU. All these security buffers would be missing if an analogous result were achieved by amending case law. In fact, it could be argued that such a path would actually reverse the outcomes brought about by the EU legislative process. The EU legislator introduced the rule (and breakthrough rule in particular), as an optional arrangement – a possibility that can be realized or not. Meanwhile, the ECJ, relying on a different reasoning, would make it mandatory. Such judicial decisions would expose the Court of Justice of European Union to accusations of judicial activism in the area where judicial restraint is a particularly valued virtue.

In all, the outcome would be a violation of the relative autonomy of corporate law as a separate branch. Typically, norm-based arguments on the autonomy of a branch or discipline of law rely on a specific set of values that are particularly treasured in that branch or discipline, thereby distinguishing it from others. What is more, such a branch or discipline can have its own specific regulatory techniques or institutions of law that underscore its distinctive nature. Typically, they include argumentation in the scope of systemic, functional or teleological interpretation. Undoubtedly, in the area of corporate law and capital market law the certainty of law, as an element crucial to business transactions, is such a distinctive value. This branch of law usually governs legal relations in which an individual bond is secondary, and the area of key concern are anonymous, mass transactions. The predictability and typicality of investors' behaviour prevails over the consideration of individual, personal context (which is the cornerstone of family and guardianship law), even if it involves a right vested by a Treaty rule. Regulatory uncertainty is a sign of market frailty; this issue has already been discussed above. Obviously, arguments based on the regulatory autonomy of a branch of law have their weaknesses. They are often raised when other arguments are missing, in order to substantiate opinions which – if such an argument is not produced – seems to be patently *contra legem*. One example of such a discussion is a debate that has continued in Polish legal sciences for over a decade, on the status of rights to shares acquired by spouses whose property in marriage is governed by the joint marital property regime[39]. Numerous researchers specialising in corporate law (including the author of this article), motivated by the willingness to protect certainty and predictability of legal transactions, for years have resisted an explicit acknowledgement that rights under shares (like any other subjective rights) make part of such a joint marital regime. The reasoning mostly relied on the specificity and autonomy of corporate law with respect to family law. Meanwhile, the objective was to avoid doubts as to who a shareholder is, how their rights can be exercised and which corporate decisions require spouse's consent. However, I am positive that these weaknesses do not apply to the argumentation against horizontal effect of the freedom of establishment and the free movement of capital in corporate law. The EU legislator seems to share this view, since whenever it modifies this discipline in a major way, such changes take the form of secondary legislation: typically, directives or, more rarely, regulations. Finally, one should point out to the fact that the values protected by the 'ban on discouraging investors' are adequately protected by other legal mechanisms (e.g. one share one vote; takeover directive; various particular compromises in national law), that were specifically introduced by such secondary legislation. The reconstruction of the legal status with respect to broadly construed shareholder preference, taking account of the EU law and ECJ case law on the one hand and the national law of member states on the other, produces a sort of a compromise between the rule of proportionality of capital contribution and the authority in the company and the autonomy of founders and shareholders who enjoy a certain degree of freedom in drafting the statutes and establishing preference attached to rights under shares. Legal scholars justly claim that the form of the compromise suggests that member states have a narrower scope of discretion than private shareholders. Certain preferences, if vested in a state, can violate the freedoms in question, while remaining completely legal when vested in private entities. In the market game, a state is a special kind of player. It has a vast array of options to influence and shape the reality. A state may be a shareholder, but it is a subject of political power itself, holding related legislative and regulatory authority on top of this, the state has access to capital (practically unlimited when compared to private investors), related to the existing resources and creditworthiness. Obviously, a state-shareholder cannot (or at least should not) exert influence on a company using other means than those typical of shareholders. However, this existing, immense disproportionality can, to a

---

39 For most recent summary of the debate see A. Opalski, in: A. Opalski (ed.), *Kodeks spółek handlowych. Vol. IIIA. Spółka akcyjna. Commentary to Articles 301–392*, Warsaw 2016, pp. 735–741.

certain extent, balance out some (certainly not prohibitive) discrimination from the perspective of preferences enjoyed by a state in the capacity of a shareholder.

Lastly, Treaty derogations (Article 65 TFEU) and case-law exceptions called 'mandatory requirements of public interest' do not seem to be applicable to private persons (e.g. public security, public order, tax law observance, systemic oversight). Obviously, this claim is not absolute. As M. Taborowski aptly reminds, the ECJ also pointed out that, in principle, individual entities may – in a horizontal relation – cite exceptions to the freedoms which could restrict the established infringement, such as public policy, public security or public health[40]. In practice, however, to rely on these derogations would be highly burdensome. Private shareholders determine specific preferences primarily with their own private financial interest in mind. Meanwhile, in its case law the ECJ has consistently emphasised that in no way can the financial interests of a state justify any restrictions of freedoms. The property of a state is to satisfy a number of protection-worthy social needs and hence its axiological rationale is stronger than that of an individual investor. To deprive (in practice) individuals of the possibility of invoking justifications would lead to their discrimination.

Literature

de Mol M., *Kücükdeveci: Mangold Revisited – Horizontal Direct Effect of a General Principle of EU Law*, 'European Constitutional Law Review' No. 6/2010;

Grundmann S., *Golden Shares – State Control in Privatised Companies: Comparative Law, European Law and Policy Aspects*, 'EUREDIA – European Banking and Financial Law Journal' No. 4/2001–2002;

Mataczyński M. (ed.), *Komentarz do ustawy z 24 lipca 2015 r. o ochronie niektórych inwestycji*, Warsaw 2016;

Mataczyński M., *Czy swoboda przepływu kapitału wywiera horyzontalny skutek? Przyczynek do dyskusji nad wpływem tej swobody na prawo spółek*, in: J. Kruczalak-Jankowska (ed.) *Wpływ europeizacji prawa na instytucje prawa handlowego*, Warsaw 2013;

Mataczyński M., *Swoboda przepływu kapitału a złota akcja Skarbu Państwa*, Warsaw 2007;

Opalski A. (ed.), *Kodeks spółek handlowych. Vol. IIIA. Spółka akcyjna. Commentary to Articles 301–392*, Warsaw 2016;

---

40 M. Taborowski, *Horizontal…*; ECJ Judgment *Bosman*, paras. 85–86.

Ringe W.G., *Company Law and Free Movement of Capital*, 'Cambridge Law Journal' Vol. 69, No. 2/2010;

Safjan M., Bosek L. (eds.), *Konstytucja. Komentarz*, Vol. II, Warsaw 2016;

Taborowski M., *Horizontal direct effect of EU internal market freedoms – current status*, in: Mataczyński M. (ed.), *Takeover of public company as a mode of exercising EU Treaty freedoms*, Warsaw 2017;

Wróbel A., Miąsik D., Półtorak N. (eds.), *Traktat o Funkcjonowaniu Unii Europejskiej. Komentarz*, Vol. 1, Warsaw 2012.

Judgments

ECJ Judgment of 8 April 1976 in case C-43/75, *Gabrielle Defrenne v Société anonyme belge de navigation aérienne Sabena*, ECLI:EU:C:1976:56;

ECJ Judgment of 27 March 1980 in case C-61/79, *Amministrazione delle finanze dello Stato v Denkavit italiana Srl*, ECLI:EU:C:1980:100;

ECJ Judgment of 26 February 1986 in case C-152/84, *M. H. Marshall v Southampton and South-West Hampshire Area Health Authority (Teaching)*, ECLI:EU:C:1986:84;

ECJ Judgment of 15 December 1995 in case C-415/93, *Union royale belge des sociétés de football association ASBL v Jean-Marc Bosman, Royal club liégeois SA v Jean-Marc Bosman and others and Union des associations européennes de football (UEFA) v Jean-Marc Bosman*, ECLI:EU:C:1995:463;

ECJ Judgment of 6 June 2000 in case C-281/98, *Roman Angonese v. Cassa di Risparmio di Bolzano SpA*, ECLI:EU:C:2000:296;

ECJ Judgment of 20 September 2001 in case C-184/99, *Rudy Grzelczyk v Centre public d'aide sociale d'Ottignies-Louvain-la-Neuve*, ECLI:EU:C:2001:458;

ECJ Judgement of 12 June 2003 in case C-222/97, *Trummer and Mayer*, ECLI:EU:C:1999:143;

ECJ Judgment of 18 May 2006 in case C-122/05, *European Commission v Italy*, ECLI:EU:C:2006:336;

ECJ Judgment of 28 September 2006 in joint cases C-282/04 and 283–04, *European Commission v The Netherlands*, ECLI:EU:C:2006:608;

ECJ Judgement of 26 March 2009 in case C-326/07, *European Commission v Italy*, ECLI:EU:U:2009:193;

ECJ Judgment of 19 January 2010 in case C-555/07 *Seda Kücükdeveci v. Swedex GmbH & Co KG* ECLI:EU:C:2010:21.

Abbreviations

Constitution – the Constitution of the Republic of Poland (*Konstytucja Rzeczypospolitej Polskiej*) (Journal of Laws of 1997 No. 78, item 483, as amended);

ECJ – European Court of Justice, Court of Justice of the European Union;

EU – European Union;

Takeover Directive – Directive 2004/25/EC of the European Parliament and the Council of 21 April 2004 on takeover bids (Official Journal of the European Community L 310 of 30 April 2004, p. 12);

TEU – Treaty on European Union (consolidated version Official Journal of the European Union C 202 of 7 June 2016, p. 13);

TFEU – Treaty on the Functioning of the European Union (consolidated version Official Journal of the European Union C 326 of 26 October 2012, p. 47);

UEFA – Union of European Football Associations.

Prof. Tomasz Sójka

Faculty of Law and Administration, Adam Mickiewicz University in Poznań

Duties of a corporate board in the context of a takeover attempt

Abstract: This paper analyzes the duties of a corporate board in the context of a takeover attempt in Polish law. The closed corporate governance model that has dominated the Polish market resulted in a rather insignificant role that civil liability for failure to meet duties by the public company's board played in Polish case law. In the case of the Polish capital market, most takeovers are 'friendly' in nature due to the control exercised over Polish public companies by strategic investors.

When it comes to the adoption of reactive defence measures by company's board faced with a threat of a hostile takeover, Polish law remains relatively permissive. Polish company law does not reserve defence measures to the exclusive competence of the general meeting. At the same time the duties of a corporate board in this area are limited and their private law enforcement remains very poor. It does not however mean that corporate board enjoys unrestrained freedom in this respect.

The discussion below will focus on the basic rules of procedure followed by a corporate board facing a hostile takeover attempt.

Key words: civil liability, corporate board's duties, hostile takeover, public company

1. Introduction

The duties of a public company's board and civil liability for failure to meet them have never played an important role in Polish case law. This is a consequence of the closed corporate governance model that has dominated the Polish market. Polish public companies are usually controlled by strategic investors, whose shareholding interest often prevents any takeovers against dominant shareholder's intent and without the consent of the corporate bodies – management and supervisory boards – appointed by them. In consequence, in the case of the Polish capital market, most takeovers are 'friendly' in nature.

The specificity of the so-called hostile takeovers in the Polish context lies in the fact that not only are the management or supervisory boards on the defence, but they are also joined by the existing controlling shareholder or shareholders, who nevertheless do not enjoy a majority sufficient to prevent a takeover of control of the company[1]. In practice, we have observed in Poland certain defence strategies commonly known in other European markets, such as the acquisition of the company's own shares, the search for a 'friendly' bidder (white knight defence) or various transactions concerning the company's property and liabilities that are to 'deter' a potential buyer[2].

In the literature the use of defence measures is associated with the concept of the so-called 'hostile takeover'[3], construed as a takeover that is viewed negatively by the existing boards of the company. As a matter of fact, this is not a legal term, but a jargon expression that has proliferated in the capital market, and I find it of little use for legal analysis. The attitude of a corporate board to the bid, being an elusive feature that additionally can vary over time, is a poor criterion for the classification of takeover bids into hostile and friendly ones, and I find it largely useless[4]. In fact, the only relatively verifiable quality of such takeovers is whether the management resorts to any defence against them, though even this criterion can be faulty, as it is not always known if such measures are undertaken purposefully or their preventive result is only a collateral effect (as in the case of a company's own share acquisition). In seems then that, for the purpose of legal analysis, one should simply focus on the takeover of control and potential measures taken by the acquired company's boards intended to impede such a takeover[5].

Polish law does not require the management board to obtain prior consent of the general meeting to initiate any defence measures against an attempted takeover. In consequence, as a rule, a potential decision to resort to such measures is made by the management board independently (Art. 368(1) CCC[6])[7]. Based on Art. 12(1) of the Takeover Directive[8], Poland did not implement the rule

1   A. Opalski, *Prawo zgrupowań spółek*, Warsaw 2012, p. 542 et seq.
2   See e.g. M. Stańczyk, *Statut spółki akcyjnej jako środek obrony przed wrogim przejęciem*, Warsaw 2014, p. et seq. and A. Opalski, *Prawo...*, p. 544.
3   Cf. C. Podsiadlik, *Wrogie przejęcie spółki*, Warsaw 2003, p. 5; A. Szumański, *Dokapitalizowanie spółki kapitałowej a obrona przed jej wrogim przejęciem*, 'Przegląd Prawa Handlowego', No. 9/2007, p. 18 et seq.
4   See, e.g. P. Davis, K. Kopt, *Control transactions*, in: R. Kraakman et al., *The anatomy of corporate law*, Oxford 2004, p. 158.
5   P. Davis, K. Kopt, *Control transactions...*, p. 157 et seq.
6   The Act of 15 September 2000 – Code of Commercial Companies and Partnerships (Polish Journal of Laws 2016, item 1578, as amended).
7   A. Opalski, *Prawo...*, p. 560 et seq.
8   Directive 2004/25/EC of the European Parliament and the Council of 21 April 2004 on takeover bids (Official Journal of the European Community L 310 of 30 April 2004, p. 12).

of management board's neutrality referred to in Art. 9 of the Takeover Directive into its legal system.

The Polish Code of Commercial Companies and Partnerships is very laconic when it comes to defining the duties of persons serving as members of a corporate board. It is even harder to find any effective legal guidelines as to the duties of the management board members when faced with a hostile takeover. Nor have such duties been examined in the Supreme Court's case law, which could consolidate the interpretation of CCC provisions in this respect. Legal literature has clearly set out to fill this lacuna, but it remains scarce and is marred by plurality of conclusions[9]. What is more, there is practically no private law path for the enforcement of these duties by companies or shareholders, because the effective laws and their interpretation by courts make it very difficult to pursue civil claims against people serving on boards of joint-stock companies[10].

Given these circumstances, Polish law remains relatively permissive when it comes to the adoption of reactive defence measures by a company's board faced with a threat of a hostile takeover. On the one hand, Polish company law does not reserve defence measures to the exclusive competence of the general meeting. Meanwhile, on the other hand, the duties of a corporate board in this area are limited and their private law enforcement remains very poor[11]. However, it does not mean that a corporate board enjoys unrestrained freedom in this respect. In consequence, the discussion below will focus on the basic rules of procedure followed by a corporate board facing a hostile takeover attempt.

2. The governing body competent to initiate defence measures

As a rule, the body competent to make decisions as to potential defence measures against any takeover of control is the company's management board (Art. 368(1) CCC). Polish law lacks a rule that would introduce a general requirement of prior general meeting's consent to take up such actions[12]. In certain cases, the potential requirement of general meeting's consent may result from the specificity of a

---

9   See e.g. M. Stańczyk, *Statut…*, p. 57 et seq. C. Podsiadlik, *Wrogie przejęcie…*, p. 5 et seq.
10   Cf. the Supreme Court judgment of 9 February 2006, file ref. No. IV CSK 128/05, 'Monitor Prawniczy' No. 5/2006, p. 226. More on this topic in: K. Oplustil, *Instrumenty nadzoru korporacyjnego (corporate governance) w spółce akcyjnej*, Warsaw 2010, p. 761 et seq.
11   Cf. comparative law comments on two models concerning the competence to institute defence measures – P. Davis, K. Kopt, *Control transactions…*, p. 164 et seq.
12   A. Opalski, *Prawo…*, p. 560 et seq.

defence measure, such as the acquisition of own shares (Art. 362(1)(8) CCC) or the disposal of the company's business (Art. 393(3) CCC). The requirement to obtain general meeting's prior consent may also follow from the company's statutes. The rule of management board's neutrality defined in Article 9 of the Takeover Directive referred to above can be adopted by a company voluntarily (based on the opt in mechanism referred to in Art. 12(2) of the Takeover Directive), in the form of inclusion of relevant provisions in the company's statutes (Art. 80a APO[13]), but in practice this possibility is not being used.

In consequence, management boards make decisions concerning defence measures on their own. A potential general meeting's resolution on the adoption of such measures does not change anything in this respect. Firstly, general meeting's consent to or recommendations on defence measures have no impact on management board's accountability for such measures[14]. Secondly, the management board is not bound by the general meeting's recommendation on defence measures (Art. 375[1] CCC)[15]. The management board must independently assess whether the defence measures being contemplated would serve the best interests of the company.

What is more, it has also been aptly emphasized in the literature that the general consent for the acquisition of own shares or the issue of shares up to the target capital limit cannot be interpreted as general meeting's consent to defence measures undertaken by the management board[16]. It has been argued that such a general mandate enjoyed by the board does not prevent the board, as a rule, from using other tools for the same purpose, should the board conclude that the company's interests require that such defence measures be initiated[17].

3. Corporate rule of management board's neutrality

Poland has opted out of the transposition of the neutrality rule laid down in Art. 9 of the Takeover Directive into its legal system. However, it is necessary to solve a problem regarding the possibility of interpreting the general rule of management board and supervisory board neutrality with respect to a takeover attempt based

---

13 Act of 29 July 2005 on Public Offerings and the Conditions Governing the Admission of Financial Instruments to an Organised Trading System and Public Companies (Journal of Laws of 2016, item 1639, as amended).
14 A. Opalski, *Prawo...*, p. 555 et seq.
15 Ibidem.
16 Ibidem.
17 Ibidem, p. 556.

on the general rules of Polish company law. Unfortunately, the answer to such a question is anything but simple, and depends to a large extent on the importance ascribed to this rule. This problem has not been examined in the Supreme Court's case law. Pursuant to the prevailing opinion in the literature, it is necessary for the management board to apply reasonable restraint to resorting to defence measures against takeover attempts and to act on the grounds of the interests of the company and its shareholders[18]. In my opinion, Polish company law does not include any rules or obligations for a corporate board to remain passive when faced with a takeover attempt nor any duties to maintain neutrality as defined in Art. 9 of the Takeover Directive. Pursuant to that provision, the board of a joint-stock company cannot initiate any defence measures without general meeting's authorization, except for seeking an alternative bid. It does not mean, however, that in this respect the board operates in a legal vacuum. It is bound by the duty to act to the benefit of the company which, despite its general and abstract character, in certain circumstances can be identified with specific rules of conduct. In my view, the corporate board's duty to pursue the company's interests (the duty of care) does entail the duty to maintain neutrality, seen as a ban on giving a substantively unjustified preference to one of the bidders trying to take over the control of the company.

Therefore, any further reasoning should start with the statement of the obvious truth that the composition of the company's shareholding structure is important for the company's interests, in particular to its capacity to generate profits in the long term. This is a simple consequence of the scope of competence of the general meeting with respect to the strategic control of the company. In abstract terms, it is possible to imagine a situation where a takeover of control by a specific shareholder would pose a real threat to the company's interests. In such a case, the defence measures will result from the general competence of the board to run the company's affairs, as broadly construed[19]. *De lege lata* the board's competence model adopted by the legislator does not assume the board's passiveness with respect to the determination of the company's shareholding structure. The board is free to make decisions to issue shares up to the target capital threshold, to purchase the company's own shares or authorize the disposal of syndicated shares[20].

---

18 Ibidem, p. 562; C. Podsiadlik, Wrogie przejęcie…, p. 84; K. Oplustil, *Obrona przed wrogim przejęciem publicznej spółki akcyjnej w prawie europejskim i polskim – uwagi de lege lata lega i de lege ferenda (part II)*, 'Prawo Spółek', No. 6/2006, p. 4.

19 See P. Memminger, *Die Revlon-Rechtsprechung in Delaware zu Übernahmetransaktionen und die Behandlung der Entsprechenden Fragestellungen im deutschen Recht*, Baden-Baden 2013, p. 45.

20 Cf. apt comments on this issue – P. Memminger, *Die Revlon…*, p. 125.

Meanwhile, it is without any doubt that the board's duty to pursue company's interests entails a ban on substantively unjustified discrimination against one of the bidders attempting to take over the control of the company[21]. Obviously, such a discrimination can take the form of applying unjustified defence measures with respect to one of the bidders, but also the preference of another bidder, for instance by disclosing corporate information to them on an exclusive basis[22].

To sum up the foregoing reasoning, it seems that *de lege lata* there are no normative grounds that would support the rule of neutrality in the Polish company law construed as an absolute duty to abstain from any defence measures. One should rather examine in what kind of situations a company's interests can speak in favor of the application of defence measures and what kind of rules of procedure should be followed by a corporate board making decisions in this respect[23]. In other words, in Polish law the defence of shareholders' interests in the context of a board's decisions on defence measures follows not so much from the duty to remain passive, but from relevant rules of due process applicable to the procedure of making such decisions[24].

4. Defence measures in company's interests only

There has been a consensus in the doctrine that potential defence measures against attempted takeovers can be undertaken in company's interests only[25]. At the same time, pursuant to the prevailing opinion, company's interests as such generally derive from all shareholders' interests[26], construed as the resultant of interests of all shareholders[27]. Company's creditors' and employees' interests are not protected independently under company's interests or the directives regarding the board's conduct[28]. However, they are of certain importance for the interpretation

---

21 Ibidem, p. 123.
22 P. Davis, K. Kopt, *Control transactions...*, p. 158.
23 Cf. on the grounds of American law – P. Memminger, *Die Revlon...*, p. 127.
24 Cf. on the grounds of American law – P. Memminger, *Die Revlon...*, p. 166.
25 A. Opalski, *Prawo...*, p. 562; C. Podsiadlik, *Wrogie przejęcie...*, p. 84; K. Oplustil, *Obrona przed wrogim przejęciem...*, p. 4;
26 A. Opalski, *Prawo...*, op. cit., p. 558 et seq., see also the Supreme Court judgment of 5 November 2009, file ref. No. I CSK 158/09; K. Oplustil, *Instrumenty nadzoru korporacyjnego...*, p. 173.
27 Ibidem.
28 A. Opalski, *Prawo...*, p. 558 et seq.

of shareholders' interests, as broadly construed, which assumes the consideration of interests of other stakeholders involved in the company's operations[29].

Polish literature does not identify any clear-cut criteria that could be used to determine the cases where a company's interests support the decision to take up defence measures. On the one hand, it is believed that a sheer threat that the bidder poses to the existing system of ownership relations or the existing form and strategy of a company's operations does not provide such a justification[30]. However, some scholars have spoken in favor of admissibility of defence measures against attempted takeovers of control 'if the existing system of ownership relations offers to shareholders a perspective of achieving better return on their investment'[31].

Nonetheless, it seems that in a typical situation the board does not have sufficient information on the bidder's detailed management strategy for the company to reliably determine which ownership structure would offer a better chance to shareholders to generate a higher return on their investments. Furthermore, in practice, an analysis of this kind would be affected by a conflict of interests arising from the loyalty bond between the corporate board and the shareholders controlling the company so far.

At the same time, it seems that, as a rule, shareholders themselves should determine the best system of ownership relations for the company when deciding to sell their shares to the bidder. Since the company's interests are a resultant of the long-term interests of all shareholders, under typical conditions the shareholders themselves are the best equipped to assess the quality of the bid for the controlling block of shares. Under normal circumstances, management board's publication of its position on the tender offer and its impact on the company's interests, as required by the law (Art. 80 APO), should be considered a completely sufficient response to a takeover bid.

However, defence measures can be classified as justified in the situation of market failures manifested by a radical discrepancy between the market price and the fair value of shares, and the lack of sufficient information that would enable the shareholders to perform a correct assessment of the bid. Such failures on a relatively small and insufficiently liquid capital market, such as the Polish one, can occur more often than in the case of large and mature markets. A traditional justification for undertaking defence measures based on the bidder's identity is the claim that the bidder is a so-called corporate looter. Pursuant to literature,

---

29 Ibidem.
30 Ibidem, p. 559.
31 Ibidem, p. 558.

this category comprises, for instance, a company's competitors whose sole purpose is to acquire a market share and restrict competition with respect to their own activity[32]. In my view, this justification can also include a radical increase in the risk of a company's operation after the takeover resulting from a bidder's features, in particular the fact that the transaction is to be financed with debt that will subsequently be 'transferred' to the acquired company, for instance by way of a merger. A radical increase in the level of debt in the acquired company is detrimental to minority shareholders, as it weakens the company's resistance to various market perturbations.

One should agree with the arguments raised in legal literature that 'corporate looters' are usually hard to identify in advance[33]. As a rule, circumstances that point to that fact are revealed *post factum*, that is after the takeover of control has taken place. For this reason, the final decision to approve a bid should be made by the shareholders, while defence measures undertaken by the board should be temporary and proportional to the threat, providing shareholders with more time to correctly assess the offer of the bidder and collect information on them. However, it is important to note that the analyzed justification for defence measures gains particular importance in countries where the protection of minority shareholders is low (such as, for instance, Poland), since once the 'looter' has taken over control, their options to pursue their rights are limited.

Yet another justification to initiate defence measures can be based on the radical discrepancy between the market price of shares and their fair value, manifested as the undervaluation of shares. This fact can be a consequence of emotional moves by market players, but also an interim market underestimation of long-term perspectives of a company, for instance as a result of initiating a major investment program or incurring significant R&D expense. Obviously this reasoning has its critics who rely on the theory of capital markets' information efficiency, pursuant to which, as a rule, market price is the only known fair value of shares, and on empirical research showing that statistically market's long-term share pricing is correct[34]. However, it is important to remember that, when considering defence measures, the board of a company is confronted not so much with a statistical, but a specific market situation, and in that specific moment the market can be

---

32 A. Opalski, *Prawo...*, p. 558 et seq.
33 F.H. Easterbrook, D.R. Fischel, *The economic structure of corporate law*, Cambrigde – London, 2006, p. 130.
34 Critical approach: F.H. Easterbrook, D. R. Fischel, *The economic structure...*, p. 201.

inefficient from the perspective of information[35]. At the same time, it seems that potential defence measures, due to the inefficiency of the price mechanism of the capital market, can be solely temporary. They should aim at a short-term price increase in order to eliminate potential inefficiencies. However, the shareholders, making a decision on the potential sale of their shares, should make the final assessment themselves[36].

5. The distribution of the burden of proof with respect to acting in company's interests

It is commonly emphasized in the literature that a takeover bid affects both the interest of the company and the interests of the members of its corporate boards, who risk losing their jobs as a result of a successful takeover. This situation results in at least a potential conflict of interests[37]. Consequently, it is necessary that there be a special justification for the corporate board to institute defence measures and a significant limitation of the scope of business risk as compared to regular dealings[38]. Bearing the potential conflict of interests in mind, one must assume that the members of a corporate board resorting to potential defence measures are liable to prove the existence of circumstances that would make the initiation of such measures necessary in the company's interests and the proportional to the potential threat[39]. In the circumstances being discussed it is reasonable to make a challengeable assumption that the board initiating defence measures acts in its own interests rather than in the interest if the company[40].

Although Polish law does not incorporate the business judgment rule directly, there is no doubt in legal literature that, when making its decisions, the management board can assume a reasonable scope of admissible business risk, and so its business decisions are deemed correct even despite their potentially negative consequences[41]. It does seem, however, given the potential conflict of interests

---

35 L.A. Cunningham, *From Random Walks to Chaotic Crashes: The Linear Genealogy of the Efficient Capital Market Hypothesis*, 'George Washington Law Review', No. 62, 1994, p. 546 et seq.

36 P. Memminger, *Die Revlon-Rechtsprechung...*, p. 45.

37 S. Barry, *Informationelle Gleichbehandlung konkurrierender Bieter bei öffentlichen Übernahmen*, Baden-Baden 2013, p. 218 et seq.

38 Ibidem.

39 In this context, cf.: *Unocal v. Mesa Petroleum Co.*, 493 A.2d 946 (Del. 1985).

40 S. Barry, *Informationelle Gleichbehandlung...*, p. 221 and 224.

41 K. Oplustil, Instrumenty nadzoru korporacyjnego..., p. 172.

involving a management board member, that such a member should not enjoy the benefits of assumption that their decision on defence measures has been correct and, in the case of a dispute, would be liable to prove that the institution of measures was in the interest of the company[42]. It is a separate issue that currently persons serving on management boards of Polish companies enjoy a specific protection against civil liability for unjustified business decisions on the grounds of an unfortunate judgment issued by the Supreme Court, which requires management board members to infringe a specific provision of an act of law or the company's statutes to be found liable before a civil court[43].

If an actual and specific conflict of interests of a company's board member occurs in the context of a bid for a takeover of control, the member, pursuant to Art. 377 CCC, is obliged to exclude themselves from any decisions on that matter, in particular from decisions on defence measures or a preference for any specific bidder[44]. Such a specific conflict of interests in the context being discussed can result from the fact that the member has signed a contract with one of the bidders offering them a right to receive a commission if the takeover takes place (finder's fee) or the member is directly involved in the acquiring entity that is taking the company over by way of a management buy-out[45]. It is also possible that such a specific conflict of interests would result from aggressive measures undertaken by the bidder who declares their intent to dismiss a specific manager and raise civil claims or criminal charges against them[46].

6. Seeking an alternative bidder as a defence strategy

One should assume that, faced with an attempt of a takeover, the management board is not obliged to seek an alternative bidder if they have grounds to conclude that the conditions of the bid are compliant with the company's interests and, in particular, the offered price corresponds to the fair value of the shares, given the current market pricing or available quotations by analysts[47]. However, if in management's view the offer is not compliant with company's interests, the duty to seek an alternative bidder could occur only if there is actual likelihood that such a

---

42 Cf. A. Opalski, *Prawo...*, p. 562 et seq.
43 Cf. the Supreme Court judgement of 9 February 2006, file ref. No. IV CSK 128/05, 'Monitor Prawniczy' 2006, No. 5, p. 226.
44 Cf. A. Opalski, *Prawo...*, p. 557.
45 Cf. on the grounds of American law – P. Memminger, *Die Revlon...*, p. 106.
46 Ibidem.
47 Cf. in the context of American law – ibidem p. 94 et seq.

bidder could be found assuming reasonable costs and outlays. As a matter of fact, the board is obliged to balance the potential costs and benefits stemming from the search from the perspective of a company's interests. It would be questionable for the company to incur significant costs of the search – for instance related to the fees of bidder's professional agents – if the chances of finding an alternative and significantly better bid were slim.

7. Acquisition of own shares as a defence mechanism

One of the possible defences against a takeover is the acquisition of a company's own shares. As a rule, the most useful legal basis for the acquisition of own shares presumes that the management board carries out such an operation authorized by a resolution of the general meeting (Art. 362(1)(5) and 362(1)(8) CCC). The decision whether to act on this authorization or not is made by the management board in compliance with a company's interests, even if authorization allows for the acquisition of a company's own shares for the purpose of defence against a hostile takeover[48]. In any case, the acquisition of own shares, if overpriced, that is above the fair value of the securities, is contradictory to a company's interests[49]. General authorization to acquire own shares, which does not specify the specific purpose for such activities, does not prevent the board, as a rule, from using this tool for the purpose of defence against a hostile takeover, should the board find that a company's interests require defence measures to be undertaken[50].

Polish law allows for the acquisition of a company's own shares without a prior resolution of the general meeting if the acquisition is to prevent an imminent direct damage to the company. There has been a relative consensus in the literature that this provision cannot be used to defend a company against a hostile takeover, as a takeover bid could hardly be classified as an imminent serious damage to the company[51]. Obviously, from a purely theoretical perspective it is possible that a takeover bid presented by a specific entity would nevertheless meet the foregoing

48 Cf. A. Opalski, *Prawo...*, p. 556.
49 On the grounds of the German law: Ch. Bank, *Präventivmassnahmen börsennotierten Gesellschaften zur Abwehr feindlicher Übernahmevershuche in Deutschland und Grossbritannien*, Frankfurt am Main 2006, p. 186 et seq.
50 Cf. A. Opalski, *Prawo...*, p. 556. Cf. also: Ch. Bank, *Präventivmassnahmen...*, p. 187.
51 For a review of literature see, e.g. S. Sołtysiński, T. Sójka, in: S. Sołtysiński, A. Szajkowski, A. Szumański, J. Szwaja, *Kodeks spółek handlowych. Komentarz. Vol. III*, Warsaw 2013, p. 508, and literature quoted therein.

criteria[52]. Nonetheless, if the management board unreasonably relies on this exceptional provision, they will risk criminal liability for illegal acquisition of a company's own shares under Art. 588 CCC.

8. Acting in company's interests in the context of multiple bidders

8.1. Preliminaries

One should assume that whenever many bidders seek to take over a company, the situation of shareholders and the corresponding duties of a corporate board are somewhat modified. Generally, most of the circumstances supporting the institution of defence measures when one bidder is seeking a takeover no longer apply. A significant underestimation of a company's shares is typically remedied as a result of the price competition between bidders. In practice, it is also very unlikely that each of the bidders would be characterized by qualities that would justify the institution of defence measures by the board. Referring to American case law in this respect, it seems that the substantial duties of the board in such a case focus rather on the organization of a 'tender' that would guarantee that the control of a company is eventually taken over in compliance with a company's interests[53].

Assuming that the bidders are acting in good faith and do not pose any threat to the company, the management board has the duty to take the steps aimed at soliciting the highest possible price for the company shares held by current shareholders[54]. This kind of 'auction-like' model of management's duties is in the company's interests, as it boosts shareholders' chances to make profit on the sale of their shares[55].

8.2. Equal treatment of bidders

Equal access to information is a precondition for the correct functioning of the pricing mechanism in the process of takeover by one of many bidders[56]. Consequently, it should be assumed that the issuer is obliged to treat all bidders equally with respect to the access to information on the issuer, enabling current

---

52 On the grounds of the German law: Ch. Bank, *Präventivmassnahmen...*, p. 187.
53 *Revlon, Inc. v. MacAndrews & Forbes Holdings, Inc.*, 506 A.2d 173 (Del. 1986).
54 S. Barry, *Informationelle Gleichbehandlung...*, p. 180 et seq.
55 Ibidem, p. 35 et seq.
56 Ibidem, p. 35 et seq.

shareholders to get the highest price for the shares to be sold[57]. In particular, this pertains to the possibility of carrying out issuer's due diligence. A bidder who has been refused access to certain information will demand a risk premium or will withdraw their bid[58]. A selective refusal to provide information is a defence measure with respect to the bidder who has been refused the information[59]. When multiple bidders compete to take over a company, the selective refusal of access to information is contradictory to the company's interests, and decreases the likelihood that the existing shareholders would receive a higher price. If the bidders are already shareholders, the duty to treat them equally in the same circumstances follows also from Art. 20 CCC (the rule of equal treatment of shareholders) and Art. 20 APO (the rule of equal treatment of investors).

However, the rule of the equal treatment of bidders is deemed violated only by unjustified discrimination of specific bidders, e.g. by failure to provide them with information. It is acceptable though to treat bidders unequally, for instance by refusing one of them the right to audit the company, if such a decision is substantively justified. Such a situation can occur, for instance, if one of the bidders is a direct competitor of the company[60].

8.3. Agreements protecting a transaction with a selected bidder

In certain cases, one of potential bidders, who has engaged the most in negotiations with the company, is willing to continue the work aiming at announcing the tender offer, providing that they are granted, for a specified time, an exclusive right to examine the company's standing and negotiate its takeover. Usually it involves the company's obligation to abstain from seeking other bidders (no-shop clauses) or the duty to pay damages if the exclusive right is breached and a takeover by another bidder is allowed. Such requirements presented by a potential bidder are not necessarily manifestations of bad faith, but often result from the need to engage in time-consuming and expensive analyses on the profitability and financial conditions of the potential tender offer.

It should be assumed that such agreements are, as a rule, incompliant with a company's interests, as they limit the price competition with respect to the takeover of control. However, in specific circumstances and in a limited scope, agreements protecting a potential deal with the bidder (deal protection devices) can

---

57   Cf. P. Memminger, *Die Revlon...*, p. 169.
58   Ibidem.
59   S. Barry, *Informationelle Gleichbehandlung...*, p. 281.
60   Cf. P. Memminger, *Die Revlon...*, p. 175.

be seen as justified from the perspective of a company's interests[61]. In particular, this is the case when a potential bidder makes their willingness to announce an attractive tender offer conditional on the possibility to carry out extensive analyses of the company's standing, while there are no signals that would suggest that an equally attractive alternative bid could be solicited from the market.

Literature analyzing American experiences in this field points out that such agreements are admissible as long as they do not prevent the involvement of other bidders completely, in particular if the penalties are low and the contracts have been made following a search for alternative bids[62]. One case quoted as an example of a situation where deal protection devices are justified is when a company in financial hardship is looking for an investor capable of providing it with quick financing, but the only realistic bidder makes further negotiations conditional upon granting them the exclusive rights[63]. In consequence, it seems that an agreement in which the board, having previously examined the market, undertakes to abstain from seeking other bidders for a specified time would be rather acceptable. Meanwhile, a contract obliging the company to carry out costly defence measures against other potential bidders or to pay high penalties for allowing a takeover by another bidder would be highly questionable.

9. Conclusions

If one wished to offer a malicious summary of Polish legislation on admissibility of reactive defence measures against hostile takeovers, the conclusion would be that the Polish model resembles the American one, but without the American system of justice, case law or the dynamic private law mechanism available to shareholders willing to enforce the duties of a corporate board. In consequence, there is a risk that the Polish capital market would be tainted with all the defects of the American model, that is the lack of shareholders' control of a corporate board's measures undertaken in the face of a takeover attempt, without corrective measures in the form of rules concerning the structure of a corporate board's duties or a mechanism that enforces compliance with them.

Polish law does not require a management board to obtain prior consent of the general meeting to undertake defence measures against an attempted takeover. In consequence, as a rule, a potential decision to resort to such measures is made by the management board independently. Poland has opted out of the transposition

---

61 S. Barry, *Informationelle Gleichbehandlung…*, p. 210 et seq.
62 Cf. on the grounds of American law – P. Memminger, *Die Revlon…*, p. 97 et seq.
63 Ibidem.

of the neutrality rule laid down in Art. 9 of the Takeover Directive into its legal system.

At the same time, The Polish Code of Commercial Companies and Partnerships is very laconic when it comes to defining the duties of persons serving as members of a company's board. It is even harder to find any guidelines in effective laws as to the duties of the management board members when faced with a hostile takeover. What is more, there is practically no private law path for the enforcement of these duties by companies or shareholders, because the effective laws and their interpretation by the courts make it very difficult to pursue civil claims with respect to people serving on boards of joint-stock companies.

Given these circumstances, Polish law remains relatively permissive when it comes to the adoption of reactive defence measures by a company's board faced with a threat of a hostile takeover. In view of the presented regulations on the duties of members of a corporate board and the lack of private law traditions of enforcing them, it would seem more appropriate for the Polish capital market to adopt the solutions based on the takeover directive, including the principle of board's neutrality with respect to a takeover bid in particular.

Literature

Bank Ch., *Präventivmassnahmen börsennotierten Gesellschaften zur Abwehr feindlicher Übernahmevershuche in Deutschland und Grossbritannien*, Frankfurt am Main 2006;

Barry S., *Informationelle Gleichbehandlung konkurrierender Bieter bei öffentlichen Übernahmen*, Baden-Baden 2013;

Cunningham L.A., *From Random Walks to Chaotic Crashes: The Linear Genealogy of the Efficient Capital Market Hypothesis*, 'George Washington Law Review', No. 62, 1994;

Davis P., Kopt K., *Control transactions*, in: Kraakman R. et al., *The anatomy of corporate law*, Oxford 2004;

Easterbrook F.H., Fischel D.R., *The economic structure of corporate law*, Cambrigde – London, 2006;

Memminger P., *Die Revlon-Rechtsprechung in Delaware zu Übernahmetransaktionen und die Behandlung der Entsprechenden Fragestellungen im deutschen Recht*, Baden-Baden 2013;

Opalski A., *Prawo zgrupowań spółek*, Warsaw 2012;

Oplustil K., *Instrumenty nadzoru korporacyjnego (corporate governance) w spółce akcyjnej*, Warsaw 2010;

Oplustil K., *Obrona przed wrogim przejęciem publicznej spółki akcyjnej w prawie europejskim i polskim – uwagi de lege lata lega i de lege ferenda (part II)*, 'Prawo Spółek', No. 6/2006;

Podsiadlik C., *Wrogie przejęcie spółki*, Warsaw 2003;

Sołtysiński S., Szajkowski A., Szumański A., Szwaja J., *Kodeks spółek handlowych. Komentarz. Vol. III*, Warsaw 2013;

Stańczyk M., *Statut spółki akcyjnej jako środek obrony przed wrogim przejęciem*, Warsaw 2014;

Szumański A., *Dokapitalizowanie spółki kapitałowej a obrona przed jej wrogim przejęciem*, 'Przegląd Prawa Handlowego', No. 9/2007.

Judgments

Unocal v. Mesa Petroleum Co., 493 A.2d 946 (Del. 1985);

Revlon, Inc. v. MacAndrews & Forbes Holdings, Inc., 506 A.2d 173 (Del. 1986);

Supreme Court judgment of 9 February 2006, file ref. No. IV CSK 128/05, 'Monitor Prawniczy' No. 5/2006;

Supreme Court judgment of 5 November 2009, file ref. No. I CSK 158/09.

Abbreviations

APO – Polish Act of 29 July 2005 on Public Offerings and the Conditions Governing the Admission of Financial Instruments to an Organised Trading System and Public Companies;

CCC – Polish Act of 15 September 2000 – Code of Commercial Companies and Partnerships;

R&D – Research and Development;

Takeover Directive – Directive 2004/25/EC of the European Parliament and the Council of 21 April 2004 on takeover bids (Official Journal of the European Community L 310 of 30 April 2004, p. 12).

Prof. Tomasz Sójka

Faculty of Law and Administration, Adam Mickiewicz University in Poznań

Preventive anti-takeover defences in Polish law

Abstract: This paper discusses preventive anti-takeover defences available to public companies in Polish law. It is limited to the methods applied in practice in the Polish capital market, such as the voting cap, or methods potentially applicable to typical situations. Anti-takeover defences that could be effectively used only in exceptional, special situations are not taken into account. The closed corporate governance model prevailing in the Polish capital market is a consequence of the construction of typical control exercised over Polish public companies by strategic investors. Nonetheless, the gradual decrease in involvement by strategic investors, typically company founders, in their businesses and their decision to sell the shares off to financial investors resulted in attempts at hostile takeovers being of a more practical nature. The main claim of this article is that, although Polish law does not allow for the application of typical poison pills based on American solutions, The Polish Code of Commercial Companies and Partnerships – as interpreted in legal literature – remains highly permissive when it comes to the application of various methods aimed at preventing any takeovers of control. The admissibility of defence mechanisms as used by Polish companies requires an extended discussion, which this paper forms a part of, and, potentially, a legislator's systemic intervention.

Key words: hostile takeovers, public company, takeover prevention, takeover defence mechanisms

1. Introduction

The corporate governance model prevailing in the Polish capital market is a closed one – on the whole, public companies are controlled by strategic investors with a qualifying holding. Nonetheless, attempts at hostile takeovers have long ceased to be a pure theory for Polish economy. This is a consequence – among other things – of the gradual decrease in involvement by strategic investors, typically company founders, in their businesses and their decision to sell off the shares to financial investors.

This study discusses preventive anti-takeover defences available to public companies in Polish law. It is limited to the methods applied in practice in the Polish capital market, such as the voting cap, or methods potentially applicable to typical situations. Anti-takeover defences that could be effectively used only in exceptional, special situations are not taken into account; such methods involve the development of mutual relationships between various companies (cross-shareholding) or making contracts between a larger number of public company shareholders (voting pool) aimed at ensuring a common response to a tender offer for company's shares[1]. Disregarding significant legal constraints applicable to such methods, such as, for instance, the potential duty of shareholders acting in concert to announce the tender offer, the possibility to apply such measures depends, among other things, on specific facts, including the existence of a partner with whom such mutual ties could be developed or a specific shareholding structure of the company[2].

The main claim of this article is that, although Polish law does not allow for the construction of typical poison pills based on American solutions, The Polish Code of Commercial Companies and Partnerships – as interpreted in legal literature – remains highly permissive when it comes to the application of various methods aimed at preventing any takeovers of control. It is also important to bear in mind that a significant part of the largest Polish companies are public companies controlled by the State Treasury holding an interest below 50% (e.g. PKN Orlen S.A., GPW S.A., PZU S.A., PKO BP S.A.). In Poland, the discussion on State Treasury's control enhancing mechanisms (CEM) has taken place in the context of – somewhat justified – fear of attempted takeovers by Russian state-owned corporations (e.g. the case of MOL in Hungary and Azoty Group in Poland). However, the excessive use of various defence mechanisms by Polish companies can be actually detrimental to Polish economy, in particular to the interests of minority shareholders holding interest in 'non-state-owned' public companies.

I am far from treating hostile takeovers as a panacea for all forms of ineffective management of companies by their officers. Hostile takeovers often serve as a weapon of mass destruction, which brings more collateral damage than benefits. The mere threat of a potential hostile takeover can also prompt executive officers to adopt an excessively short-term management perspective (short-termism). However, the disproportionally strong protection of managers against the incentivizing mechanisms of the market for corporate control also seems to be harmful to the interests of public company shareholders and the economy as a whole. It can lead to excessive and unjustified reinforcement of management board's position with respect to shareholders[3]. In consequence, it seems that the admissibility of

---

1   Cf. more on the topic in: Ch. Bank, *Präventivmassnahmen börsennotierten Gesellschaften zur Abwehr feindlicher Übernahmevershuche in Deutschland und Grossbritannien*, Frankfurt am Main 2006, p. 148 et seq.
2   Ibidem.
3   S. Sołtysiński, *Golden Shares: Recent Developments in E.C.J. Jurisprudence and Member States Legislation*, in: S. Grundmann, B. Haar, H. Merkt (eds.), *Festschrift für Klaus J. Hopt zum 70. Geburtstag am 24. August 2010*, Berlin/New York 2010, p. 2592.

defence mechanisms as used by Polish companies requires an extended discussion and, potentially, a legislator's systemic interference.

2. Typical mechanisms increasing the dominant shareholders' control

Obviously, typical mechanisms increasing the control of public companies exercised by dominant shareholders include the preference for their shares in terms of voting rights. Polish law in general allows for such shares to be issued (Art. 351(2) CCC), introducing a cap of two votes per share (the first sentence of Art. 352 CCC). At the same time, the legislator explicitly determined that '*the preference with respect to voting rights does not apply to public companies*'. In consequence, we may assume that a legislator's intent was to implement the rule of '*one share one vote*'. In this way Polish law would follow German solutions, many of which were used as a model for Polish legislation. However, practice has taken a slightly different direction. The Polish capital market regulator – the Polish Financial Supervision Authority – allows for companies that have issued shares with voting preference, typically for the founders of such companies, before their initial public offering (IPO), to be traded on the market. This is a consequence of the fact that when the preferred shares were issued the companies had not been public yet. Therefore, Polish law prevents public companies from issuing preferred shares, meaning that they can no longer do so once the shares have been dematerialized for the purposes of IPO. Meanwhile, PFSA and a significant part of legal scholars have assumed the interpretation that shares with voting preference issued before IPO can continue as such once the company goes public[4]. Given the explicit wording of the second sentence of Art. 352 CCC, I find this interpretation disputable. In practice, the only authority that can enforce a ban on shares with voting preference in public companies is the PFSA. This is done at the stage of approval of the IPO-related prospectuses[5], but the Authority has adopted a narrowing interpretation of the said provision.

One should also add that, in the context of the Polish capital market, serious arguments speak in favour of limited exemptions from the narrowly interpreted rule of the proportionality of contribution and voting rights (i.e. the 'one share one vote' rule). If one disregarded companies owned by the State Treasury, the Polish capital market would be dominated by small and medium enterprises,

---

4   A. Opalski, in: A. Opalski (ed.), *Kodeks spółek handlowych. Vol. IIIA. Spółka akcyjna. Commentary to Articles 301–392*, Warsaw 2016, p. 957.

5   Cf. M. Rodzynkiewicz, *Kodeks spółek handlowych. Komentarz*, Warsaw 2012, p. 693.

often controlled by their founders. The rigorously observed proportionality rule could discourage founders of companies that are small, but have a large growth potential, from seeking capital on the stock exchange[6].

Another traditional mechanism reinforcing shareholders' control of the company, and thereby protecting it against a hostile takeover, is shareholders' vested rights (Art. 354 CCC). These rights apply to a specific shareholder regardless of the number of shares held and they expire not later than when they cease to be the shareholder of the company. However, in practice they often take the form of a specific shareholder's right to appoint management or supervisory board members. This right enables the shareholder who has sold the majority of the shares they have had to continue to exert influence on the composition of those corporate authorities[7]. However, the scope of these privileges is limited. In line with Art. 354 CCC, restrictions concerning the scope of rights under preferred shares and their execution are applicable to vested rights accordingly. This pertains in particular to corporate preference awarded to a specific shareholder, such as the right to appoint management or supervisory board members who directly 'compete' with shareholders' voting rights. In consequence, there should be no doubt that no vested corporate rights can be established in public companies, and, as a result, public companies' statutes cannot contain such provisions (Art. 354(3) CCC in conjunction with the second sentence of Art. 351(2)). However, in practice, the functioning of certain types of corporate vested rights in public companies has been accepted, in particular if such rights had been established before the IPO took place (before the company went public) and their scope is moderate.

There has been a lot of controversy in legal literature concerning the issue of appropriate application of restrictions on voting privileges under preferred shares with respect to vested rights (Art. 354(3) in conjunction with Art. 352 CCC). It is not easy to limit the preference to the maximum of two votes per share when it comes to the rights ascribed to a specified shareholder regardless of the number of shares held and when such rights are exercised substantially outside the general meeting's ballot[8]. Nonetheless, pursuant to a legislator's explicit instruction laid down in Art. 354(3) CCC, such privileges should be subject to fair and reasonable restrictions on terms and conditions similar to the restrictions applicable to the shares awarding voting preference. The rationale for this solution is the same as

---

6   See also: W.G. Ringe, *Deviations from Ownership-Control Proportionality*, in: U. Bernitz, W.G. Ringe, *Company Law and Economic Protectionism*, Oxford 2010, p. 219.

7   S. Sołtysiński, M. Mataczyński, in: S. Sołtysiński, A. Szajkowski, A. Szumański, J. Szwaja (eds.), *Kodeks spółek handlowych. Vol. III. Spółka akcyjna*, Warsaw 2013, p. 434 et seq.

8   A. Opalski, *Kodeks...*, p. 976 et seq.

in the case of restrictions of voting preference – a departure from the rule of proportionality between the contribution and the scope of corporate rights should be exceptional and subject to reasonable restrictions. As a matter of fact, the reason behind the requirement to use corporate vested rights in a highly limited manner also follows from the rule that requires provisions of a company's statutes to be compliant with the nature of a joint-stock company (Art. 304(4) CCC), which assumes that the scope of corporate rights and the scope of capital risk incurred must be proportionate. The exact restrictions applicable to shareholder's vested rights can be determined only on a case by case basis, in reference to specific vested rights which are being proposed. There is no doubt in legal literature that the object of vested rights – the rights vested in a shareholder regardless of the number of shares held – cannot consist in the appointment of the entire management or supervisory boards, or even the majority of members of those authorities[9]. However, this does not change the fact that a minority shareholder's right to appoint a significant part of management or supervisory board members can pose a major hindrance for a takeover of full operating control of a company by the buyer of the controlling interest, and in consequence can discourage entities potentially interested in taking over the company.

3. *Voting cap*

In Poland, the voting cap, that is a selective restriction of voting rights, is a commonly used legal structure enabling the State Treasury to retain control of public companies, partially privatized by way of public offering. The voting cap prevents shareholders whose stake in the company exceeds a determined threshold from exercising voting rights under shares above that threshold. The State Treasury is exempted from this rule. The voting cap has been included in the statutes of eleven out of thirteen public companies in which State Treasury's interest is higher than 20% (Energa S.A., PGE S.A., JSW S.A., Grupa Lotos S.A., PGNiG S.A., PKN Orlen S.A., PZU S.A., PKO BP S.A., Tauron Polska Energia S.A., Grupa Azoty S.A.)[10].

The mechanism of asymmetric restriction of voting rights (voting cap) is based on Art. 411(3) CCC. Pursuant to this provision, "*statutes may restrict the voting rights of shareholders holding more than one tenth of the total number of shares in a company*". This solution is based on the pre-war Commercial Code of 1934 (the

---

9   Ibidem. See also: S. Sołtysiński, M. Mataczyński, in: S. Sołtysiński, A. Szajkowski, A. Szumański, J. Szwaja (eds.), *Kodeks...*, p. 434 et seq.

10 A.M. Weber, *Wpływ instytucji prawa rynku kapitałowego na spółki Skarbu Państwa*, a PhD dissertation accepted at the University of Warsaw in 2015, p. 130.

second sentence of Art. 404 of the Commercial Code of 1934), but traditionally it was rather perceived as an instrument aimed at the protection of minority shareholders against domination by a specific shareholder[11]. The basic function of this legal institution was seen as ensuring the appropriate fragmentation of shareholding in a company by discouraging dominant shareholders from acquiring shares above a specified threshold, by way of preventing them from exercising their voting rights above this limit[12]. We must add though that before the war this institution had been used in this form extremely rarely. Usually, it was applied in companies that were privatized by the allocation of shares to their employees, which did not foster effective management. In this context, the use of the voting cap mechanism to reinforce largest shareholder's control of the company seems to be a major distortion of this institution[13]. In fact, the mechanism of selective capping of voting rights is rather harmful to minority shareholders affected by it, as it effectively discourages entities interested in increasing their shareholding in the company from buying its shares, and in consequence prevents the remaining minority shareholders from benefiting from the related share price increase. The situation would be different only if, due to the specific nature of the shareholder exempted from the voting cap, the reinforcement of its control of the company were in the company's – and, in consequence, all shareholders' – interests[14].

The selective capping of voting rights of certain shareholders forms an extremely strong instrument protecting the company against hostile takeovers. It gives preference to shareholders exempted from the cap, awarding them a relatively sustained control of the company despite having only 20–30% interest in its capital[15]. However, there are doubts as to the legality of including voting cap provisions in public companies' statutes. I disregard here the issue of potential compliance of such provisions with the freedom of movement of capital enshrined in the Treaty in cases where the actual beneficiary of the cap is the State Treasury (as it is the case). At this point one should only mention the fact that, in view of the

---

11 M. Allerhand, *Kodeks handlowy. Komentarz*, reprint, Warsaw 1997, p. 628 (item 6, commentary on Art. 404 of the Commercial Code). See also: T. Dziurzyński in: T. Dziurzyński, Z. Fenichel, M. Honzatko, *Kodeks handlowy. Komentarz*, reprint, Warsaw 1992, p. 419 (item 2, commentary on Art. 404 of the Commercial Code).

12 Cf. opinions by scholars commenting on the law before the Second World War – ibidem.

13 Similarly: A. Opalski, in: S. Sołtysiński (ed.), *System prawa prywatnego. Vol. 17B – Prawo spółek kapitałowych*, Warsaw 2010, p. 358.

14 See also: W.G. Ringe, *Deviations from Ownership-Control Proportionality...*, p. 220.

15 A. Opalski, in: S. Sołtysiński (ed.), *System...*, p. 358.

Court of Justice's judgement in the case involving the Netherlands, there are some doubts as to the assessment of the voting cap provisions as used in Poland from the perspective of the free movement of capital[16]. Pursuant to this judgement, also a measure taken by the state as a market participant on the basis of contractual institutions arising out of a "regular" application of a company law can be classified as a state measure infringing the principle of the free movement of capital[17].

The application of voting cap can be hardly reconciled with the systemic interpretation of Art. 411(3) CCC in the context of the entirety of CCC provisions on the exemptions from the principle of proportionality between the contribution (and thus the level of risk inherent to holding an interest in a company) and the scope of shareholder's rights. In fact, the acceptability of a selective voting cap does not explicitly follow from Art. 411(3) CCC. What the provisions allow for is the introduction of measures restricting the voting rights of shareholders with more than 10% of votes in the company. However, they do not explicitly allow for any differentiation of the level of this cap between shareholders. Meanwhile, if the Polish legislator introduces selective, that is shareholder-specific exemptions from the principle of proportionality between contribution and rights in a company, as in the case of preferred shares (Art. 351 and 352 CCC) and vested rights (Art. 354 CCC), they do so explicitly, imposing clear-cut limits for such exemptions, e.g. in the form of maximum voting preference per one share. The interpretation of Art. 411(3) CCC as a provision that allows for a selective restriction of voting rights would mean a sort of "back door" implementation of a radical and unlimited exemption from the proportionality rule, outside the system of restrictions that CCC stipulates for any exemptions from this rule. One could not claim that a rational legislator intended to restrict voting preference to two votes per share while allowing selective voting caps in the same company, since the latter has much far-reaching effects for the distribution of forces at the general meeting than share preference entitling shareholders to cast two votes per share.

Even if we assumed that Art. 411(3) CCC allows for selective voting caps, the introduction of such measures to the statutes of an existing joint-stock company

---

16 ECJ Judgment of 28 September 2006 in joined cases C-282/04 and C-283/04 *Commission v. Kingdom of Netherlands*, ECLI:EU:C:2006:608. See also: W.G. Ringe, *Deviations from Ownership-Control Proportionality...*, p. 215 et seq.

17 Ibidem. Cf. S. Sołtysiński, in: S. Grundmann, B. Haar, H. Merkt (eds.), *Festschrift...*, p. 2579 et seq.; M. Mataczyński, *Ograniczenia wykonywania prawa głosu akcjonariuszy w orzecznictwie Europejskiego Trybunału Sprawiedliwości*, in: Z. Kuniewicz, K.A. Dadańska (eds.), *Węzłowe problemy prawa handlowego, VI Ogólnopolski Zjazd Katedr Prawa Handlowego*, Szczecin/Międzyzdroje 2007, p. 187.

is subject to limitation from the perspective of the principle of equal treatment of shareholders[18]. Given this interpretation, selective voting caps, just as the issuance of preferred shares, would form an exemption from the principle of proportionality between contribution and rights in a company, and would be subject to control from the perspective of the principle of equal treatment of shareholders construed as a legal norm applicable to a company, and its authorities in particular[19]. It happens this way as selective voting caps are manifestations of objectively unequal treatment of shareholders. Obviously, the principle of equal treatment of shareholders is not absolute as such – it applies only to shareholders whose circumstances are the same. Unequal treatment of shareholders must be justified by different circumstances of the preferred shareholder, assessed from the perspective of the company's best interests. However, even a justified infringement of the principle of equal treatment should be appropriate and proportional to the purpose it is to serve[20]. A classic example of a justified infringement of the equal treatment principle is the emergency issuance of preferred shares subscribed by one shareholder by a company undergoing serious financial distress.

When it comes to the introduction of the voting cap in an existing joint-stock company, it is impossible to conclude in advance that such an amendment to the statutes would not be substantively justified by special circumstances of a specific shareholder. However, such justification would be much more difficult than in the case of the issuance of preferred shares referred to above, as the shareholder exempted from the cap is awarded a preferred position free of charge. As a matter of fact, they gain actual preference at the expense of limiting rights that other shareholders enjoy. Such a preference would need to be justified by special qualities of that shareholder, making the reinforcement of their position among other shareholders beneficial to the company, and thus the remaining shareholders, in the long term. Nonetheless, these special circumstances should be specific enough to justify awarding such a far-reaching preference to one shareholder in a company. The interest of such a shareholder on its own is insufficient to justify

---

18 A. Opalski, in: S. Sołtysiński (ed.), *System...*, p. 361.

19 A. Opalski, *Prawo zgrupowań spółek*, Warsaw 2012, p. 360 et seq.; cf. the Supreme Court judgement of 20 June 2007, file ref. No. V CSK 154/07, 'Orzecznictwo Sądów Gospodarczych' No. 3/2009, item 20.

20 A. Opalski, *Prawo zgrupowań...*, p. 361; M. Romanowski, *Zasada jednakowego traktowania udziałowców spółki kapitałowej, część I*, 'Przegląd Prawa Handlowego' No. 1/2005, p. 10 et seq. Cf. M. Rodzynkiewicz, *Kodeks...*, p. 844. See also: A. Bieri, *Statutarische Beschränkungen des Stimmrechts bei Gesellschaften mit börsenkotierten Aktien*, Zürich 2011, p. 197.

such a move. As a result, the introduction of the voting cap, because of its specific nature, should be in the objective interest of the company, and not its dominant shareholder.

Pursuant to the prevailing trend in case law and doctrine, company's interest, as a rule, is a resultant of the interest of its shareholders and is not completely autonomous from their interest[21]. At the same time, there is no doubt that company's interest does not coincide with majority shareholder's interest, but it is a function of justified interest of majority and minority shareholders alike. The legal structure of the company's interest suggests its mediatory role between minority and majority interests[22]. This role requires that the company's interest be objectivised with respect to any current interest of the majority shareholder in order to protect minority shareholders' interests. In my opinion, the more dominated a company by the majority, the more weight-justified interest of minority shareholders should bear.

The protection of justified interest of company shareholders does not mean the consideration of any subjective shareholders' interests, but their objective interests, interpreted on the grounds of the company's statutes and law. Consequently, if a public company's statutes provide that the company was established to run a specified business and generate profits, non-business interest of a shareholder should play no role when interpreting the company's interest.

4. *Poison pill*

The use of defence strategies based on American poison pills, more aptly referred to as shareholder rights plans, is prohibited under Polish law. A poison pill enables the Board of Directors to dilute the shareholding by issuing a significant number of shares to be subscribed by existing shareholders or third parties supportive of a company's management at a price significantly discounted in comparison to

---

21 K. Oplustil, *Instrumenty nadzoru korporacyjnego (corporate governance) w spółce akcyjnej*, Warsaw 2010, p. 147–181; A. Opalski, *O pojęciu interesu spółki handlowej*, 'Przegląd Prawa Handlowego' No. 11/2008, p. 16–23; A. Opalski, *Prawo zgrupowań…*, p. 145–227; A. Opalski, *Rada nadzorcza w spółce akcyjnej*, Warsaw 2006, p. 150–160; S. Sołtysiński, in: S. Sołtysiński (ed.) *System prawa prywatnego. Vol. 17A. – Prawo spółek kapitałowych*, Warsaw 2010, p. 32–37. See also the Supreme Court judgment of 5 November 2009, file ref. No. I CSK 158/09, 'Orzecznictwo Sądu Najwyższego Izba Cywilna' No. 4/2010, item 63; Supreme Court judgement of 22 October 2009, file ref. No. III CZP 63/09, 'Orzecznictwo Sądu Najwyższego Izba Cywilna' No. 4/2010, item 55.

22 See the Constitutional Court judgment of 21 June 2005, file ref. No. P 25/02, 'Orzecznictwo Trybunału Konstytucyjnego A' No. 6/2005, item 65.

the market price, thereby preventing the unwanted shareholder from taking over control of the company[23]. Pursuant to Polish law, the decision on the issuance of new shares, as a rule, is made by the general meeting (Art. 430(1) CCC), while the existing shareholders have the priority right to the newly issued shares. In consequence, in practice no defence measures whose structure would be similar to the American version of shareholder rights plans are used.

Nonetheless, one should mention the fact that in certain cases Polish law allows for the capital increase and the issuance of new shares in a special procedure, where the decision on the date of the issue and the group at which the issue is targeted is made by the management board. Company's statutes may authorise the board to issue shares up to the amount of target capital (Art. 444 et seq. CCC) and to waive the related pre-emptive rights (Art. 447(1) CCC)[24]. Meanwhile, the general meeting's resolution amending the statutes to authorize the board to issue shares up to the target capital, and to waive the related pre-emptive rights at supervisory board's consent, must meet the requirements applicable to the resolution on the waiver of pre-emptive rights (Art. 447(2) CCC). It means that the resolution should be adopted by the majority of 80% of votes, its adoption must be in the company's interests and the management board should submit a written opinion laying down the reasons for awarding them such authority (Art. 433(2) CCC). When a company faces a threat of hostile takeover, the management board holding such an authority could issue – at supervisory board's consent – shares to the shareholders supportive of the company's management.

What is more, the management board can be authorized to issue, to a selected group of existing shareholders, subscription warrants for the shares to be issued within conditional share capital increase (Art. 448 et seq. CCC)[25]; shareholders' pre-emptive right under such warrants can be also waived on terms and conditions already mentioned above, i.e. under Art. 433(2) CCC. The Code of Commercial Companies does not specify the moment when subscription warrants should be issued to subjects who are to be granted the right to take up shares within conditional share capital increase. In consequence, it seems theoretically admissible for the general meeting to adopt a resolution on the issue of subscription warrants authorising the management board to issue the warrants with the

---

23 W. Underhill, A. Austmann, in: J. Payne (ed.), *Takeovers in English and German law*, Oxford 2002, p. 105.

24 M. Romanowski, in: S. Sołtysiński (ed.) *System…*, *Vol. 17B*, p. 730.

25 Ibidem, p. 769 et seq.

waiver of pre-emptive rights to the existing shareholders in case a tender offer for the company's shares is announced (Art. 453(2) CCC)[26].

However, the basic problem inherent to this defence mechanism lies in the fact that once the management board is authorized to issue shares up to the target capital value or to issue subscription warrants, and – in my opinion – also when the resolution on conditional share capital increase is adopted, the waiver of existing shareholders' pre-emption rights is necessary. Meanwhile, the pre-emptive right can be waived only in the interest of the company (Art. 433(2) CCC). It is highly doubtful that a defence against abstractly construed, unspecified hostile takeover could be classified as a justified reason in the company's interest to waive the pre-emptive rights. From a company's perspective, a potential and unspecific hostile takeover is rather a neutral event, which, in the case of the announcement of a tender offer, can be favourable or not, depending on the identity of the subject effecting the takeover and the price they are willing to pay[27].

5. Restrictions on changes to management board composition

Partial, gradual rotation of the management board composition (staggered board), whose members practically cannot be dismissed, is sometimes used as a preventive measure of defence against hostile takeover. It prevents the subject who acquired the controlling interest in a company from obtaining operating control of its business in a relatively short time[28]. However, in the Polish context this solution will have limited applicability, since, as a rule, the general meeting is competent to dismiss or suspend a management board member before their term expires (the second sentence of Art. 368(4) CCC). What is more, the general meeting is not bound by the planned duration of the term held by a specific person or the fact that the default rule laid down in the first sentence of Art. 368(4) CCC awards the competence to appoint and dismiss management board members to the supervisory board[29]. Pursuant to these provisions, the general meeting as such is not competent to appoint management board members, but the sole possibility to dismiss them can be sufficient to exert pressure on the supervisory

---

26 M. Goszczyk, in: A. Opalski (ed.), *Kodeks spółek handlowych. Vol. IIIB. Spółka akcyjna. Commentary to Articles 393–490*, Warsaw 2016, p. 1148 and 1182.

27 In this respect see the discussion on the grounds of German law – Ch. Bank, *Präventivmassnahmen...*, p. 148 et seq.

28 W. Underhill, A. Austmann, in: J. Payne (ed.), *Takeovers...*, p. 98 et seq.

29 A. Opalski, in: A. Opalski (ed.), *Kodeks... Vol. IIIA*, p. 1216 et seq.

board to cooperate with the subject who has gained the dominant position at the general meeting.

The general meeting adopts resolution on the dismissal of management board members and resolutions on the appointment and dismissal of supervisory board members by an absolute majority of votes (Art. 414 CCC). Obviously, the company's statutes may stipulate stricter requirements applicable to such resolutions, but such solutions are fairly inconvenient since also in typical circumstances, where no threat of hostile takeover exists, they prevent the general meeting from exercising its competence with respect to the determination of the company's authorities' composition.

This competence of the general meeting to dismiss management board members cannot be waived on the basis of the statutes (*ius cogens*)[30]. However, the statutes can make the admissibility of a management board member's dismissal dependent on the existence of an "important reason", irrespective of the fact whether the dismissal of the management board member takes place on the grounds of the general meeting's resolution or in a standard procedure, on the basis of the supervisory board's resolution. In theory, the general meeting's resolution dismissing management members without an "important reason" required by the statutes can be appealed against under Art. 442 CCC. However, the general meeting's resolution dismissing management board members remains in force until repealed by a court's judgement as incompliant with the statutes[31]. Given the slow pace at which litigation proceeds in Poland, challenging the resolution in court does not seem to be effective as a defence measure against a hostile takeover.

The two-tier model of corporate authorities in itself poses a certain barrier to acquitting operating control of a company by a hostile takeover[32]. First, the acquirer needs to take over control of a supervisory board which, in the default model, appoints and dismisses the management board (the first sentence of Art. 368(4) CCC). As a rule, there are no explicit obstacles preventing one from introducing restrictions on the dismissability of supervisory board members, e.g. limiting such options to important reasons or delegating the competence to appoint or dismiss supervisory board members to other subjects than a general meeting, for instance to single shareholders (Art. 385(2) CCC)[33]. However,

30 Ibidem, p. 1216.
31 Ibidem, p. 1258. See also W. Popiołek, in: J. Strzępka (ed.), *Kodeks spółek handlowych. Komentarz*, Warsaw 2015, p. 952.
32 Cf. also the discussion on the grounds of German law – Ch. Bank, *Präventivmassnahmen…*, p. 96 et seq.
33 A. Opalski, in: A. Opalski (ed.), *Kodeks… Vol. IIIA*, p. 1515 et seq.

substantially, the irrevocable competence of the general meeting to dismiss the management board seriously weakens the importance of a potentially strong position of a supervisory board with respect to shareholders. It is also disputable whether a supervisory board, acting in company's interest, can re-appoint to the management board persons who have been dismissed from it by the general meeting. In practice, it is also quite rare to adopt provisions which would significantly hinder a general meeting's ability to change a supervisory board's composition, as in typical circumstances, that is outside the context of hostile takeover bids, they would constitute a major hindrance to exercising corporate oversight[34]. Furthermore, a shareholder with 20% of votes at the general meeting can request the supervisory board members to be appointed by way of cumulative voting, a procedure to which the specific rules for supervisory board member appointments do not apply (Art. 385(3) CCC)[35].

6. Conclusions

In this article I have attempted to prove that, although Polish law does not allow for the application of typical poison pill solutions based on American practice, CCC provisions, as currently interpreted in legal literature, remain relatively permissive when it comes to the use of various methods of preventing hostile takeovers. This problem is exacerbated by the fact that Poland has failed to implement the breakthrough rule laid down in Art. 11 of the Takeover Directive, and, in consequence, no mechanism allowing for a waiver of legally constructed defence measures in the context of a tender offer for shares exists. Secondly, the defence measures of disputable legality can be challenged mostly when established or at the stage of approval of the IPO-related prospectus by the Polish Financial Supervision Authority. Pursuant to the Supreme Court case law, a general meeting's resolution that is incompliant with law, including resolutions that amend a company's statutes, remains in force until declared invalid by a final court judgement[36]. As a result, there is a serious risk that even legally dubious statutory defence mechanisms will remain effective for a longer time in a situation when a tender offer for a company's shares has been announced. Judiciary mechanisms, slow and insufficiently equipped to settle complex company law disputes, offer

---

34 Cf. Ch. Bank, *Präventivmassnahmen…*, p. 100.

35 A. Opalski, in: A. Opalski (ed.), *Kodeks… Vol. IIIA*, p. 1521 et seq.

36 Supreme Court resolution of 18 September 2013, file ref. No. III CZP 13/13, 'Orzecznictwo Sądu Najwyższego Izba Cywilna' No. 3/2014, item 23.

a rather poor protection for the interest of those shareholders who welcome the offer to sell their shares.

In consequence, it seems that the issue of admissibility of various mechanisms employed by Polish companies in defence against hostile takeovers requires an extended discussion and a potential systemic action on the part of the legislator. The disproportionally strong protection of managers against incentivizing mechanisms of the market for corporate control can be detrimental to the interest of public companies' shareholders and the economy as a whole[37]. At the same time, boosting the power of the largest shareholder may intensify their appetite to derive private benefits of control[38].

Literature

Allerhand M., *Kodeks handlowy. Komentarz*, reprint, Warsaw 1997;

Bank Ch., *Präventivmassnahmen börsennotierten Gesellschaften zur Abwehr feindlicher Übernahmevershuche in Deutschland und Grossbritannien*, Frankfurt am Main 2006;

Bieri A., *Statutarische Beschränkungen des Stimmrechts bei Gesellschaften mit börsenkotierten Aktien*, Zürich 2011;

Dziurzyński T., Fenichel Z., Honzatko M., *Kodeks handlowy. Komentarz*, reprint, Warsaw 1992;

Mataczyński M., *Ograniczenia wykonywania prawa głosu akcjonariuszy w orzecznictwie Europejskiego Trybunału Sprawiedliwości*, in: Kuniewicz Z., Dadańska K.A. (eds.), *Węzłowe problemy prawa handlowego, VI Ogólnopolski Zjazd Katedr Prawa Handlowego*, Szczecin/Międzyzdroje 2007;

Opalski A. (ed.), *Kodeks spółek handlowych. Vol. IIIA. Spółka akcyjna. Commentary to Articles 301–392*, Warsaw 2016;

Opalski A. (ed.), *Kodeks spółek handlowych. Vol. IIIB. Spółka akcyjna. Commentary to Articles 393–490*, Warsaw 2016;

Opalski A., *O pojęciu interesu spółki handlowej*, 'Przegląd Prawa Handlowego' No. 11/2008;

Opalski A., *Prawo zgrupowań spółek*, Warsaw 2012;

Opalski A., *Rada nadzorcza w spółce akcyjnej*, Warsaw 2006;

Oplustil K., *Instrumenty nadzoru korporacyjnego (corporate governance) w spółce akcyjnej*, Warsaw 2010;

---

37 S. Sołtysiński, in: S. Grundmann, B. Haar, H. Merkt (eds.), *Festschrift…*, p. 2592.
38 W.G. Ringe, *Deviations from Ownership-Control Proportionality…*, p. 221 et seq.

Payne J. (ed.), *Takeovers in English and German law*, Oxford 2002;

Ringe W.G., *Deviations from Ownership-Control Proportionality*, in: Bernitz U., Ringe W.G., *Company Law and Economic Protectionism*, Oxford 2010;

Rodzynkiewicz M., *Kodeks spółek handlowych. Komentarz*, Warsaw 2012;

Romanowski M., *Zasada jednakowego traktowania udziałowców spółki kapitałowej, część I*, 'Przegląd Prawa Handlowego' No. 1/2005;

Sołtysiński S. (ed.) *System prawa prywatnego. Vol. 17A. – Prawo spółek kapitałowych*, Warsaw 2010;

Sołtysiński S. (ed.), *System prawa prywatnego. Vol. 17B – Prawo spółek kapitałowych*, Warsaw 2010;

Sołtysiński S., *Golden Shares: Recent Developments in E.C.J. Jurisprudence and Member States Legislation*, in: Grundmann S., Haar B., Merkt H. (eds.), *Festschrift für Klaus J. Hopt zum 70. Geburtstag am 24. August 2010*, Berlin/New York 2010;

Sołtysiński S., Szajkowski A., Szumański A., Szwaja J. (eds.), *Kodeks spółek handlowych. Vol. III. Spółka akcyjna*, Warsaw 2013;

Strzępka J. (ed.), *Kodeks spółek handlowych. Komentarz*, Warsaw 2015;

Weber A.M., *Wpływ instytucji prawa rynku kapitałowego na spółki Skarbu Państwa*, a PhD dissertation accepted at the University of Warsaw in 2015.

Judgments

Constitutional Court judgment of 21 June 2005, file ref. No. P 25/02, 'Orzecznictwo Trybunału Konstytucyjnego A' No. 6/2005;

ECJ Judgment of 28 September 2006 in joined cases C-282/04 and C-283/04 *Commission v. Kingdom of Netherlands*, ECLI:EU:C:2006:608;

Supreme Court judgment of 20 June 2007, file ref. No. V CSK 154/07, 'Orzecznictwo Sądów Gospodarczych' No. 3/2009;

Supreme Court judgment of 22 October 2009, file ref. No. III CZP 63/09, 'Orzecznictwo Sądu Najwyższego Izba Cywilna' No. 4/2010;

Supreme Court judgment of 5 November 2009, file ref. No. I CSK 158/09, 'Orzecznictwo Sądu Najwyższego Izba Cywilna' No. 4/2010;

Supreme Court resolution of 18 September 2013, file ref. No. III CZP 13/13, 'Orzecznictwo Sądu Najwyższego Izba Cywilna' No. 3/2014.

Abbreviations

CCC – Polish Act of 15 September 2000 – Code of Commercial Companies and Partnerships;

CEM – Control Enhancing Mechanisms;

Commercial Code of 1934 – Act of 27 June 1934 – Commercial Code (Journal of Laws from 1934 No. 57, item 102, as amended);

ECJ – European Court of Justice; Court of Justice of the European Union;

IPO – Initial Public Offering;

PFSA – Polish Financial Supervision Authority;

S.A. – spółka akcyjna (Polish joint-stock company);

Takeover Directive – Directive 2004/25/EC of the European Parliament and the Council of 21 April 2004 on takeover bids (Official Journal of the European Community L 310 of 30 April 2004, p. 12).

Prof. Florian Möslein

University of Marburg, Faculty of Law

Rethinking European takeover law after Brexit: a German perspective

Abstract: The rethinking of European Takeover Law is a current challenge as well as an ongoing task. The economic and political landscape has changed considerably since the Directive was enacted, and these changes have had an impact on the evaluation of takeover law with its obvious socio-economic implications. Above all, the imminence of Brexit is currently set to trigger such fundamental changes. The UK vote to leave the EU will not only lead to the detachment of Europe's most important takeover market. It also implies that the jurisdiction of origin of the City Code on Takeovers and Mergers – the rulebook which has provided nothing less than the role model for the entirety of European Takeover Law – will no longer form part of the harmonized laws.

From an EU integrationist perspective, this raises an interesting question of principle: what is the impact of one jurisdiction's exit on existing harmonization measures, especially if that jurisdiction once provided the yardstick and bedrock of this harmonization? In order to evaluate the need for a reform of the Takeover Directive after Brexit, this paper focuses on analysing the impact of the Takeover Directive on German Law, in particular by assessing whether, and to what extent, the regulatory approach of the City Code on Takeovers and Mergers has been adopted in German national legislation due to the transposition of the Takeover Directive. While some substantive differences, for example, those regarding the passivity rule and mandatory bids, are well-known and much discussed, it seems crucial to review the overall structure, system and general regulatory "style". This paper will therefore concentrate on the scope, the general principles and the taxonomy of German Takeover Law, and assess its respective peculiarities in comparison to the original UK approach.

Key words: Takeover Directive, Brexit, German Takeover law, European harmonization, regulatory approach

1. Introduction

The rethinking of European Takeover Law is a current challenge as well as an ongoing task[1]. The Takeover Directive itself provides for its own revision, as Art. 20

---

[1] On the reform discussion in general cf. K. Hopt, *European Takeover Reform of 2012/2013 – Time to Re-Examine the Mandatory Bid*, 'European Business Organization Law Review' No. 15/2014, p. 143; idem, *Europäisches Übernahmerecht: eine rechtsvergleichende, rechtsdogmatische und rechtspolitische Untersuchung*, Tübingen 2013; idem,

requires the Commission to examine the said Directive in the light of the experience acquired in applying it and, if necessary, to propose its revision[2]. The point in time provided for this revision – five years after transposition was due – elapsed a while ago without any formal amendment. Despite various reform proposals[3] and due to political resistance[4], the Commission left it to the European Securities and Market Authority to issue nothing more than an informal public statement that aimed to clarify some of the most controversial issues, namely with respect to shareholder cooperation and acting in concert[5].

Today, however, there are far more fundamental reasons to discuss and consider a reform of the Takeover Directive: the economic and political landscape has changed considerably since the Directive was enacted, and these changes have had an impact on the evaluation of takeover law with its obvious socio-economic implications. Above all, the imminence of Brexit is currently set to trigger such fundamental changes[6]. The UK vote to leave the EU will not only lead to the

---

Stand der Harmonisierung der europäischen Übernahmerechte – Bestandsaufnahme, praktische Erfahrungen und Ausblicke, in: P. Mülbert, R. Kiem, A. Wittig (ed.), *10 Jahre WpÜG: Entwicklungsstand – Praktische Erfahrungen – Reformbedarf – Perspektiven*, Frankfurt am Main 2011, p. 43; Ch.H. Seibt, *Reform der EU-Übernahmerichtlinie und des deutschen Übernahmerechts*, 'Zeitschrift für Wirtschaftsrecht' No. 1/2012; J.A. McCahery, E.P.M. Vermeulen, *The Case Against Reform of the Takeover Bids Directive*, 'European Business Law Review' No. 22/2011, p. 541; G. Tsagas, *The Revision of the EU Takeover Directive in Light of the 2011 UK Takeover Law Reform*, 'International and Comparative Company Law Journal' No. 10/2013, p. 21.

2   For more detail on this provision: H. Krause, *Die EU-Übernahmerichtlinie – Anpassungsbedarf im Wertpapiererwerbs- und Übernahmegesetz*, 'Der Betriebs-Berater' 2004, pp. 113, 119; S. Maul, D. Muffat-Jeandet, *Die EU-Übernahmerichtlinie – Inhalt und Umsetzung in nationales Recht*, 'Die Aktiengesellschaft' 2004, p. 306, 317 et seq.

3   Report from the Commission to the European Parliament, the Council, the European Economic and Social Committee and the Committee of the Regions – Application of Directive 2004/25/EC on takeover bids, 28 June 2012, COM 2012 (347) fin.

4   Cf. J. Mukwiri, *Reforming EU Takeover Law Remains on Hold*, 'European Company Law' No. 12/2015, p. 186.

5   Information on shareholder cooperation and acting in concert under the Takeover Bids Directive, revised version as of 20 June 2014, available for download at: https://www.esma.europa.eu/sites/default/files/library/2015/11/2014-677.pdf (last visited 30 November 2016).

6   On Brexit in general, for instance: P. Craig, *Brexit: A Drama in Six Acts*, 'European Law Review' No. 41/2016, p. 447; on its manifold business law implications: E. Ferran, *The UK as a Third Country Actor in EU Financial Services Regulation*, Working Paper, available for download at: https://papers.ssrn.com/sol3/papers.cfm?abstract_id=2845374;

detachment of Europe's most important takeover market. It also implies that the jurisdiction of origin of the City Code on Takeovers and Mergers[7] – the rulebook which has provided nothing less than the role model for the entirety of European Takeover Law – will no longer form part of the harmonized laws. For the time being, different forms of Brexit are under discussion, ranging from a softer version which maintains the UK's access to the Single Market, to harder versions where the UK would become a genuine third country whose trade with the EU would be based either on specific agreements or merely on its membership in the World Trade Organization (WTO)[8]. Both of the consequences mentioned will arise, however, regardless of Brexit's final intensity.

From the EU integrationist perspective, any form of Brexit raises an interesting question of principle: what is the impact of one jurisdiction's exit on existing harmonization measures, especially if that jurisdiction once provided the yardstick and bedrock of this harmonization? On a formal level, harmonization measures remain in force and are, as such, unaffected by Brexit. In substance, however, the perspective is different: once the leading jurisdiction ceases to be a Member State, the very fundament of harmonization changes, and the critical question arises as to whether a Directive based on a henceforth external model still qualifies as a legitimate harmonization measure. According to its competence provisions, the TFEU aims to approximate (Art. 114 TFEU) or coordinate (Art. 44(2)(g) TFEU) the respective provisions of Member States – which is different from approaching the rules of a third country. That difference is negligible if, at the time of the respective Member State's withdrawal, harmonization has already caused a Union-wide comprehensive acceptance of the regulatory regime that was once provided

---

M. Lehmann, D. Zetzsche, *Brexit and the Consequences for Commercial and Financial Relations between the EU and the UK*, 'European Business Law Review' No. 27/2016 on the Impact of Brexit on UK and European Business Law, Working Paper available for download at https://papers.ssrn.com/sol3/papers.cfm?abstract_id=2841333; M. Schillig, *Corporate Law after Brexit*, Working Paper, available for download at: https://papers.ssrn.com/sol3/papers.cfm?abstract_id=2846755 (all last visited 30 November 2016).

7   The Takeover Code of the Panel on Takeovers and Mergers (current version 12th edn. 12 September 2016), available for download at www.thetakeoverpanel.org.uk (last visited 30 November 2016); printed copies can be ordered from the Panel on Takeovers and Mergers, 10 Paternoster Square, London EC4M 7DY. On UK Takeover Law in general: H. Baum, *Funktionale Elemente und Komplementaritäten des britischen Übernahmerechts*, 'Recht der Internazionalen Wirtschaft' 2003, p. 421; J. Payne (ed.) *Takeovers in English and German Law*, Oxford 2002.

8   For a survey of different scenarios see M. Lehmann, D. Zetzsche, *Brexit and the Consequences…*, sub I.

by the withdrawing Member State. In that case, a large degree of uniformity will persist among the remaining Member States, regardless of the loss of the former role model. The situation is different, however, where substantial divergences persist despite the harmonization measure. European Takeover Law characteristically belongs to that latter category. For various reasons, national legislators enjoy a great deal of flexibility in transposing the Takeover Directive: the Directive contains various options for Member States, it contains many general principles that need interpretation and at times it simply mandates that a specific question be regulated without any substantive indications (cf. in particular Art. 13)[9]. In consequence, Member States are left with considerable regulatory discretion. It is therefore crucial to analyse how legislators of the Member States have exercised that discretion in order to assess the degree of convergence of European Takeover Law. The more divergences persist, the more pressing the question becomes of whether the Directive will lose its internal justification once Britain has left the EU – and the greater the need emerges to rethink European Takeover Law.

As a prerequisite for such a discussion of the reform, it is necessary to assess and evaluate the Directive's impact on national law. In this respect, a broad comparative analysis might seem preferable at first sight (and has indeed been attempted in the studies and reports that were published on the occasion of the Commission's assessment of the Directive according to Art. 20)[10]. Yet such a macro-level approach would not be capable of revealing the more fundamental systemic connections within specific national laws. Instead, a micro-level approach, focusing on one single national jurisdiction, is more likely to provide such insights and might at least serve as the first step. German Takeover Law promises to be a good candidate for such an analysis – not so much due to the economic importance of German capital markets, but mainly because of the original entanglement of

9 In general: F. Möslein, *Grenzen unternehmerischer Leitungsmacht im marktoffenen Verband*, Berlin 2007, p. 317–322; on the Directive's options in particular: M. Gatti, *Optionality Arrangements and Reciprocity in the European Takeover Directive*, 'European Business Organization Law Review', No. 6/2005, p. 553.

10 Cf. Marccus Partners (in collaboration with the Centre for European Policy Studies, June 2012), *Study on the Application of Directive 2004/25/EC on Takeover Bids*, available for download at: http://ec.europa.eu/internal_market/company/docs/takeoverbids/study/study_en.pdf (last visited 30 November 2016). See also the Commission's Report on the implementation of the Directive on Takeover Bids, 21 February 2007, SEC (2007) 268, fin., available for download at: http://ec.europa.eu/internal_market/company/docs/takeoverbids/2007-02-report_en.pdf (last visited 30 November 2016).

the emergence of German and European Takeover Law. The German Law on Takeovers, the so-called Wertpapiererwerbs- und Übernahmegesetz (WpÜG), was enacted in 2001, i.e., before the enactment of the European Takeover Directive and only a few months after a previous proposal for such a Directive had been rejected in the European Parliament by a parity of votes – not least because of the pressure from the German government[11]. Given that just a year earlier, that same government had still backed the respective Common Position in the European Council[12], the failure of the Directive proposal was quite spectacular. It also illustrates Germany's difficulties at that time, in the aftermath of Vodafone's takeover of Mannesmann and with the European harmonization of takeovers[13], thereby explaining why the Directive, when it was finally adopted, left so much regulatory discretion to the Member States. The German regulatory approach to takeovers, even though of rather recent origin, was therefore probably the most important antagonist of the UK approach once the Directive had emerged. Consequently, German law might seem particularly resistant to the adoption of respective legislative solutions, even after the transposition of the Directive.

In order to evaluate the need for the reform of the Takeover Directive after Brexit, this paper focuses on analysing the impact of the Takeover Directive on German Law, in particular by assessing whether, and to what extent, the regulatory approach of the City Code on Takeovers and Mergers has been adopted in German national legislation due to the transposition of the Takeover Directive.

---

11 On the reasons for and consequences of this rejection cf. S. Pluskat, *Das Scheitern der europäischen Übernahmerichtlinie*, 'WM Wirtschtafts- und Bankrecht' 2001, p. 1937; K.H. Lehne, *Die 13. Richtlinie auf dem Gebiet des Gesellschaftsrechts betreffend Übernahmeangebote – gescheitert, aber dennoch richtungsweisend für das künftige europäische Übernahmerecht*, in: H. Hirte (ed.), *Wertpapiererwerbs- und Übernahmegesetz*, Cologne 2002, p. 32, 41–43.

12 Common Position (EC) No 1/2001 of 19 June 2000 adopted by the Council, acting in accordance with the procedure referred to in Art. 251 of the Treaty establishing the European Community, with a view to adopting a Directive of the European Parliament and of the Council on company law concerning takeover bids, OJ 2001 C 23/1; for more detail on its substance, see, for instance, K. Hopt, *Auf dem Weg zum deutschen Übernahmegesetz – Gemeinsamer Standpunkt des Rates zur 13. Richtlinie und Diskussionsentwurf des Übernahmegesetzes*, in: *Festschrift für Hans-Georg Koppensteiner zum 65. Geburtstag*, Vienna 2001, p. 61, 65–70.

13 For more details on the systemic change brought about by this takeover in German capital markets: M. Höpner, G. Jackson, *Revisiting the Mannesmann takeover: How markets for corporate control emerge*, 'European Management Review', No. 3/2006, p. 142.

While some substantive differences, for example, those regarding the passivity rule and mandatory bids, are well-known and much discussed, it seems crucial to review the overall structure, system and general regulatory 'style'. This paper will therefore concentrate on the scope, the general principles and the taxonomy of German Takeover Law, and assess its respective peculiarities in comparison to the original UK approach.

2. Scope

The first two provisions of the German Takeover Code define the scope of this law from a substantive, functional and territorial perspective[14]. Both provisions are closely intertwined, because the rules on the scope of this law (§ 1 WpÜG) frequently refer back to the definitions provided by § 2 WpÜG. Nonetheless, § 1 WpÜG also has an independent meaning: by requiring the securities that are subject of a takeover offer to be admitted to a regulated market, the provision lays down an additional condition for the law's application which goes beyond the content of § 2 WpÜG. More generally, § 1 WpÜG provides for the substantive and international scopes, whereas the personal scope of application stems from the specific provisions of the law.

2.1. Substantive scope of application

In accordance with § 1 (1), the WpÜG applies to offers for the acquisition of securities issued by a target company and admitted to trading on an organized market. This wording makes clear that the application of German Takeover Law does not depend on the acquisition of control, but on the making of a (public) offer. German law thus follows a formal, not functional, concept[15]. In a comparative perspective, this is quite remarkable: prior to the implementation of the Directive, the City Code had followed the opposite approach by focusing exclusively on the acquisition of control. In consequence, corporate transformations, certain forms of contractual agreements between companies and schemes of arrangement were

---

14 K. Hopt, *Grundsatz- und Praxisprobleme nach dem Wertpapiererwerbs- und Übernahmegesetz*, 'Zeitschrift für das gesamte Handels- und Wirtschaftsrecht' No. 166/2002, p. 383, 393.

15 More extensively, on a broader comparative basis: F. Möslein, *Grenzen...*, p. 471–480; also on this point: H. Baum, *"Öffentlichkeit" des Erwerbsangebots als Anwendungsvoraussetzung des Übernahmerechts – Eine rechtsvergleichende Analyse*, 'Die Aktiengesellschaft' No. 2003, p. 144, 145–150.

also subject to its rules[16]. In contrast, according to current German law, the takeover provisions do not apply to every change of control, nor do they require such change. This is because not every public offer necessarily leads to an acquisition of control or even to a reinforcement of a control position[17]. § 1 (1) WpÜG focuses on public offers, and § 2 (1) WpÜG defines this notion as voluntary or mandatory public purchase or exchange offers for the acquisition of securities of an offeree company[18]. As in many other jurisdictions, the term 'public' is deliberately not defined by law[19]. According to the prevailing opinion, the size of the group of persons to whom the offer is made is crucial, whereas factors such as standardization or negotiability of the contractual conditions only play a subordinate role[20].

In accordance with § 1 (1) WpÜG, the public offer must aim to acquire securities, which includes, according to § 2 (1) WpÜG, purchase as well as exchange offers. It all depends on whether an offer aims at the acquisition of securities in exchange for a pecuniary advantage. Whether share buy-backs are also covered is controversial: while the wording seems to speak in favour of subjecting them to takeover law, its systematic structure is based on a personal difference between the bidder and the target company. Moreover, shareholders are already protected in such situations by provisions of corporate law (cf. § 71 (1) no. 8 of the German Stock Corporation Act (AktG), as well as § 53a of that law)[21]. The interpretation

---

16 Cf. F. Möslein, *Grenzen...*, p. 477 et seq. On the functional legitimation, see P.L. Davies, *The Regulation of Takeovers and Mergers*, London 1976, p. 21: 'From the point of view of government concern at the possible consequences of such transactions for the efficient conduct of the enterprises involved, however, it makes little difference in what particular way the enterprises are brought under common ownership or control'; similarly, see A. Johnston, *The City Take-Over Code*, Oxford 1980, p. 153 (functional equivalence).

17 This approach conforms to a broad Continental European tradition, see F. Möslein, *Grenzen...*, p. 472–477. Similar, for instance, is the recommendation of the Swiss takeover panel in its decision *Zurich Allied AG*, 12.6.1998, recital 1 ('The scope of the takeover rules is not limited to transactions which may lead to a shift of control over the offeree').

18 For a survey, see H. Fleischer, *Zum Begriff des öffentlichen Angebots im Wertpapiererwerbs- und Übernahmegesetz*, 'Zeitschrift für Wirtschaftsrecht' No. 2001, p. 1653, 1653–1655.

19 Criticized, for instance, by H. Baum, *"Öffentlichkeit"...*, p. 144, 145. For a comparative survey, see F. Möslein, *Grenzen...*, p. 473 et seq.

20 Similar, for instance, is H. Fleischer, *Zum Begriff...*, p. 1653, 1658–1660.

21 In favour of subjecting buy-backs to takeover law, namely H. Fleischer, T. Körber, *Der Rückerwerb eigener Aktien und das Wertpapiererwerbs- und Übernahmegesetz*, 'Der Betriebs-Berater' No. 2001, p. 2589, 2592 et seq.; K. Hopt, *Grundsatz...*, p. 383, 393; W.G. Paefgen, *Die Gleichbehandlung beim Aktienrückerwerb im Schnittfeld von*

of this provision suddenly changed in that respect in 2006 when the supervisory authority announced, without any further justification, that Takeover Law would no longer be applied to share buy-backs[22]. The City Code, on the other hand, also applies to share buy-backs, albeit with important exceptions[23]. These variations illustrate the differences between formal and functional approaches, since a share buy-back is difficult to reconcile with the concept of a public offer (which seems to exclude the personal identities of a bidder and a target company), as well as with the concept of a change of control. Finally, according to § 2 (2), the concept of securities includes shares and similar securities representing corporate membership rights (no. 1), as well as derivatives which confer a right to acquire such membership rights (no. 2). This focus on membership rights implies a considerable limitation of the substantive scope, since it excludes, in particular, offers for the purchase of profit participation certificates or bonds[24]. Conversely, the offer does not need to aim to vote shares; this again proves the formal, non-functional approach of German takeover law, distinguishing it clearly from the original City Code approach[25].

In addition, these respective securities must be issued by a target company, according to § 1 (1). Some clarification is again provided by § 2, which defines target companies in para. 3 as 'Aktiengesellschaften oder Kommanditgesellschaften' (stock companies or limited commercial partnerships, cf. no. 1) based in Germany, or as companies based in another state of the European Economic

---

Gesellschafts- und Übernahmerecht, 'Zeitschrift für Wirtschaftsrecht' No. 2002, p. 1509, 1513 et seq.; see, on the other hand, H. Baum, *Rückerwerbsangebote für eigene Aktien: übernahmerechtlicher Handlungsbedarf?*, 'Zeitschrift für das gesamte Handels- und Wirtschaftsrecht' No. 167/2003, p. 580, in particular at 588 et seq.; T. Baums, M. Stöcker, *Rückerwerb eigener Aktien und WpÜG*, in: *Festschrift für Herbert Wiedemann zum 70. Geburtstag*, Munich 2002, p. 703, 704–716; C. Berrar, Y. Schnorbus, *Rückerwerb eigener Aktien und Übernahmerecht*, 'Zeitschrift für Unternehmens- und Gesellschaftsrecht' No. 2003, p. 59, 68–86; J. Koch, *Der Erwerb eigener Aktien – kein Fall des WpÜG*, 'Neue Zeitschrift für Gesellschaftsrecht' No. 2003, p. 61, 64 et seq.

22 Circular of 9 August 2006, available for download at https://www.bafin.de/SharedDocs/
    Veroeffentlichungen/DE/Auslegungsentscheidung/WA/ae_060809_rueckerwerb.html
    (last visited 30 November 2016).

23 In detail E. Ferran, *Principles of Corporate Finance Law*, Oxford 2008, p. 226.

24 Cf. the government draft for the WpÜG, reprinted in the legislative materials, Bundestagsdrucksache (BT-Drs.) 14/7034, p. 34 ('die ein Mitgliedschaftsrecht verkörpern' – embodying a membership right.).

25 See, for instance, H. Fleischer, S. Kalss, *Das neue Wertpapiererwerbs- und Übernahmegesetz*, Munich 2002, p. 59 et seq.

Area (no. 2). Both alternatives aim to limit both the substantive and international scopes of application. In substance, however, the provision does not effectively restrict the scope of application, because these two types of companies are nonetheless the only ones whose membership rights can be admitted to trading on an organized market (in addition to European Companies, included by virtue of Art. 9 SE regulation). Accordingly, it does not make any difference in substance that the second alternative is not restricted to specific types of companies: foreign target companies are also only subject to the law if their shares are eligible for a (domestic) organized market, which in turn requires a legal form comparable to a stock company. Whether domestic companies of foreign legal form, as recognized by the ECJ jurisprudence, are subject to the law is therefore primarily a question of the international scope of application[26].

Finally, the respective securities must be admitted to trading on an organized market, according to § 1 (1) WpÜG. What is to be understood as being an organized market is again defined in § 2 WpÜG: (7) and refers, on the one hand, to the notion of a regulated market as defined in § 32 et seq. of the German Stock Exchange Act (BörsG), and, on the other, to the concept of regulated markets as defined in the former Art. 4 (1) no. 14 Directive 2004/39/EC (MiFID I), now replaced by Art. 4 (1) no. 21 Directive 2014/65/EU (MiFID II). In any event, Art. 56 MiFID II provides that the respective markets are enumerated in a continuously updated list, available on the website of the European Securities and Markets Authority (ESMA)[27]. Over-the-counter markets such as the German Freiverkehr, organized under private law (§ 48 BörsG), are in any event outside of the scope of application of the WpÜG. Even though its market participants might seem to require similar protection, this differentiation corresponds to usual market practice and is foreseeable for these participants. Since the wording refers to the authorization, it is irrelevant whether or not the securities concerned are actually traded on the market in question[28]. The applicability of the WpÜG does not end before the authorization is revoked in accordance with § 39 BörsG. According to the latest reform of the German Stock Exchange Law in 2015, however, such a delisting in turn requires

---

26 Cf. J. Oechsler, *Der ReE zum Wertpapiererwerbs- und Übernahmegesetz*, 'Neue Zeitschrift für Gesellschaftsrecht' No. 2001, p. 817 (discussing analogous application); most standard commentaries argue against such a substantive application.

27 Https://registers.esma.europa.eu/publication/searchRegister?core=esma_registers_mifid_rma (last visited 30 November 2016).

28 In a similar vein on the legislative materials, see Bundestagsdrucksache (BT-Drs.) 14/7034, p. 35 (on § 2 Abs. 7).

a public offer, at least in principle[29]. Note that such delistings are not harmonized by European law, and that, again, the UK's approach is quite different, requiring a shareholder vote with a two-tier 'majority-of-the-minority' requirement[30].

2.2. International scope of application

These two criteria, i.e., the issuance of the respective securities by a target company and the market admission of the said securities, not only define the substantial, but also the international scope of application of the WpÜG. This does not follow from § 1 (1) itself, but from the corresponding definitions contained in § 2. According to this provision, the decisive connecting criteria for the international applicability of the WpÜG (but not necessarily for the applicable law of the contract between bidders and offerees!) are the domicile of a target company and the place where its securities are admitted. On the other hand, the residence or nationality of the offerees - or even of the offeror - is irrelevant. In comparison, the approach of the London City Code was partially different, for its application originally did not

---

29 For more detail on the new provisions, see H. Bungert, B.E. Leyendecker-Langner, *Die Neuregelung des Delisting*, 'Zeitschrift für Wirtschaftsrecht' No. 2016, 49; F. Gegler, *Die Neuregelung des Delistings – Angemessener Aktionärsschutz oder „Dolchstoß"?*, 'Zeitschrift für Bank- und Kapitalmarktrecht' No. 2016, p. 273; R. Harnos, *Aktionärsschutz beim Delisting*, 'Zeitschrift für das gesamte Handels- und Wirtschaftsrecht' No. 179/2015, p. 750; K. Hasselbach, M. Pröhl, *Delisting mit oder ohne Erwerbsangebot nach neuer Rechtslage*, 'Neue Zeitschrift für Gesellschaftsrecht' No. 2015, p. 209; D. Kocher, E. Seiz, *Das neue Delisting nach § 39 Abs. 2–6 BörsG*, 'Der Betrieb' No. 2016, 153; U. Wackerbarth, *Das neue Delisting-Angebot nach § 39 BörsG oder: Hat der Gesetzgeber hier wirklich gut nachgedacht?*, 'Zeitschrift für Wirtschafts- und Bankrecht – Wertpapier-Mitteilungen' No. 2016, p. 385.

30 For an extensive comparison of UK and German delisting rules, cf. P. Maume, *The Parting of the Ways – Delisting under German and UK Law*, 'European Business Organization Law Review' No. 16/2015, p. 255 (however, it refers to the rules that were applicable in Germany prior to the latest legislative reform).

even require the market admission of the target's securities[31]. However, it also referred to the 'nationality' of the target company[32]. The German WpÜG applies, on the one hand, to all companies with registered offices in Germany (§ 2 (3) no. 1), and, on the other hand, to companies with their registered office in any other country in the European Economic Area (no. 2). Yet, the law does not clarify whether it depends on the statutory or the administrative seat. This distinction is of particular relevance when a target company whose shares are admitted to a German organized market has been established under the law of a state outside of the European Economic Area, but who has moved its administrative seat to Germany, while retaining its foreign legal form – a constellation that is possible, for instance, in the case of companies from the USA. If, however, the company in question was established (in otherwise identical circumstances) under foreign law but within the European Economic Area, the WpÜG is in any case applicable. Even in this constellation, the distinction between statutory and administrative seats plays at least a certain role, namely with respect to the specific rules in § 1 (3) and § 11a WpÜG (only applicable if the law applies according to § 2 (3) no. 2 - not no. 1 - of the WpÜG. The concept of corporate residency that applies to takeover law does not necessarily need to be congruent with the principles that apply to conflicting corporate laws[33]. Even the ECJ fundamental freedoms jurisprudence is not decisive, since the application of takeover law does not concern the questions of the recognition of foreign companies, or

---

31 Cf. the original version of Introduction, No. 4 lit. a) City Code (applicable to all listed and unlisted public companies, potentially even to private companies); for more detail, see R. Pennington, *Corporate Takeovers Through the Public Markets – United Kingdom*, in: J. Kozyris (ed.), *Corporate Takeovers Through the Public Markets*, London 1996, p. 305, 315; M.A. Weinberg, M.V. Blank, *Takeovers & Mergers*, 5th edn., London 2003, para. 4-1005.

32 See again the original version of Introduction, No. 4 lit. a) City Code; for more detail, see M.A. Weinberg, M.V. Blank, *Takeovers…*, para. 4-1006.

33 For instance, the applicability of the City Code used to require domestic 'residence', but contrary to corporate conflict rules, this required domestic registration as well as domestic central management, cf. T. Ogowewo, *New Takeover Code Rules on Exchange Offers and Auctions*, 'The Company Lawyer' No. 23/2002, p. 216 et seq. See also P. Lee, *Takeover Regulation in the United Kingdom*, in: Institut für europäisches und internationales Wirtschafts- und Sozialrecht (ed.), *Erwerb von Beteiligungen am Beispiel der öffentlichen Übernahmeangebote*, Lausanne 1990, p. 660 ('We have learnt that it is crazy to bite off more than we can chew.'); more extensively P. Lee, *Takeovers – The UK experience*, in: J.H. Farrar (ed.), *Takeovers, Institutional Investors and the Modernization of Corporate Laws*, Auckland 1993, p. 192, 195.

of superimposing them with domestic corporate law[34]. Correspondingly, and in accordance with the prevailing view in the German literature, one can solely focus on the existence of a domestic statutory seat, not on their place of central management and control[35]. This connecting criterion is based on historical and systematic arguments, as well as on practical considerations[36]. In addition, it corresponds to the wording of § 2 (3) no. 1 WpÜG, which is based on a correspondence of registered office and German legal form ('Aktiengesellschaft'). Last but not least, this interpretation rule also appears to be compatible with the respective provision in the European Directive[37]. As a consequence, the WpÜG does not apply to the US company described by way of example, and only partially applies to the 'EEA-foreign' company. The City Code takes a somewhat different view by explicitly referring to the place of central management and control[38].

On the other hand, with respect to the place where the target company's securities are admitted, a geographical restriction results from § 1 (1) in conjunction with § 2 (7) WpÜG: according to these provisions, 'organized markets' are only those within the European Economic Area. Target companies whose shares are admitted exclusively outside of this market area (for example, on a US stock exchange) are therefore not subject to the WpÜG. In the case of an authorization within the EEA, however, the WpÜG is in principle applicable. Just as they do in the case of an 'EEA-foreign' (statutory) seat, however, special rules apply in the case of an authorization in another EEA country. Where this authorization exists exclusively in the foreign EEA country, § 1 (2) WpÜG only provides for a partial application of German law, namely 'insofar as it rules the control, the obligation to submit a Bid or any deviating provisions, the information of the employees of the Offeree Company or the Offeror, the actions of the Board Members of the Offeree Company, by which the success of such Bid could be prevented, or any other corporate law issues'. A subordinated ordinance derives the applicability from §§ 1–9, 29 et seq., 30, 33–33d, 34, 35 (partial), 36–39c and 40–68 WpÜG, but

---

34 F. Möslein, *Grenzen...*, p. 497.

35 Most leading German commentaries argue to this effect; see also F. Möslein, *Grenzen...*, p. 496 et seq.; R. Steinmeyer, *Der übernahmerechtliche Sitzbegriff*, in: *Wirtschafts- und Privatrecht im Spannungsfeld von Privatautonomie, Wettbewerb und Regulierung, Festschrift für Ulrich Immenga zum 70. Geburtstag*, Munich 2004, p. 743, 745–749; for a different view, however, see, J. von Hein, *Grundfragen des europäischen Übernahmekollisionsrechts*, 'Die Aktiengesellschaft' No. 2001, p. 213, 231.

36 Cf. R. Steinmeyer, *Der übernahmerechtliche...*, p. 743, 747 et seq.

37 For more detail, see F. Möslein, *Grenzen...*, p. 316 et seq.

38 See Introduction, No. 3 lit. a) (ii) City Code in its current version.

this provision is criticized because not all of these regulations are of a corporate nature[39]. In practice, however, this rule has not yet become relevant in the absence of any corresponding case constellation[40]. Finally, § 1 (5) WpÜG provides for a second special provision for constellations with a 'double' EEA-foreign relationship, namely for cases of EEA-foreign target companies whose voting rights are not admitted in their respective home country, but are in both Germany and another EEA country (e.g., French law company with admission in Germany and Luxembourg). In such cases with multiple admission outside of the seat of residence, § 1 (5) the decision on the competent supervisory authority is left to a target company itself, but also requires appropriate notification and publication.

§ 24 WpÜG provides for a substantive law provision that is closely related to these conflict-of-law rules[41]. It does not decide on the international scope of application, but concerns constellations where the takeover laws of different states apply at the same time. Such constellations are conceivable because foreign jurisdictions outside of the European Economic Area may well define different application criteria, due to the lack of international harmonization regarding the conflict-of-law rules on takeovers. As a result, a cumulative application of domestic and foreign takeover laws may well arise[42], which can lead to severe problems for bidders who can consequently be subject to duplicate and potentially conflicting obligations. As a consequence, § 24 WpÜG provides for the possibility of restricting the offer by excluding certain security holders whose domicile, seat or residence falls outside of the European Economic Area. Yet such restrictions are contrary to the basic principle of equal treatment provided for in § 3 (1) WpÜG, and therefore require an authorization by the supervisory authority, which in turn requires unreasonableness (in addition to the existence of a cross-border offer, and to the obligation under a foreign takeover regime outside the European Economic Area). According to the prevailing interpretation,

---

39 Cf. leading German commentaries, for instance P. Versteegen, in: H. Hirte, Ch. von Bülow (eds.) *Kölner Kommentar zum WpÜG*, Cologne 2010, § 1 para. 52–54; U. Wackerbarth, in: W. Goette et al. (eds.) *Münchener Kommentar zum AktG (und WpÜG)*, Munich 2011, § 1, para. 32.

40 Obviously, there are simply no German companies with securities admitted exclusively in EEA countries, see J. Van Kann, C. Just, *Der Regierungsentwurf zur Umsetzung der europäischen Übernahmerichtlinie*, 'Deutsches Steuerrecht' No. 2006, p. 328.

41 J. von Hein, *Zur Kodifikation des europäischen Übernahmekollisionsrechts*, 'Zeitschrift für Unternehmens- und Gesellschaftsrecht' No. 2005, pp. 528, 543.

42 More generally on the cumulative application of capital market laws U.H. Schneider, *Internationales Kapitalmarktrecht*, 'Die Aktiengesellschaft' No. 2001, pp. 269, 273.

such unreasonableness presupposes a substantial conflict of duties which would otherwise make it impossible for the bidder to comply with both national and foreign mandatory requirements at the same time[43].

3. General principles

With respect to the structure of German Takeover Law, the general principles enumerated in § 3 WpÜG play an important role. To incorporate such a catalogue of general principles at the very outset of a law is a very unusual legislative technique in German law. Indeed, this incorporation originates from the example set in the City Code and other foreign takeover laws[44], and also complies with the European Directive (Art. 3 Takeover Directive), but it is worth noting that such a catalogue – similar to some kind of preamble – is rather unusual in Continental Europe and indeed in civil law jurisdictions. According to the legislative materials, these principles aim to replicate the intentions of the rule-maker[45]. Methodologically, these principles have two different purposes: on the one hand, they provide a legal point of reference for lawyers, in particular to supervisory authorities and courts, whenever more specific provisions must be interpreted or developed in the case of unavoidable legal uncertainties or even regulatory gaps. On the other hand, they provide a yardstick for the formulation of subordinated rules, in particular in supervisory decrees[46]. In any event, according to their character as legal principles, these rules do not as such provide for any specific legal implications; rather, their effect is restricted to their interaction with other, more specific legal rules[47]. Only some specific provisions within § 3, such as the equal treatment provision in para. 1, are sufficiently concrete to claim immediate validity[48].

43　The legislative material stresses that any additional financial burden alone will not suffice, see Bundestagsdrucksache (BT-Drs.) 14/7034, p. 51.

44　Cf. the 'General Principles' in section B of the City Code; similar provisions are found in Art. 1 of the Swiss Takeover Regulation (Verordnung der Übernahmekommission über öffentliche Kaufangebote) and in § 3 of the Austrian Takeover Law (Übernahmegesetz).

45　Bundestagsdrucksache (BT-Drs.) 14/7034, p. 35.

46　Covered extensively by H. Fleischer, S. Kalss, *Das neue…*, p. 70 et seq.

47　More generally on the effects of legal principles: F. Bydlinski, *Juristische Methodenlehre und Rechtsbegriff*, Berlin 1982, p. 132 et seq.; K. Larenz, *Methodenlehre der Rechtswissenschaft*, 2nd edn. Berlin 1992, p. 362; cf. also the seminal work of R. Dworkin, *Taking Rights Seriously*, Cambridge 1977. From a legal and economic perspective cf. L. Kaplow, *Rules Versus Standards: An Economic Analysis*, 'Duke Law Journal' No. 42/1992, p. 557.

48　Cf. P. Versteegen, in: *Kölner Kommentar zum WpÜG*, § 3 para. 4.

Finally, it follows from the principle character that there is no hierarchy between the different general principles; as an optimization concept, these should rather be brought into harmony with each other, as equally relevant rules, by means of their mutual balancing[49].

The first principle is laid down in § 3 (1) WpÜG and requires equal treatment. Security holders of a target company, which are of the same class, must accordingly be treated equally. Since the principle does not specify to whom it is addressed, it remains unclear whether it only commits the bidder, or the target company and/or the supervisory authority as well[50]. Yet, the latter two addressees are already under similar obligations under § 53a of the German Stock Corporation Act (AktG) and Art. 3 of the Basic Law (Grundgesetz – GG). However, this does not speak against their obligation, since the range, infringements and possibilities of enforcement differ[51]. Moreover, the central importance of this principle, sometimes described as the 'Magna Carta' of takeover law[52], as well as its systematic comparison with other principles, which at least partly explicitly name the norm addressees (cf. § 3 (3) and (4)), speak against restricting the personal scope of the equality principle. On the other hand, only shareholders of the target company, or, more precisely, security holders of the same type, are protected. The decisive factor is whether the securities in question enjoy the same rights, which is not the case, in particular, in the case of ordinary and non-voting preference shares[53]. However, the provision does not give an answer to the question of whether competing bidders are to be treated equally, for instance, with respect to their access to information, precisely because it is exclusively aimed at the protection of shareholders[54]. In substance,

---

49 Similarly, see H. Fleischer, S. Kalss, *Das neue...*, p. 70 et seq.; more generally, see R. Alexy, *Recht, Vernunft, Diskurs*, Frankfurt am Main 1995, p. 216 (describing the balancing of interests as typical for the application of legal interests).

50 See, on the one hand (only with respect to the bidder): P. Versteegen, in: *Kölner Kommentar zum WpÜG*, § 3 para. 16; K. Hopt, *Grundsatz- und Praxisprobleme...*, pp. 383, 399 et seq.; on the other hand (also the target company and supervisory authority): H. Fleischer, S. Kalss, *Das neue...*, p. 72.

51 For more detail, see U. Wackerbarth, in: *Münchener Kommentar zum AktG*, § 3, paras. 5–7, 12 et seq.

52 M. Peltzer, *Übernahmeangebote nach künftigem Europarecht und dessen Umsetzung in deutsches Recht*, in: H.D. Assmann, F. Bozenhardt, N. Basaldua, M. Peltzer (eds.), *Übernahmeangebote*, Berlin 1990, p. 179, 187.

53 Covered more extensively, for instance, in P. Versteegen, in: *Kölner Kommentar zum WpÜG*, § 3 para. 17.

54 Similarly, see H. Fleischer, *Konkurrenzangebote und Due Diligence*, 'Zeitschrift für Wirtschaftsrecht' No. 2002, pp. 651, 654; T. Drygala, *Deal Protection in Verschmelzungs- und*

the principle formulates a strict criterion by not restricting itself to a mere prohibition of arbitrary action, but - positively - by laying down an obligation to treat
the addressees equally[55]. Accordingly, the bidder must offer the same offer price
to security holders of the same class, which in particular excludes premiums for
block shareholders or time preferences in favour of faster sellers. This requirement, which also forms the basis of § 31 (4) and (5) WpÜG (without being explicitly stated there), prevents the payment of control premiums, for instance[56]. Apart
from price discrimination, § 3 (1) WpÜG also prohibits informational inequality,
which prevents both earlier, as well as more comprehensive, information being
provided to individual shareholders[57]. Finally, the general principle of equality of
treatment can also be applied to the allocation of shares, even if a more specific
provision in this respect is contained in § 19 WpÜG[58].

The second principle in § 3 (2) WpÜG aims to ensure the possibility of making
an informed decision, and requires that security holders of the target company
have sufficient time and information to make a decision on the offer in light of
the facts. This requirement, which is not only addressed to the bidder[59], goes
beyond the duty of equal treatment laid down in § 3 (1) WpÜG, because it collectively protects shareholders by acknowledging their need for information, as
well as their competence to decide. In contrast to the principle of equal treatment,
however, this so-called transparency requirement[60] is not sufficiently concrete to
be directly applied, since restrictions can arise from conflicting legal principles
and legitimate interests, in particular the acceleration requirement according to

---

Unternehmenskaufverträgen, 'Zeitschrift für Wirtschafts- und Bankrecht – Wertpapier-
Mitteilungen' No. 2004, pp. 1421, 1457, 1463; K.H. Liekefett, *Bietergleichbehandlung bei
öffentlichen Übernahmeangeboten*, 'Die Aktiengesellschaft' No. 2005, pp. 802, 803. Such
a principle may, however, be based on other legal provisions, namely on corporate law
fiduciary duties, cf. F. Möslein, *Grenzen...*, p. 525–529, 600 et seq.

55 P. Versteegen, in: *Kölner Kommentar zum WpÜG*, § 3 para. 13; with some restrictions,
for instance: G. Bachmann, *Der Grundsatz der Gleichbehandlung im Kapitalmarktrecht*,
'Zeitschrift für das gesamte Handels- und Wirtschaftsrecht' No. 170/2006, pp. 144, 174,
177 (unequal treatment in exceptional cases).

56 In detail P. Versteegen, in: *Kölner Kommentar zum WpÜG*, § 3 para. 22 et seq.

57 H. Fleischer, S. Kalss, *Das neue...*, p. 72 et seq.

58 Similarly, see H. Fleischer, S. Kalss, *Das neue...*, p. 73.

59 For more detail, see U. Wackerbarth, in: *Münchener Kommentar zum AktG*, § 3 WpÜG,
para. 14.

60 In this sense, for instance, see T.M.J. Möllers, *Verfahren, Pflichten und Haftung, insbesondere der Banken, bei Übernahmeangeboten*, 'Zeitschrift für Unternehmens- und
Gesellschaftsrecht' No. 2002, pp. 664, 668 et seq.

Art. § 3 (4) WpÜG, as well as from business secrecy interests[61]. Instead, this principle is expressed in numerous, more specific rules.

§ 3 (3) WpÜG provides for an interest-based principle: the standard obliges the Management Board and Supervisory Board of the target company to act in the interest of the company. Parallels to company law provisions, as expressly stated in §§ 93, 116 AktG and § 76 AktG, are obvious[62]. It is questionable, however, how the company and takeover law duties interact, and the extent to which they limit the management of a company[63]. This question is particularly important, because the organs of the target company decide in situational conflicts of interest. However, the more specific provision in § 33 WpÜG, which regulates defence measures, does not provide for a strict neutrality obligation, but allows considerable scope for - potentially self-interested - managerial decisions. In addition, there is no specific regulation on the question of whether bodies of a target company are allowed to promote friendly takeover offers, even though such a promotion may be detrimental to the target company's shareholders, for example, in cases where potentially higher offers from competitive bidders are prevented[64]. In both situations - the prevention of hostile takeovers and the encouragement of friendly takeovers - the question arises as to whether, even if it is not excluded by specific takeover rules in limine, the power of the management bodies is restricted by these more general company and takeover law obligations and principles. Even if the necessary decision-making competence exists, the respective decision-making bodies can, for example, be subjected to a more intensive after-the-fact review, and may possibly not enjoy exemption from judicial control as laid down in the Business Judgment Rule (§ 93 (1) sentence 2 AktG). As § 3 (3) WpÜG provides for an interest-based principle, the standard makes it clear that company law obligations to act in the interest of the company are not superseded during takeovers[65]. The respective principles in takeover and company law may use different wording – 'interests of

61 H. Fleischer, S. Kalss, *Das neue...*, p. 73; similarly, see P. Versteegen, in: *Kölner Kommentar zum WpÜG*, § 3 para. 30–34 (also on specific issues); for a different view see U. Wackerbarth, in: *Münchener Kommentar zum AktG*, § 3 WpÜG, para. 17.
62 H. Fleischer, S. Kalss, *Das neue...*, p. 74.
63 For a detailed discussion, see F. Möslein, *Grenzen...*.
64 Covered extensively in M. Winner, *Die Zielgesellschaft in der freundlichen Übernahme*, Vienna 2002; see also P. Versteegen, in: *Kölner Kommentar zum WpÜG*, § 3 para. 37; M. Hippeli, M. Diesing, *Business Combination Agreements bei M&A-Transaktionen*, 'Die Aktiengesellschaft' No. 2015, p. 185.
65 In a similar vein, see Bundestagsdrucksache (BT-Drs.) 14/7034, p. 35; see also P. Versteegen, in: *Kölner Kommentar zum WpÜG*, § 3 para. 35 (clarification).

the target company' instead of 'interests of the undertaking' (Unternehmensinteresse) - but according to the legislative materials, this does not imply any difference in substance[66]. Rather, both principles are equally multi-faceted ('pluralist interest'), even if this necessarily reduces the intensity of control[67]. However, by referring to corporate interests, § 3 (3) WpÜG may well open up additional possibilities for enforcement, for example, by supervisory authorities. It is precisely this procedural effect which constitutes the decisive added value of the duplication of interest-based standards in company and takeover law.

The fourth principle (§ 3 Abs. 4 WpÜG) provides for an acceleration of takeovers. It targets both the bidder and the target company, obliging them to act as quickly as possible. According to its wording, the purpose of the provision is to hinder target companies in their business activities for no longer than a reasonable period of time[68]. Moreover, takeovers should not be used as a means of preventing competition[69]. Since this principle of acceleration stands in opposition to § 3 (2) WpÜG, which grants the holder sufficient time to make his decision, both principles need to be balanced[70]. This balance is largely provided for by the law itself, which sets various detailed deadlines, therefore specifying not only minimum,

<hr>

66 Cf. again Bundestagsdrucksache (BT-Drs.) 14/7034, p. 35, referring to business interests ('im Interesse des Unternehmens'), but also to the interests of various shareholders ('Interessen der Aktionäre, der Arbeitnehmer und die Interessen der Gesellschaft insgesamt zu berücksichtigen'); see also P. Versteegen, in: *Kölner Kommentar zum WpÜG*, § 3 paras. 36–38; H. Fleischer, S. Kalss, *Das neue...*, p. 74; with doubts, however, U. Wackerbarth, in: *Münchener Kommentar zum AktG*, § 3 WpÜG, para. 19 et seq.

67 Similarly, see U. Wackerbarth, in: *Münchener Kommentar zum AktG*, § 3 WpÜG, para. 19, referring to an indefinable cloud of interests ('undefinierbare Interessenwolke'). The legislator postulates only that the board balances these different interests through practical concordance ('im Wege praktischer Konkordanz'), cf. Bundestagsdrucksache (BT-Drs.) 14/7034, p. 52 (referring to § 27 (1) WpÜG); similarly already, see K. Hopt, *Aktionärskreis und Vorstandsneutralität*, 'Zeitschrift für Unternehmens- und Gesellschaftsrecht' No. 1993, pp. 534, 536.

68 Some argue that the second sentence has wider implications, cf. P. Versteegen, in: *Kölner Kommentar zum WpÜG*, § 3 para. 46; for a different view, see U. Wackerbarth, in: *Münchener Kommentar zum AktG*, § 3 WpÜG, para. 29.

69 On the second point cf. Bundestagsdrucksache (BT-Drs.) 14/7034, p. 35.

70 Similarly, see U. Wackerbarth, in: *Münchener Kommentar zum AktG*, § 3 WpÜG, para. 28; H. Fleischer, S. Kalss, *Das neue...*, 2002, p. 76.

but also maximum periods[71]. Against the background of these more specific provisions, this general principle is generally considered to be of low importance[72].

The fifth and final principle, laid down in § 3 (5) WpÜG, serves to avoid market distortions. It provides that no such market distortions shall be created in the trading of securities of the target or bidding company, or any other company affected by the offer. While the other principles serve the interests of individual shareholders, the interests of shareholders collectively or the interests of the target company, this last principle aims to protect the well-functioning of the capital market in general. It therefore extends beyond the WpÜG, and is not only expressed in various specific expressions within this law, but also, more importantly, in general capital market law, in particular in the insider trading and market manipulation prohibitions, but also in the various disclosure requirements[73]. Moreover, it does not only address those directly involved in the takeover, but also all those who may cause market distortions through trading securities of the companies referred to in the provision[74]. The question is, however, whether this general principle has its own importance beyond all specific provisions, and whether it can be directly applied, for example, in cases where these specific provisions do not apply (for instance, in the cases of the so-called matched orders)[75]. While the question has not yet been decided[76], such an application of the general principle seems quite conceivable and even methodically possible. For systematic reasons, it is questionable whether this specific principle could otherwise be of any relevance at all: since the more specific provisions are part of regulations outside of the WpÜG,

---

71 Examples are the provisions limiting the offer period to 10 weeks (§ 10 (1) WpÜG) and requiring immediate disclosure of the change of control (§ 35 (1) WpÜG). For more detail, see P. Versteegen, in: *Kölner Kommentar zum WpÜG*, § 3 para. 47; see also U. Hamann, *Die Angebotsunterlage nach dem WpÜG – Ein praxisorientierter Überblick*, 'Zeitschrift für Wirtschaftsrecht' No. 2001, pp. 2249, 2250.

72 In a similar vein, see P. Versteegen, in: *Kölner Kommentar zum WpÜG*, § 3 para. 48; U. Wackerbarth, in: *Münchener Kommentar zum AktG*, § 3 WpÜG, para. 28 (describing the difficulties of recognizing a specific meaning).

73 For more detail, see U. Wackerbarth, in: *Münchener Kommentar zum AktG*, § 3 WpÜG, para. 31; H. Fleischer, S. Kalss, *Das neue…*, p. 76.

74 K.D. Stephan, in: H.D. Assmann, T. Pötzsch, U.H. Schneider (eds.), *WpÜG-Kommentar*, 2ⁿᵈ edn., Cologne 2013, § 3, para. 63.

75 For more detail, see U. Wackerbarth, in: *Münchener Kommentar zum AktG*, § 3 WpÜG, para. 32; see also K. Altenhain, *Die Neuregelung der Marktpreismanipulation durch das Vierte Finanzmarktförderungsgesetz*, 'Der Betriebs-Berater' No. 2002, pp. 1874, 1877.

76 Cf. K.D. Stephan, in: H.D. Assmann, T. Pötzsch, U.H. Schneider (eds.), *WpÜG-Kommentar*, § 3, paras. 62, 68 (criticizing this deficit).

their interpretation would appear to be unaffected by this general principle. In particular, such an influence is excluded where the relevant prohibitions are governed by directly applicable European law, as is henceforth the case with the rules on market manipulation and insider trading[77]. If there is a lack of interpretative relevance, the principle would be practically meaningless if its direct application were also to be rejected altogether. Such insignificance would contradict both the prominent position of this principle and its presumed legislative intention[78]. All of this shows the difficulties of applying such general principles in codified legal systems. In comparison, their application seems to be much easier in a common law jurisdiction such as the UK.

4. Taxonomy

Besides the scope of application and the general principles, a thorough analysis is required of a third key characteristic of German Takeover Law, namely the structure and taxonomy of this legislation. Due to the codified nature of German law and the great importance of systematic considerations in German legal thinking, this third aspect seems to be of particular importance and well worth comparing with other legislations, in particular the European and UK approaches. While the scope of application of the law depends merely on whether a public takeover offer has been made (cf. § 2 (1) WpÜG), the architecture of the German Takeover Code reveals further differentiations, since different provisions of this law apply to different forms of takeover offer: the Act is structured like a layer model, and distinguishes between simple acquisition offers (Chapter 3, §§ 10–28 WpÜG), takeover offers (Chapter 4, §§ 29–34 WpÜG) and mandatory bids (Chapter 5, §§ 35–39 WpÜG). This structure is a distinctive feature of German law, since it is not prescribed by the European Directive. As opposed to the formal approach decisive for the applicability of the law as such, the functional distinction building on the change of control gains importance at this second, structural level: while the rules on simple acquisition offers apply to all public offers, the rules on takeover offers require the

---

77 For more detail on the recent reform, see K. von der Linden, *Das neue Marktmiss-brauchsrecht im Überblick*, 'Deutsches Steuerrecht' No. 2016, p. 1036; D. Poelzig, *Insider- und Marktmanipulationsverbot im neuen Marktmissbrauchsrecht*, 'Neue Zeitschrift für Gesellschaftsrecht' No. 2016, p. 528; K.U. Schmolke, *Das Verbot der Markt-manipulation nach dem neuen Marktmissbrauchsregime*, 'Die Aktiengesellschaft' No. 2016, p. 434.

78 In this sense, however, see K.D. Stephan, in: H.D. Assmann, T. Pötzsch, U.H. Schneider (eds.), *WpÜG-Kommentar*, § 3, para. 68.

offer to be directed at the acquisition of control, whereas the rules on mandatory bids only apply once control has already been acquired.

4.1. Simple acquisition offer (§§ 10–28 WpÜG)

The third chapter of the WpÜG, which covers §§ 10 to 28, applies to all offers falling within the meaning of § 2 (1) WpÜG. As opposed to the two other chapters which require offers to be directed at the acquisition of control (takeover offers, chapter 4) or control to already have been acquired (mandatory bids, chapter 5), the application of the rules in this chapter does not depend on any further conditions. Only certain specific rules within this chapter explicitly require a takeover or mandatory offer (see §§ 16 (2), 23 (1) 1 no. 3, 23 (2) WpÜG). While from a systematic point of view, these rules belong to the other two chapters, they nonetheless form part of this part, due to their substantive content. Conversely, the rules of this second chapter apply irrespective of such additional qualifications, because they also apply to takeover offers and mandatory bids. At least, the final rules of the other two chapters provide for such an application, at least in principle: § 34 WpÜG provides that the rules of the third section must apply 'unless otherwise specified in the preceding provisions'[79], whereas § 39 WpÜG exempts specific provisions from this corresponding application[80]. Overall, the regulatory structure of the WpÜG thus resembles the structure of the German Civil Code (BGB), since this third chapter forms a kind of general part with rules that are generally applicable to all kinds of offers[81]. However, there is an important systematic difference to the BGB, which reduces the clarity of the law by requiring the exceptions mentioned. This difference consists of the fact that the third section is not only a general part, but also, at the same time, forms the special part for the specific form of the voluntary offer, which is not directed at the acquisition of

---

79 This particularly refers to the provision of § 32 WpÜG on partial offers, which deviates from the general rule in § 19 WpÜG, cf. the legislative materials Bundestagsdrucksache (BT-Drs.) 14/7034, p. 59; see also M.G. Kremer, H. Oesterhaus, in: *Kölner Kommentar zum WpÜG*, § 34 para. 4.

80 Explicitly excluded from the third chapter are, namely, § 10 (1) 1 (disclosure of the decision to make an offer), § 14 (1) 1 (submission of the offer document), § 16 Abs. 2 (additional acceptance period), § 18 (1) (conditions), § 19 (allocation), § 25 (resolution of the meeting between shareholders and offeror) and § 26 WpÜG (blocking period); for more detail, see K. Hasselbach, in: *Kölner Kommentar zum WpÜG*, § 39 paras. 41–78.

81 Similar H.D. Assmann, in: H.D. Assmann, T. Pötzsch, U.H. Schneider (eds.), *WpÜG-Kommentar*, § 10 WpÜG, para. 1.

control. As opposed to the structure of the BGB, the general rules are therefore not consistently placed before the brackets, but are contained in the chapter on the most basic form, namely the simple acquisition offer[82]. This 'modular system' is similar to the regulatory approach that has already been used in the German law on corporate transformations (UmwG)[83].

This specific structure of German Takeover Law has significance for its application, but it is also important from the perspective of European harmonization. Only takeover offers and mandatory bids, not simple acquisition offers, are covered by the European Takeover Directive (see Art. 1(1) in conjunction with Art. 2(1) lit. as of this Directive). An interpretation in conformity with the Directive is only necessary within its scope of application[84]. Since the provisions of the third chapter apply to both simple acquisitions offers not covered by the Directive and - as the 'general part' - to takeover offers and mandatory bids which are subject to it, interpretation of the rules contained in this chapter must follow different patterns. In the second case, that is, when applying these rules to takeover offers and mandatory bids, an interpretation in accordance with the Directive is required, and, in the case of interpretative doubts, a preliminary ruling procedure to the ECJ is mandatory[85]. In the first case, however, when the rules are applied to simple acquisition offers, European law does not require such an interpretation. The regulatory technique, with which the legislature intended to regulate the different types of the offer as uniformly as possible, nevertheless provides a systematic argument in favour of interpreting these rules in accordance with the Directive, but this is just an argument at the level of national law. This so-called quasi-in-accordance-with-the-Directive interpretation ('quasi-richtlinienkonforme Auslegung') is therefore not a requirement of European law, meaning that a split interpretation is also possible whenever any contradicting considerations

82 In a similar vein, for instance, see K. Langenbucher, *Aktien- und Kapitalmarktrecht*, 3rd ed., Munich 2015, § 18 para. 20 ('Basistypus' – basic type); H. Hirte, T.A. Heinrich, in: *Kölner Kommentar zum WpÜG*, Introduction, para. 85 ('Grundfall' – basic case).

83 T. Pötzsch, in: H.D. Assmann, T. Pötzsch, U.H. Schneider (eds.), *WpÜG-Kommentar*, Introduction, para. 39; cf. also H. Hirte, T.A. Heinrich, in: *Kölner Kommentar zum WpÜG*, Introduction, para. 85.

84 In general on the requirement to interpret the WpÜG in accordance with the European Directive, see H. Hirte, T.A. Heinrich, in: *Kölner Kommentar zum WpÜG*, Introduction, paras. 99–99c.

85 Similarly (but rather generally), see H. Hirte, T.A. Heinrich, in: *Kölner Kommentar zum WpÜG*, Introduction, para. 99c; see also M. Lutter, *Die Auslegung angeglichenen Rechts*, 'Juristen Zeitung' No. 1992, pp. 593, 602.

suggest that, in the case of simple acquisition offers, the provisions should not be interpreted in accordance with the Directive[86]. This difference can be relevant, for example, within the framework of § 24 WpÜG, which allows restrictions on be placed on the offer with regard to certain foreign addressees. Such restrictions raise questions of European law: they are not explicitly provided for in the Takeover Directive, but conflict with the principle of equal treatment as required by Art. 3(1)(a) of that Directive[87]. Accordingly, the concept of 'unreasonableness', the central prerequisite for such a limitation under German law, requires an interpretation in accordance with the Directive and may need to be referred to the ECJ – but only within the scope of the Takeover Directive, that is, when applied to takeover offers and mandatory bids, but not in the case of simple acquisition offers.

In substance, there have been criticisms of the fact that this regulatory technology leads to the over-regulation of simple acquisition offers[88]. In fact, the interests that Takeover Law is designed to protect largely depend on the change of control, not on the mere existence of a public offer. As far as the acquisition of an initial holding is concerned, there are also alternative possibilities in the form of a step-by-step purchase of shares on the stock exchange or of a package acquisition, which in turn are not subject to comparable regulation[89]. On the other hand, simple acquisition offers can also be directed at increasing already existing control interests[90]. Since they are not directed at, or do not lead to, a change in control,

---

86 More generally, see P. Hommelhoff, *Die Rolle der nationalen Gerichte bei der Europäisierung des Privatrechts*, in: C.W. Canaris et. al (eds.) *50 Jahre Bundesgerichtshof, Festgabe aus der Wissenschaft*, Munich 2000, p. 889, 915 et seq.; cf. also C.W. Canaris, *Die richtlinienkonforme Auslegung und Rechtsfortbildung im System der juristischen Methodenlehre*, in: H. Koziol, P. Rummel (eds.), *Im Dienste der Gerechtigkeit: Festschrift für Franz Bydlinski*, Berlin 2002, p. 47, 74 ('Ausstrahlungswirkung der Richtlinie auf das richtlinienfreie Recht' – spillover effects of the Directive on national law not subject to the said Directive).

87 U.H. Schneider, J. Rosengarten, in: H.D. Assmann, T. Pötzsch, U.H. Schneider (eds.), *WpÜG-Kommentar*, § 24 WpÜG, para. 7; P. Versteegen, in: *Kölner Kommentar zum WpÜG*, § 24 para. 4; see also T. Behnke, *Erste praktische Erfahrungen mit dem Ausschluss ausländischer Anteilsinhaber nach § 24 WpÜG*, 'Zeitschrift für Wirtschafts- und Bankrecht – Wertpapier-Mitteilungen' No. 2002, p. 2229; J. von Hein, *Zur Kodifikation...*, pp. 528, 560.

88 See, for instance, the position of the German Bar Association: *DAV-Handelsrechtsausschusses* zum RegE, 'Neue Zeitschrift für Gesellschaftsrecht' No. 2001, p. 1003.

89 K. Langenbucher, *Aktien- und Kapitalmarktrecht*, § 18 para. 22.

90 H.D. Assmann, T. Pötzsch, in: H.D. Assmann, T. Pötzsch, U.H. Schneider (eds.), *WpÜG-Kommentar*, § 34 WpÜG, para. 8; on this notion, see also P. Versteegen, in: *Kölner Kommentar zum WpÜG*, § 2 para. 15.

such increasing control offers are neither subject to the rules on takeover offers nor those of mandatory bids, i.e., they would otherwise remain unregulated. Yet, such offers can certainly affect the interests of minority shareholders. While the control threshold of the WpÜG pursuant to § 29 (2) WpÜG is 30% of the voting rights, the actual decision-making power in stock companies often requires higher participation quotas. This is partly due to economic reasons (participation of other shareholders), but it is primarily the result of company law provisions containing stricter majority or participation requirements for many structural decisions, for example, for the conclusion of company agreements (§ 293 (1) 2 AktG: three quarters of the represented share capital), for integration (§ 319 (2) p. 2 AktG: same requirement) or for a squeeze-out (§ 327a (1) AktG and § 39a (1) WpÜG: 95% of the capital representing voting rights)[91].

For simple acquisition offers, in particular for offers aiming for initial holdings, the provision on partial offers in § 19 WpÜG is particularly important. Since such offers, in contrast to takeover offers and mandatory bids, are neither directed at nor leading to a change in control, the offeror must effectively be able to ensure that his offer does not have exactly that effect: if before the offer, the offeror's participation is below the control threshold, then this threshold must not be exceeded after the offer as well[92]. However, when he makes a public offer, the case may arise that too many shareholders accept this offer. Consequently, the offeror needs to have the possibility of only acquiring a certain proportion of the target company or only a certain number of shares. For simple acquisition offers, § 19 WpÜG also presupposes the possibility of a partial offer, and provides that only declarations of acceptance are generally taken into consideration (pro rata allocation). Conversely, § 19 WpÜG does not apply to takeover offers and mandatory bids (cf. §§ 32 and 39 WpÜG), meaning that such offers must necessarily be full offers[93]. § 19 WpÜG is therefore indeed an example of the third chapter, not as the general, but as a 'special part', of that law. Due to the actual binding effect of declarations of intent, partial offers are not easy to classify in terms of German contract law, because the final agreement applies to a smaller number of shares than for which acceptance has been declared. One can most fittingly interpret partial offers as containing a provisional condition making the final agreement dependent on the fact that no more (or just as many) shareholders accept the offer

91 Similar H.D. Assmann, T. Pötzsch, in: H.D. Assmann, T. Pötzsch, U.H. Schneider (eds.), *WpÜG-Kommentar*, § 34 WpÜG, para. 8.
92 K. Langenbucher, *Aktien- und Kapitalmarktrecht*, § 18 para. 23.
93 D. Favoccia, in: H.D. Assmann, T. Pötzsch, U.H. Schneider (eds.), *WpÜG-Kommentar*, § 19 WpÜG, para. 2; K. Hasselbach, in: *Kölner Kommentar zum WpÜG*, § 19 paras. 2, 13.

as determined in the offer document; in the event that this threshold is exceeded, there is an inverse (again conditional) agreement with a corresponding reduction of the contract scope[94]. The scope for the formulation of such conditions in the offer document is limited by § 19 WpÜG in several respects. On the one hand, the restriction may relate only to the proportion of the share capital or the number of securities, but not to certain shareholders or shareholder types[95]. On the other hand, the offeror may only deviate from the principle of pro rata allocation under exceptional circumstances, and must justify any such deviation. For example, round or de minimis clauses are considered permissible in order to avoid the allocation of share fractions or fragmentation. Conversely, allocation procedures decided by lot or the declaration of acceptance date are deemed to be invalid, because they also do not comply with the general principles in § 3 (1) and (2) WpÜG[96]. Finally, it is a matter of dispute as to whether the offeror can nonetheless accept declarations of acceptance even if they exceed the threshold laid down in the offer[97]. For dogmatic as well as teleological reasons, however, such a possibility is to be rejected. On the one hand, the mentioned condition is not fulfilled, and so the shareholder's declaration cannot therefore be interpreted as a new offer[98]; an (implicit) change to the original offer would in any event go against § 21 WpÜG[99]. On the other hand, it would go against the prohibition of *invitatio ad offerendum*,

---

94 In the same vein, see D. Favoccia, in: H.D. Assmann, T. Pötzsch, U.H. Schneider (eds.), *WpÜG-Kommentar*, § 19 WpÜG, para. 9; K. Langenbucher, *Aktien- und Kapitalmarktrecht*, § 18 para. 23; similarly, see K. Hasselbach, in: *Kölner Kommentar zum WpÜG*, § 19 paras. 15 et seq. (legal fiction); for a different view, however, see J. Oechsler, *Rechtsgeschäftliche Anwendungsprobleme bei öffentlichen Übernahmeangeboten*, 'Zeitschrift für Wirtschaftsrecht' No. 2003, pp. 1330, 1335 (unilateral act *sui generis*, comparable to precontractual arrangements).

95 D. Favoccia, in: H.D. Assmann, T. Pötzsch, U.H. Schneider (eds.), *WpÜG-Kommentar*, § 19 WpÜG, para. 4; K. Hasselbach, in: *Kölner Kommentar zum WpÜG*, § 19 para. 12.

96 Cf. the legislative materials, Bundestagsdrucksache (BT-Drs.) 14/7034, p. 48; extensively also D. Favoccia, in: H.D. Assmann, T. Pötzsch, U.H. Schneider (eds.), *WpÜG-Kommentar*, § 19 WpÜG, paras. 12 et seq.; K. Hasselbach, in: *Kölner Kommentar zum WpÜG*, § 19 paras. 22–27.

97 Affirmative K. Hasselbach, in: *Kölner Kommentar zum WpÜG*, § 19 paras. 28–32; negating, however D. Favoccia, in: H.D. Assmann, T. Pötzsch, U.H. Schneider (eds.), *WpÜG-Kommentar*, § 19 WpÜG, para. 15.

98 In this sense, however, K. Hasselbach, in: *Kölner Kommentar zum WpÜG*, § 19 para. 2 (acceptance by the offeror in accordance with § 151 BGB).

99 Cf. D. Favoccia, in: H.D. Assmann, T. Pötzsch, U.H. Schneider (eds.), *WpÜG-Kommentar*, § 19 WpÜG, para. 15.

as defined in § 17 WpÜG, if the subsequent acceptance was at the sole discretion of the offeror. Such discretion would also contradict the principles of equal treatment and the obligation to make an offer, because it would open possibilities for circumventing such requirements[100]. Altogether, the rule on partial offers shows the extent to which takeover law is embedded in (national) contract law. These strong links between takeover law and contract law need to be taken into account when (re-)considering the European harmonization of takeover law.

The remainder of the third chapter essentially reflects the chronological sequence of the bidding process. In fact, these provisions form the 'general part', because they are largely independent of the specific peculiarities of simple acquisition offers. For instance, § 10 WpÜG provides for certain disclosure obligations before an offer is made; §§ 11 and 12 WpÜG refer to the offer document and correlated liability (with a financing requirement in § 13 WpÜG); §§ 14 et seq. WpÜG concern the supervisory procedure and §§ 17 et seq. WpÜG regulate the binding effect of offers (with advertising rules in § 28 WpÜG; see also § 25 WpÜG). After the publication of the offer, the management of the target company is obliged to issue an opinion (§ 27 WpÜG); the acceptance period, which starts from the same moment, is subject to the provisions of §§ 21–23 WpÜG (provisions on amendments to the offer, competing offers and disclosure requirements of the offeror)[101].

4.2. Takeover offers (§§ 29–34 WpÜG)

The fourth chapter, which covers §§ 29 to 34 of the WpÜG, regulates takeover offers and defines them as 'offers directed at the acquisition of control' (§ 29 (1) WpÜG). Since the concept of control is thus a fundamental condition for the existence of a takeover offer, its definition (§ 29 (2) WpÜG), supplemented by ancillary rules (§ 30 WpÜG), constitutes a substantial part of this chapter. At the same time, the acquisition of control is also a constitutive feature of mandatory bids, which are regulated in the fifth chapter (cf. § 35 (1) WpÜG). For this reason, these provisions can be systematically understood as a kind of 'small general part', which could be placed before the bracket of both chapters, since they apply to both types of offer. Similarly, the provisions on consideration (§ 31 WpÜG) and defensive measures (§§ 33–33d WpÜG) also apply analogously to mandatory bids according to the reference in § 39 WpÜG. Even though (voluntary) takeover

100 Even D. Favoccia, in: H.D. Assmann, T. Pötzsch, U.H. Schneider (eds.), *WpÜG-Kommentar*, § 19 WpÜG, paras. 31 et seq., admits that such risks exist.
101 § 24 WpÜG falls somewhat outside of this range, and concerns cross-border offers - see above, sub. II.2.

offers and mandatory offers are arranged in separate chapters, they follow largely uniform rules. This synchronism is based on the legislative consideration[102] that anyone who gains control as a result of a voluntary takeover offer should not be required to submit another, additional (mandatory) offer[103]. The offeror should therefore be spared the time and cost of a 'double offer'. At the same time, the avoidance of such double offers complies with the general principle of acceleration as laid down in § 3 (4) WpÜG, since it is also in the interest of the target company to avoid interference in its business activities by additional offers. However, voluntary takeover offers can only have the effect of exemption from a mandatory bid (cf. explicitly § 35 (3) WpÜG) if they essentially meet the same requirements as mandatory offers. Otherwise, the respective protective mechanisms, in particular the minimum price rule as laid down in § 31 WpÜG, would risk being circumvented by submitting a voluntary offer[104].

The definition of the takeover offer in § 29 (1) WpÜG is the notion of offer in turn defined in § 2 (1) WpÜG as a public purchase or exchange offer for the acquisition of securities of a target company. As an additional qualifying condition, this offer needs to be 'directed at the acquisition of control'. The meaning of control is defined in para. 2. The concept of acquisition includes, in a broad sense, all transactions leading to the achievement or crossing of the control threshold. In addition to the acquisition of voting share ownership, this definition therefore also includes offers which cannot result in the acquisition of control *per se* (e.g., the purchase of non-voting shares) but which are subjected to respective conditions (e.g., the parallel purchase of a control share)[105]. Finally, the criterion that the offer must be 'directed' at the acquisition of control also requires judicial

---

102   Cf. legislative materials, Bundestagsdrucksache (BT-Drs.) 14/7034, p. 30; for a sceptical view, however, see P. Mülbert, *Übernahmerecht zwischen Kapitalmarktrecht und Aktien(konzern)recht – Die konzeptionelle Schwachstelle des WpÜG*, 'Zeitschrift für Wirtschaftsrecht' No. 2001, pp. 1221, 1223, 1229.

103   Similarly, see H.D. Assmann, in: H.D. Assmann, T. Pötzsch, U.H. Schneider (eds.), *WpÜG-Kommentar*, § 29 WpÜG, para. 3; Ch. von Bülow, in: *Kölner Kommentar zum WpÜG*, § 29 paras. 25 et seq.; see also J. Tyrolt, Ch. Cascante, *Pflichtangebotsbefreiung durch Übernahmeangebot und Mindestpreiseregelungen*, in: P. Mülbert, R. Kiem, A. Wittig (eds.), *10 Jahre Wertpapiererwerbs- und Übernahmegesetz (WpÜG). Entwicklungsstand - praktische Erfahrungen - Reformbedarf - Perspektiven*, Frankfurt am Main 2011, pp. 110, 111–113.

104   See, once again, the legislative materials Bundestagsdrucksache (BT-Drs.) 14/7034, p. 30.

105   In the same sense, see Ch. von Bülow, in: *Kölner Kommentar zum WpÜG*, § 29 paras. 41 et seq.

interpretation. With regard to the protection to be provided by the rules on takeover offers, this criterion neither presupposes a subjective element (intention of the offeror) nor requires actual success (achievement of the control threshold). Rather the objective suitability of an offer to acquire control is sufficient to be assessed from an ex-ante point of view[106]. Whether the acquisition of control is likely or not is irrelevant, so that the rules apply, for example, to offers where the purchase price is below the current market price (the so-called low ball offers)[107]. On the other hand, the mere increase of control is not subject to these rules. The same applies to initial acquisitions which cannot objectively lead to the acquisition of control, for example, because the offer takes the form of a partial offer (see § 55 WpÜG)[108]. Conversely, takeover offers in the sense of § 29 (1) WpÜG are only permissible as full offers (§ 32 WpÜG), because the shareholders of the target company would otherwise be subject to unacceptable pressure to sell their shares, which would also contradict the equal treatment principle as laid down in § 3 (1) WpÜG[109]. If a bidder, on the other hand, wants to make sure that he only needs to acquire the shares if he actually gains control, § 18 (1) WpÜG allows for a suspensive condition that a sufficient number of shareholders must accept the offer. By this means, the offeror can avoid paying the control premium without actually acquiring control in return[110]. On the other hand, such a condition is not a necessary precondition for the bid to be qualified as a takeover offer, because § 27 (1) WpÜG does not require the actual acquisition of control ('directed at')[111].

---

106 H.D. Assmann, in: H.D. Assmann, T. Pötzsch, U.H. Schneider (eds.), *WpÜG-Kommentar*, § 29 WpÜG, para. 4; Ch. von Bülow, in: *Kölner Kommentar zum WpÜG*, § 29 para. 44; K. Langenbucher, *Aktien- und Kapitalmarktrecht*, § 18 para. 26; not very meaningful, on the other hand, in the legislative materials, Bundestagsdrucksache (BT-Drs.) 14/7034, p. 53.

107 Ch. von Bülow, in: *Kölner Kommentar zum WpÜG*, § 29 para. 45.

108 H.D. Assmann, in: H.D. Assmann, T. Pötzsch, U.H. Schneider (eds.), *WpÜG-Kommentar*, § 29 WpÜG, para. 6; Ch. von Bülow, in: *Kölner Kommentar zum WpÜG*, § 29 paras. 18 et seq.; S. Harbarth, *Kontrollerlangung und Pflichtangebot*, 'Zeitschrift für Wirtschaftsrecht' No. 2002, pp. 321, 324; T. Liebscher, *Das Übernahmeverfahren nach dem neuen Übernahmegesetz*, 'Zeitschrift für Wirtschaftsrecht' No. 2001, 853, 857.

109 K. Langenbucher, *Aktien- und Kapitalmarktrecht*, § 18 para. 29.

110 Cf. again K. Langenbucher, *Aktien- und Kapitalmarktrecht*, § 18 para. 27.

111 Ch. von Bülow, in: *Kölner Kommentar zum WpÜG*, § 29 para. 44; for a different view, see M. Santelmann, *Notwendige Mindesterwerbsschwellen bei Übernahmeangeboten*, 'Die Aktiengesellschaft' No. 2002, p. 497.

4.3. Mandatory bids (§§ 35–39 WpÜG)

The fifth chapter, which covers §35 to 39 WpÜG, concerns mandatory bids as a third form of a public offer. It differs from the other two forms since it is not voluntary, but compulsory: the offer must be made in accordance with the offer obligation provided for in § 35 (2) 1 WpÜG. This respective obligation is triggered by the (direct or indirect) acquisition of control in the target company, which in turn refers to the rules on the control threshold as laid down in the fourth chapter[112]. In addition, such an acquisition of control also triggers another obligation, which chronologically and logically precedes the first one, namely the obligation to disclose the acquisition of control according to § 35 (1) 1 WpÜG. In addition to these two obligations which form its core, this fifth chapter contains some ancillary rules (regarding the timing, procedure and content of the mandatory bids), several exemptions from and exceptions to the offer obligation, sanctions, as well as the reference to the two preceding chapters in § 39 WpÜG.

a) Obligation to disclose the acquisition of control

The obligation to disclose the acquisition of control pursuant to § 35 (1) 1 WpÜG forms the counterpart to § 10 WpÜG, which provides the obligation to disclose the decision to make a simple acquisition or a takeover offer[113]. However, since the mandatory bid, as opposed to the other two forms, is not based on a voluntary decision of the offeror but on a legal duty, the trigger of this obligation differs. Nonetheless, both obligations form the first stage of the bidding process. Moreover, they serve the same purpose of informing the public at an early stage of the imminence of an offer, and therefore forming specific expressions of the ad-hoc publicity (and are therefore subject to § 15 WpÜG as *lex specialis*)[114]. They

---

112   H. Krause, in: H.D. Assmann, T. Pötzsch, U.H. Schneider (eds.), *WpÜG-Kommentar*, § 35 WpÜG, para. 3.

113   H. Krause, in: H.D. Assmann, T. Pötzsch, U.H. Schneider (eds.), *WpÜG-Kommentar*, § 35 WpÜG, para. 7.

114   Cf. § 35 (1) 4 in conjunction with § 10 (6) WpÜG; on the interplay of these provisions (as well as on their interplay with the disclosure duties in § 21 WpÜG); for more detail, see H. Krause, in: H.D. Assmann, T. Pötzsch, U.H. Schneider (eds.), *WpÜG-Kommentar*, § 35 WpÜG, paras. 182–184; K. Hasselbach, in: *Kölner Kommentar zum WpÜG*, § 35 paras. 181–183, 189.

correlate with the prohibition of insider trading, as they aim at preventing the exploitation of insider knowledge as far as possible[115].

The disclosure obligation is addressed to every person who directly or indirectly obtains control over a target company. In the case of joint or parallel acquisitions, it is more difficult to identify the addressee, but wording, legislative history and the respective provisions of the Directive speak in favour of individual and independent obligations instead of mutual absorption[116]. While the term 'control' refers to the definition in § 29 (2) WpÜG, the criterion of its direct or indirect acquisition requires further interpretation. In addition to the acquisition of voting shares via purchase or exchange, immediate control can also be obtained by other means, e.g., through inheritance, change of legal form or conversions. Such cases, however, may then be exempted by the supervisory authority according to § 36 WpÜG[117]. Indirect control is acquired by an intermediary of companies either on the part of a bidder or a target company (e.g., acquisition by subsidiaries or acquisition of a company which in turn controls a subsidiary)[118]. The concept corresponds to the provision in § 30 WpÜG, which contains additional situations of such attribution, such as the granting of options or acting in concert, which may then lead to the application of § 35 WpÜG[119]. It is noteworthy that even the temporary or passive acquisition of control (e.g., due to the allocation of voting rights, the acquisition of one's own shares or the reduction of capital) is in principle subject to the obligation of § 35 (1) 1 WpÜG, but again, exemptions

---

115   Covered extensively in K. Hasselbach, in: *Kölner Kommentar zum WpÜG*, § 35 para. 5; similarly, see H. Krause, in: H.D. Assmann, T. Pötzsch, U.H. Schneider (eds.), *WpÜG-Kommentar*, § 35 WpÜG, para. 7.

116   Cf. P.O. Mülbert, *Umsetzungsfragen der Übernahmerichtlinie – Änderungsbedarf bei den heutigen Vorschriften des WpÜG*, 'Neue Zeitschrift für Gesellschaftsrecht' No. 2004, pp. 633, 641; K. Hopt, P.O. Mülbert, Ch. Kumpan, *Reformbedarf im Übernahmerecht*, 'Die Aktiengesellschaft' No. 2005, pp. 109, 113; K. Hopt, *Grundsatz- und Praxisprobleme…*, pp. 383, 416 et seq.

117   More extensive information on such other (direct) forms of acquisition: H. Krause, in: H.D. Assmann, T. Pötzsch, U.H. Schneider (eds.), *WpÜG-Kommentar*, § 35 WpÜG, paras. 79 et seq.; K. Hasselbach, in: *Kölner Kommentar zum WpÜG*, § 35 paras. 82 et seq.

118   In detail: H. Krause, in: H.D. Assmann, T. Pötzsch, U.H. Schneider (eds.), *WpÜG-Kommentar*, § 35 WpÜG, paras. 88–102; K. Hasselbach, in: *Kölner Kommentar zum WpÜG*, § 35 paras. 84–90.

119   H. Krause, in: H.D. Assmann, T. Pötzsch, U.H. Schneider (eds.), *WpÜG-Kommentar*, § 35 WpÜG, paras. 103–109; K. Hasselbach, in: *Kölner Kommentar zum WpÜG*, § 35 para. 91.

according to § 37 WpÜG may apply[120]. Thus, the concept of acquisition in German Law, at least in principle, reaches further than the same concept in the UK Takeover Code, which states somewhat fuzzily that in the case of gifts, shares or interests in shares, the Panel must be consulted[121]. § 35 (3) WpÜG exempts the acquisition of control by a previous takeover offer so as to avoid multiple offers[122].

§ 35 (1) WpÜG also provides for the duration, procedure and content of the disclosure obligation, but contains extensive references. The disclosure has to be made within seven calendar days, starting from the date on which the offeror was or is required to be aware of their own control position. Namely in the cases of = passive acquisition of control, or where shares are attributed according to legal rules, the acquisition date and the start of the notice period may therefore diverge. The procedure follows similar rules as those governing the disclosure of the decision to make a voluntary offer. In the disclosure document, the number of voting rights must be stated, in addition to the information about the target company and the offeror.

b) Obligation to make an offer

The centrepiece of the fifth chapter is the obligation to make an offer, pursuant to § 35 (2) 1 WpüG. This obligation is based on the core idea that as many shareholders as possible should participate in the control premium. It therefore aims to protect minority shareholders of a target company, while at the same time safeguarding the equal treatment principle laid down in § 3 (1) WpÜG. This possibility of equal participation is given once an offer is comprehensively made to all voting shareholders; accordingly, the obligation to make an offer does not apply when control has been acquired on the basis of a takeover offer according to § 35 (3) WpÜG. However, the obligation as such does not yet ensure the equal distribution of the control premium, since it is conceivable that single blockholders have been paid higher premiums for previous or subsequent over-the-counter

---

120   The triggers are always company law operations with the potential to shift voting power (which, for instance, does not happen in the case of a forfeiture of shares); for more detail, see H. Krause, in: H.D. Assmann, T. Pötzsch, U.H. Schneider (eds.), *WpÜG-Kommentar*, § 35 WpÜG, paras. 110–132; *Hasselbach*, in: Kölner Kommentar zum WpÜG, § 35 paras. 92–105.

121   See Note 12 on Rule 9.1 of the City Code.

122   For more extensive information on § 35 (3) WpÜG, see H. Krause, in: H.D. Assmann, T. Pötzsch, U.H. Schneider (eds.), *WpÜG-Kommentar*, § 35 WpÜG, paras. 270–284; K. Hasselbach, in: *Kölner Kommentar zum WpÜG*, § 35 paras. 241–256.

purchases[123]. The risks of 'lowballing' or 'creeping in' are, however, taken into account by specific rules on the consideration to be paid, according to § 31 (3) and (5) WpÜG[124]. In any event, the obligation to make an offer gives minority shareholders an exit option. Within the framework of German law, this raises the perpetual question of how this option, provided by Takeover Law, correlates with the minority protection offered by the law of groups (Konzernrecht). A great deal depends on its qualification as group-related or capital-market-related protection[125], but this qualification is just as controversial as the respective economic assessment[126].

§ 35 (2) WpÜG itself provides for a two-step procedure. In the first step, the offeror is obliged to submit an offer document within four weeks following the

---

123   K. Langenbucher, *Aktien- und Kapitalmarktrecht*, § 18 para. 31.

124   The scope of these provisions is limited, however, due to their time restrictions. Extensions have been discussed for specific cases (namely in the case of *ACS* and *Hochtief AG*), but did not become law. See the legislative proposal of the SPD parliamentary group, Bundestagsdrucksache (BT-Drs.) 17/3481; for more detail, see T. Baums, *Low Balling, Creeping in und deutsches Übernahmerecht*, 'Zeitschrift für Wirtschaftsrecht' No. 2010, p. 2374; J. Tyrolt, Ch. Cascante, *10 Jahre WpÜG – Reformbedarf im Übernahmerecht?*, 'Die Aktiengesellschaft' No. 2012, pp. 97, 104; J. Tyrolt, Ch. Cascante, *Pflichtangebotsbefreiung...*, pp. 110, 140–144.

125   On the one hand, for instance, see J. Reul, *Die Pflicht zur Gleichbehandlung der Aktionäre bei privaten Kontrolltransaktionen. Eine juristische und ökonomische Analyse*, Tübingen 1991, p. 303 et seq.; K. Hopt, *Konzernrecht - Die europäische Perspektive*, 'Zeitschrift für das gesamte Handels- und Wirtschaftsrecht' No. 171/2007, pp. 199, 233; K. Hopt, *Grundsatz- und Praxisprobleme...*, pp. 383, 386, 415; P. Mülbert, *Übernahmerecht...*, pp. 1221, 1226; H. Fleischer, *Schnittmengen des WpÜG mit benachbarten Rechtsmaterien – eine Problemskizze*, 'Neue Zeitschrift für Gesellschaftsrecht' No. 2002, pp. 545, 548; on the other hand, see K.J. Heiser, *Interessenkonflikte in der Aktiengesellschaft und ihre Lösung am Beispiel des Zwangsangebots*, Hamburg 1999, pp. 47–51, 350–396; E. Houben, *Die Gestaltung des Pflichtangebots unter dem Aspekt des Minderheitenschutzes und der effizienten Allokation der Unternehmenskontrolle*, 'Zeitschrift für Wirtschafts- und Bankrecht – Wertpapier-Mitteilungen' No. 2000, pp. 1873, 1877; D. Kleindiek, *Funktion und Geltungsanspruch des Pflichtangebots nach dem WpÜG*, 'Zeitschrift für Unternehmens- und Gesellschaftsrecht' No. 2002, pp. 546, 558–561.

126   For an overview, see H. Fleischer, S. Kalss, *Das neue...*, p. 38 et seq.; K. Hopt, *Europäisches und deutsches Übernahmerecht*, 'Zeitschrift für das gesamte Handels- und Wirtschaftsrecht' No. 161/1997, pp. 368, 385; see also E. Houben, *Die Gestaltung...*, 1873; H. Rau-Bredow, *Ökonomische Analyse obligatorischer Übernahmeangebote*, 'Die Betriebswirtschaft' No. 59/1999, p. 763. Seminally on the negative view, put forward namely by representatives of the *Chicago School*: F.H. Easterbrook, D.R. Fischel, *Corporate Control Transactions*, 'Yale Law Journal' No. 91/1982, p. 698.

disclosure of the acquisition of control. The term 'offeror' covers the same persons as § 35 (1) 1 WpÜG, i.e., anyone who directly or indirectly acquires control over a target company[127]. While the deadline for submitting the offer document corresponds to the publication according to § 35 (1) 1 WpÜG, in the case of omitted or delayed publication, the rule has to be adapted so that the date on which the publication would have had to be made is decisive[128]. Conversely, if that first disclosure has been made by mistake, there is no obligation to submit the offer document[129]. The submission of such a document includes an (implicit) application for its publication to be authorized, and the supervisory authority will subsequently examine this document in accordance with the general standards (cf. § 39 WpÜG, which refers to § 15 (1) no. 1 and 2 WpÜG)[130]. The examination period also follows the general rules, and generally lasts for 10 working days (§ 35 (2) 1 WpüG, referring to § 14 (2) 1 WpÜG)[131].

In the second step, § 35 (2) 1 WpÜG obliges the offeror to publish the offer. The publication must be effected without delay (cf. § 14 (2) 1 WpÜG, to which the provision refers)[132]. The publication follows the general rules, since § 35 (2) 2 WpÜG refers to § 14 WpÜG: in addition to the actual announcement (on the Internet, as well as either in the Federal Gazette or by making it available

---

127 H. Krause, in: H.D. Assmann, T. Pötzsch, U.H. Schneider (eds.), *WpÜG-Kommentar*, § 35 WpÜG, para. 186; K. Hasselbach, in: *Kölner Kommentar zum WpÜG*, § 35 para. 192.

128 H. Krause, in: H.D. Assmann, T. Pötzsch, U.H. Schneider (eds.), *WpÜG-Kommentar*, § 35 WpÜG, para. 188; K. Hasselbach, in: *Kölner Kommentar zum WpÜG*, § 35 para. 174.

129 H. Krause, in: H.D. Assmann, T. Pötzsch, U.H. Schneider (eds.), *WpÜG-Kommentar*, § 35 WpÜG, paras. 190 et seq.; on the other hand, differentiating in accordance with the various contents of mandatory disclosure, see K. Hasselbach, in: *Kölner Kommentar zum WpÜG*, § 35 paras. 194–199.

130 For more detail, see H. Krause, in: H.D. Assmann, T. Pötzsch, U.H. Schneider (eds.), *WpÜG-Kommentar*, § 35 WpÜG, paras. 209 et seq.; K. Hasselbach, in: *Kölner Kommentar zum WpÜG*, § 35 paras. 211, 214.

131 The possibility of § 14 (2) 3 WpÜG providing for the supervisory authority to extend the deadline is given, even though § 35 (2) 1, 2 WpÜG does not refer to it, because it applies correspondingly according to § 39 WpÜG; cf. H. Krause, in: H.D. Assmann, T. Pötzsch, U.H. Schneider (eds.), *WpÜG-Kommentar*, § 35 WpÜG, para. 211; K. Hasselbach, in: *Kölner Kommentar zum WpÜG*, § 35 para. 216.

132 According to the legal definition in § 121 (1) 1 BGB, this means without undue delay, cf. H. Krause, in: H.D. Assmann, T. Pötzsch, U.H. Schneider (eds.), *WpÜG-Kommentar*, § 35 WpÜG, para. 214; K. Hasselbach, in: *Kölner Kommentar zum WpÜG*, § 35 para. 219.

for distribution free of charge at a suitable location), its immediate communication to the supervisory authority, as well as its submission to the management board of the target company, is required[133]. The content of the offer is also essentially based on the general rules; in particular, a full offer to all shareholders, for all of their shares, is required (§ 32 in conjunction with § 39 WpÜG), and it may not be subject to any conditions (§§ 31 in conjunction with § 39 WpÜG)[134]. Specific questions arise with respect to the securities which must be covered by the mandatory bid, namely with regard to the category of securities concerned: while (even non-voting) shares must be included regardless of their admission to the stock exchange, the obligation does not extend to economically comparable securities which do not constitute membership rights, and which therefore do not form part of the definition of securities in § 2 (2) WpÜG (such as convertible bonds, options, American depositary receipts or tracking stocks). On the other hand, § 35 (2) 3 WpÜG provides for a specific exception with respect to the person of the shareholder, namely for their own shares of the target company, shares belonging to a subsidiary or majority-owned company of the target company, as well as shares owned by a third party but held for the account of the target company or a company which is its subsidiary or majority-owned. The reason for this exception is that the respective persons lack the specific need for protection that is otherwise typical of minority shareholders.

5. Conclusion

Our in-depth analysis of German Takeover Law has focused on its scope of application, its general principles and its taxonomy – rather than reproducing the usual descriptions of single legal institutions such as defensive measures or mandatory bids. While those legal institutions may be particularly controversial, the topics covered by this paper are crucial to the fundamental structure, architecture and very 'anatomy' of Takeover Law. Our analysis has revealed several characteristic features of German law that deviate either from the original UK City Code or even from the European Directive. To begin with, the scope of application follows a formal, not functional, approach: rather than focusing on the acquisition

---

133 Covered extensively in H. Krause, in: H.D. Assmann, T. Pötzsch, U.H. Schneider (eds.), *WpÜG-Kommentar*, § 35 WpÜG, paras. 215–218; K. Hasselbach, in: *Kölner Kommentar zum WpÜG*, § 35 paras. 220–224.
134 For more detail, see H. Krause, in: H.D. Assmann, T. Pötzsch, U.H. Schneider (eds.), *WpÜG-Kommentar*, § 35 WpÜG, paras. 224, 229–234; M. Schlitt, Ch. Ries, in: *Münchener Kommentar zum AktG*, § 35, paras. 195–198, 203 et seq., 216.

of control, the respective German rules focus on the making of a public offer. This approach has far-reaching structural effects insofar as German law also covers simple acquisition offers that do not aim to acquire control. The respective provisions form part of one (of three) specific chapters on the various forms of takeover, and do indeed constitute the 'general part' of German takeover law. In contrast, such offers are not subject to either the European Directive or the UK City Code. A second observation concerns the general principles. In accordance with the Directive (and following the UK role model), such principles are effectively provided for in German Takeover Law, but they are quite alien to legal tradition and thinking in this country. In consequence, they raise various problems of application, and their relationship to more specific provisions is very heavily debated in various respects.

These two fragmentations in particular illustrate that European Takeover Law – as the European harmonization in general – is based on compromises. They also demonstrate that the antithesis to the German (and indeed Continental European) approach stems from the UK City Code. While we do not claim that any single approach is superior in substance, we are simply observing that major discrepancies exist between these two opposing approaches. With the UK leaving the EU, however, these discrepancies will increasingly lose significance. If the takeover law approaches in the remaining Member States are much closer to each other, Brexit will fundamentally change the very foundation of the harmonization of European Takeover Law. Since the Takeover Directive in its current version leaves such a wide margin of discretion to Member States that it may not even qualify as 'true harmonization', Brexit therefore promises to offer new prospects for the more intensive harmonization of European Takeover Law: it might finally make a level playing field possible. Even though detrimental to European integration in so many respects, there is at least one advantage to Brexit – making it worthwhile to rethink European Takeover Law.

Literature

Alexy R., *Recht, Vernunft, Diskurs*, Frankfurt am Main 1995;

Altenhain K., *Die Neuregelung der Marktpreismanipulation durch das Vierte Finanzmarktförderungsgesetz*, 'Der Betriebs-Berater' No. 2002;

Assmann H.D., Pötzsch T., Schneider U.H. (eds.), *WpÜG-Kommentar*, 2nd edn., Cologne 2013;

Bachmann G., *Der Grundsatz der Gleichbehandlung im Kapitalmarktrecht*, 'Zeitschrift für das gesamte Handels- und Wirtschaftsrecht' No. 170/2006;

Baum H., *"Öffentlichkeit" des Erwerbsangebots als Anwendungsvoraussetzung des Übernahmerechts – Eine rechtsvergleichende Analyse*, 'Die Aktiengesellschaft' No. 2003;

Baum H., *Funktionale Elemente und Komplementaritäten des britischen Übernahmerechts*, 'Recht der Internazionalen Wirtschaft' 2003;

Baum H., *Rückerwerbsangebote für eigene Aktien: übernahmerechtlicher Handlungsbedarf?*, 'Zeitschrift für das gesamte Handels- und Wirtschaftsrecht' No. 167/2003;

Baums T., *Low Balling, Creeping in und deutsches Übernahmerecht*, 'Zeitschrift für Wirtschaftsrecht' No. 2010;

Baums T., Stöcker M., *Rückerwerb eigener Aktien und WpÜG*, in: *Festschrift für Herbert Wiedemann zum 70. Geburtstag*, Munich 2002;

Behnke T., *Erste praktische Erfahrungen mit dem Ausschluss ausländischer Anteilsinhaber nach § 24 WpÜG*, 'Zeitschrift für Wirtschafts- und Bankrecht – Wertpapier-Mitteilungen' No. 2002;

Berrar C., Schnorbus Y., *Rückerwerb eigener Aktien und Übernahmerecht*, 'Zeitschrift für Unternehmens- und Gesellschaftsrecht' No. 2003;

Bungert H., Leyendecker-Langner B.E., *Die Neuregelung des Delisting*, 'Zeitschrift für Wirtschaftsrecht' No. 2016;

Bydlinski F., *Juristische Methodenlehre und Rechtsbegriff*, Berlin 1982;

Canaris C.W., *Die richtlinienkonforme Auslegung und Rechtsfortbildung im System der juristischen Methodenlehre*, in: Koziol H., Rummel P. (eds.), *Im Dienste der Gerechtigkeit: Festschrift für Franz Bydlinski*, Berlin 2002;

Craig P., *Brexit: A Drama in Six Acts*, 'European Law Review' No. 41/2016, p. 447;

Davies P.L., *The Regulation of Takeovers and Mergers*, London 1976;

Drygala T., *Deal Protection in Verschmelzungs- und Unternehmenskaufverträgen*, 'Zeitschrift für Wirtschafts- und Bankrecht – Wertpapier-Mitteilungen' No. 2004;

Dworkin R., *Taking Rights Seriously*, Cambridge 1977;

Easterbrook F.H., Fischel D.R., *Corporate Control Transactions*, 'Yale Law Journal' No. 91/1982;

Ferran E., *Principles of Corporate Finance Law*, Oxford 2008;

Ferran E., *The UK as a Third Country Actor in EU Financial Services Regulation*, Working Paper, available for download at: https://papers.ssrn.com/sol3/papers.cfm?abstract_id=2845374;

Fleischer H., Kalss S., *Das neue Wertpapiererwerbs- und Übernahmegesetz*, Munich 2002;

Fleischer H., *Konkurrenzangebote und Due Diligence*, 'Zeitschrift für Wirtschaftsrecht' No. 2002;

Fleischer H., Körber T., *Der Rückerwerb eigener Aktien und das Wertpapiererwerbs- und Übernahmegesetz*, 'Der Betriebs-Berater' No. 2001;

Fleischer H., *Schnittmengen des WpÜG mit benachbarten Rechtsmaterien – eine Problemskizze*, 'Neue Zeitschrift für Gesellschaftsrecht' No. 2002;

Fleischer H., *Zum Begriff des öffentlichen Angebots im Wertpapiererwerbs- und Übernahmegesetz*, 'Zeitschrift für Wirtschaftsrecht' No. 2001;

Gatti M., *Optionality Arrangements and Reciprocity in the European Takeover Directive*, 'European Business Organization Law Review', No. 6/2005;

Gegler F., *Die Neuregelung des Delistings – Angemessener Aktionärsschutz oder „Dolchstoß"?*, 'Zeitschrift für Bank- und Kapitalmarktrecht' No. 2016;

Goette W. et al. (eds.) *Münchener Kommentar zum AktG und WpÜG*, Munich 2011;

Hamann U., *Die Angebotsunterlage nach dem WpÜG – Ein praxisorientierter Überblick*, 'Zeitschrift für Wirtschaftsrecht' No. 2001;

Harbarth S., *Kontrollerlangung und Pflichtangebot*, 'Zeitschrift für Wirtschaftsrecht' No. 2002;

Harnos R., *Aktionärsschutz beim Delisting*, 'Zeitschrift für das gesamte Handels- und Wirtschaftsrecht' No. 179/2015;

Hasselbach K., Pröhl M., *Delisting mit oder ohne Erwerbsangebot nach neuer Rechtslage*, 'Neue Zeitschrift für Gesellschaftsrecht' No. 2015;

Heiser K.J., *Interessenkonflikte in der Aktiengesellschaft und ihre Lösung am Beispiel des Zwangsangebots*, Hamburg 1999;

Hippeli M., Diesing M., *Business Combination Agreements bei M&A-Transaktionen*, 'Die Aktiengesellschaft' No. 2015;

Hirte H., von Bülow Ch. (eds.) *Kölner Kommentar zum WpÜG*, Cologne 2010;

Höpner M., Jackson G., *Revisiting the Mannesmann takeover: How markets for corporate control emerge*, 'European Management Review', No. 3/2006;

Hopt K., *Konzernrecht - Die europäische Perspektive*, 'Zeitschrift für das gesamte Handels- und Wirtschaftsrecht' No. 171/2007;

Hopt K., *Aktionärskreis und Vorstandsneutralität*, 'Zeitschrift für Unternehmens- und Gesellschaftsrecht' No. 1993;

Hopt K., *Auf dem Weg zum deutschen Übernahmegesetz – Gemeinsamer Standpunkt des Rates zur 13. Richtlinie und Diskussionsentwurf des Übernahmegesetzes*, in: *Festschrift für Hans-Georg Koppensteiner zum 65. Geburtstag*, Vienna 2001;

Hopt K., *Europäisches Übernahmerecht: eine rechtsvergleichende, rechtsdogmatische und rechtspolitische Untersuchung*, Tübingen 2013;

Hopt K., *Europäisches und deutsches Übernahmerecht*, 'Zeitschrift für das gesamte Handels- und Wirtschaftsrecht' No. 161/1997;

Hopt K., *European Takeover Reform of 2012/2013 – Time to Re-Examine the Mandatory Bid*, 'European Business Organization Law Review' No. 15/2014;

Hopt K., *Grundsatz- und Praxisprobleme nach dem Wertpapiererwerbs- und Übernahmegesetz*, 'Zeitschrift für das gesamte Handels- und Wirtschaftsrecht' No. 166/2002;

Hopt K., Mülbert P.O., Kumpan Ch., *Reformbedarf im Übernahmerecht*, 'Die Aktiengesellschaft' No. 2005;

Hopt K., *Stand der Harmonisierung der europäischen Übernahmerechte – Bestandsaufnahme, praktische Erfahrungen und Ausblicke*, in: Mülbert P., Kiem R., Wittig A. (ed.), *10 Jahre WpÜG: Entwicklungsstand – Praktische Erfahrungen – Reformbedarf – Perspektiven*, Frankfurt am Main 2011;

Houben E., *Die Gestaltung des Pflichtangebots unter dem Aspekt des Minderheitenschutzes und der effizienten Allokation der Unternehmenskontrolle*, 'Zeitschrift für Wirtschafts- und Bankrecht – Wertpapier-Mitteilungen' No. 2000;

Johnston A., *The City Take-Over Code*, Oxford 1980;

Kaplow L., *Rules Versus Standards: An Economic Analysis*, 'Duke Law Journal' No. 42/1992;

Kleindiek D., *Funktion und Geltungsanspruch des Pflichtangebots nach dem WpÜG*, 'Zeitschrift für Unternehmens- und Gesellschaftsrecht' No. 2002;

Koch J., *Der Erwerb eigener Aktien – kein Fall des WpÜG*, 'Neue Zeitschrift für Gesellschaftsrecht' No. 2003;

Kocher D., Seiz E., *Das neue Delisting nach § 39 Abs. 2–6 BörsG*, 'Der Betrieb' No. 2016;

Krause H., *Die EU-Übernahmerichtlinie – Anpassungsbedarf im Wertpapiererwerbs- und Übernahmegesetz*, 'Der Betriebs-Berater' 2004;

Langenbucher K., *Aktien- und Kapitalmarktrecht*, 3rd ed., Munich 2015;

Larenz K., *Methodenlehre der Rechtswissenschaft*, 2nd edn. Berlin 1992;

Lee P., *Takeover Regulation in the United Kingdom*, in: Institut für europäisches und internationales Wirtschafts- und Sozialrecht (ed.), *Erwerb von Beteiligungen am Beispiel der öffentlichen Übernahmeangebote*, Lausanne 1990;

Lee P., *Takeovers – The UK experience*, in: Farrar J.H. (ed.), *Takeovers, Institutional Investors and the Modernization of Corporate Laws*, Auckland 1993;

Lehmann M., Zetzsche D., *Brexit and the Consequences for Commercial and Financial Relations between the EU and the UK*, 'European Business Law Review' No. 27/2016;

Lehne K.H., *Die 13. Richtlinie auf dem Gebiet des Gesellschaftsrechts betreffend Übernahmeangebote – gescheitert, aber dennoch richtungsweisend für das künftige europäische Übernahmerecht*, in: Hirte H. (ed.), *Wertpapiererwerbs- und Übernahmegesetz*, Cologne 2002;

Liebscher T., *Das Übernahmeverfahren nach dem neuen Übernahmegesetz*, 'Zeitschrift für Wirtschaftsrecht' No. 2001;

Liekefett K.H., *Bietergleichbehandlung bei öffentlichen Übernahmeangeboten*, 'Die Aktiengesellschaft' No. 2005;

Lutter M., *Die Auslegung angeglichenen Rechts*, 'Juristen Zeitung' No. 1992;

Maul S., Muffat-Jeandet D., *Die EU-Übernahmerichtlinie – Inhalt und Umsetzung in nationales Recht*, 'Die Aktiengesellschaft' 2004;

Maume P., *The Parting of the Ways – Delisting under German and UK Law*, 'European Business Organization Law Review' No. 16/2015;

McCahery J.A., Vermeulen E.P.M., *The Case Against Reform of the Takeover Bids Directive*, 'European Business Law Review' No. 22/2011;

Möllers T.M.J., *Verfahren, Pflichten und Haftung, insbesondere der Banken, bei Übernahmeangeboten*, 'Zeitschrift für Unternehmens- und Gesellschaftsrecht' No. 2002;

Möslein F., *Grenzen unternehmerischer Leitungsmacht im marktoffenen Verband*, Berlin 2007;

Mukwiri J., *Reforming EU Takeover Law Remains on Hold*, 'European Company Law' No. 12/2015;

Mülbert P.O., *Übernahmerecht zwischen Kapitalmarktrecht und Aktien(konzern)recht – Die konzeptionelle Schwachstelle des WpÜG*, 'Zeitschrift für Wirtschaftsrecht' No. 2001;

Mülbert P.O., *Umsetzungsfragen der Übernahmerichtlinie – Änderungsbedarf bei den heutigen Vorschriften des WpÜG*, 'Neue Zeitschrift für Gesellschaftsrecht' No. 2004;

Oechsler J., *Der ReE zum Wertpapiererwerbs- und Übernahmegesetz*, 'Neue Zeitschrift für Gesellschaftsrecht' No. 2001;

Oechsler J., *Rechtsgeschäftliche Anwendungsprobleme bei öffentlichen Übernahmeangeboten*, 'Zeitschrift für Wirtschaftsrecht' No. 2003;

Ogowewo T., *New Takeover Code Rules on Exchange Offers and Auctions*, 'The Company Lawyer' No. 23/2002;

P. Hommelhoff, *Die Rolle der nationalen Gerichte bei der Europäisierung des Privatrechts*, in: Canaris C.W. et. al (eds.) *50 Jahre Bundesgerichtshof, Festgabe aus der Wissenschaft*, Munich 2000;

Paefgen W.G., *Die Gleichbehandlung beim Aktienrückerwerb im Schnittfeld von Gesellschafts- und Übernahmerecht*, 'Zeitschrift für Wirtschaftsrecht' No. 2002;

Payne J. (ed.) *Takeovers in English and German Law*, Oxford 2002;

Peltzer M., *Übernahmeangebote nach künftigem Europarecht und dessen Umsetzung in deutsches Recht*, in: Assmann H.D., Bozenhardt F., Basaldua N., Peltzer M. (eds.), *Übernahmeangebote*, Berlin 1990;

Pennington R., *Corporate Takeovers Through the Public Markets – United Kingdom*, in: Kozyris J. (ed.), *Corporate Takeovers Through the Public Markets*, London 1996;

Pluskat S., *Das Scheitern der europäischen Übernahmerichtlinie*, 'WM Wirtschafts- und Bankrecht' 2001;

Poelzig D., *Insider- und Marktmanipulationsverbot im neuen Marktmissbrauchsrecht*, 'Neue Zeitschrift für Gesellschaftsrecht' No. 2016;

Rau-Bredow H., *Ökonomische Analyse obligatorischer Übernahmeangebote*, 'Die Betriebswirtschaft' No. 59/1999;

Reul J., *Die Pflicht zur Gleichbehandlung der Aktionäre bei privaten Kontrolltransaktionen. Eine juristische und ökonomische Analyse*, Tübingen 1991;

Santelmann M., *Notwendige Mindesterwerbsschwellen bei Übernahmeangeboten*, 'Die Aktiengesellschaft' No. 2002;

Schillig M., *Corporate Law after Brexit*, Working Paper, available for download at: https://papers.ssrn.com/sol3/papers.cfm?abstract_id=2846755;

Schmolke K.U., *Das Verbot der Marktmanipulation nach dem neuen Marktmissbrauchsregime*, 'Die Aktiengesellschaft' No. 2016;

Schneider U.H., *Internationales Kapitalmarktrecht*, 'Die Aktiengesellschaft' No. 2001;

Seibt Ch.H., *Reform der EU-Übernahmerichtlinie und des deutschen Übernahmerechts*, 'Zeitschrift für Wirtschaftsrecht' No. 1/2012;

Steinmeyer R., *Der übernahmerechtliche Sitzbegriff*, in: *Wirtschafts- und Privatrecht im Spannungsfeld von Privatautonomie, Wettbewerb und Regulierung, Festschrift für Ulrich Immenga zum 70. Geburtstag*, Munich 2004;

Tsagas G., *The Revision of the EU Takeover Directive in Light of the 2011 UK Takeover Law Reform*, 'International and Comparative Company Law Journal' No. 10/2013;

Tyrolt J., Cascante Ch., *10 Jahre WpÜG – Reformbedarf im Übernahmerecht?*, 'Die Aktiengesellschaft' No. 2012;

Tyrolt J., Cascante Ch., *Pflichtangebotsbefreiung durch Übernahmeangebot und Mindestpreiseregelungen*, in: Mülbert P., Kiem R., Wittig A. (eds.), *10 Jahre Wertpapiererwerbs- und Übernahmegesetz (WpÜG). Entwicklungsstand - praktische Erfahrungen - Reformbedarf - Perspektiven*, Frankfurt am Main 2011;

Van Kann J., Just C., *Der Regierungsentwurf zur Umsetzung der europäischen Übernahmerichtlinie*, 'Deutsches Steuerrecht' No. 2006;

von der Linden K., *Das neue Marktmissbrauchsrecht im Überblick*, 'Deutsches Steuerrecht' No. 2016;

von Hein J., *Grundfragen des europäischen Übernahmekollisionsrechts*, 'Die Aktiengesellschaft' No. 2001;

von Hein J., *Zur Kodifikation des europäischen Übernahmekollisionsrechts*, 'Zeitschrift für Unternehmens- und Gesellschaftsrecht' No. 2005;

Wackerbarth U., *Das neue Delisting-Angebot nach § 39 BörsG oder: Hat der Gesetzgeber hier wirklich gut nachgedacht?*, 'Zeitschrift für Wirtschafts- und Bankrecht – Wertpapier-Mitteilungen' No. 2016;

Weinberg M.A., Blank M.V., *Takeovers & Mergers*, 5th edn., London 2003;

Winner M., *Die Zielgesellschaft in der freundlichen Übernahme*, Vienna 2002.

Abbreviations

AktG – Aktiengesetz (German Act on joint-stock companies) of 6 September 1965 (BGBl. I S. 1089);

BGB – Bürgerliches Gesetzbuch (German Civil Code) of 18 August 1896 (BGBl. I S. 42, ber. S. 2909, ber. 2003 I S. 738);

BörsG – Börsengesetz (German Act on stock exchange) of 22 June 1897 (BGBl. I S. 2010);

City Code, London City Code – The Takeover Code of the Panel on Takeovers and Mergers (current version 12th edn. 12 September 2016);

Commission – the European Commission;

ECJ – European Court of Justice;

EEA – European Economic Area;

ESMA – European Securities and Markets Authority;

EU – European Union;

GG – Grundgesetz für die Bundesrepublik Deutschland (Constitution or Basic Law for the Federal Republic of Germany) of 23 May 1949 (BGBl. S. 1);

MiFID I – directive 2004/39/EC of the European Parliament and of the Council of 21 April 2004 on markets in financial instruments amending Council Directives 85/611/EEC and 93/6/EEC and Directive 2000/12/EC of the European Parliament and of the Council and repealing Council Directive 93/22/EEC (Official Journal of the European Community L 145 of 30 April 2004, p. 1, as amended);

MiFID II – directive 2014/65/EU of the European Parliament and of the Council of 15 May 2014 on markets in financial instruments and amending Directive 2002/92/EC and Directive 2011/61/EU (Official Journal of the European Union L 173 of 12 July 2014, p. 349, as amended);

RegE – Regierungsentwurf (Governmental Bill of the Act of Parliament);

SE – Societas Europea (European Company);

Takeover Directive – directive 2004/25/EC of the European Parliament and of the Council of 21 April 2004 on takeover bids (Official Journal of the European Community L 310 of 30 April 2004, p. 12, as amended);

TFEU – Treaty on the Functioning of the European Union (consolidated version Official Journal of the European Union C 326 of 26 October 2012, p. 47, as amended);

WpÜG – Wertpapiererwerbs- und Übernahmegesetz (German Act on the acquisition of securities and the takeovers) of 20 December 2001 (BGBl. I S. 3822);

WTO – World Trade Organization.

Prof. Mariusz Golecki & Prof. Maciej Mataczyński

University of Łódź, Faculty of Law and Administration
Adam Mickiewicz University in Poznań, Faculty of Law and Administration

'National Champions' between corporate and political governance. Institutional analysis of the forms of protectionism in the strategic sectors in EU Law

Abstract: The concept of the so-called 'national champions' refers to companies which are perceived as of vital importance to the national interest. Generally, there are two sources of their particular importance. Firstly, the companies may have access to unique resources relevant to economic and security considerations. Secondly, the lack of control of a given company may result in the externality effect for the national economy. Typically, the situation results from the so-called spin-off effect in terms of specific assets such as infrastructure. Both situations usually lead to a form of protectionism and state control. The paper aims to scrutinize the ways in which control is exercised by the state. It seems that, at least in Europe, corporate ownership structure is still used by governments, whereas some new forms of implicit control and state influence are emerging. In some states such as France, Germany or Poland special administrative procedures have been implemented in response to the evolution of the EU Law. Secondly, the question remains which of these two strategies, based on private or public law respectively, is more effective and less inefficient. We intend to apply a wider concept of dynamic efficiency, taking the potential systemic effects into account. The third dimension concerns the impact of the 'national champions' strategy upon political systems, democratic control, transparency and other public choice considerations such as the agency problem.

Key words: evolution of company law, corporate governance, public management, state capitalism, state ownership, neoinstitutional economics, critical infrastructures

1. The evolution of corporate governance and the rise of national champions: from the 'the end of history' to 'the end of free market'

In their intriguing paper from 2001 entitled *The End of History for Corporate Law*[1], Henry Hansmann and Rainier Kraakman observed that due to the common agreement pertaining to a corporate form, the model of corporation has already achieved a high degree of uniformity, and in the long run will become a common denominator for different legal systems and economies reflecting the normative assumption and priorities motivated by the need to protect shareholders who are residual claimants and real principal controlling managers. Meanwhile, the authors put forward a claim according to which the other models were going to die out in a process of natural selection, observing that the other models were simply inefficient. Thus, the end of history would mark the evolution of the models of corporate control, where competitive models such as the manager-oriented model, the labour-oriented and the state-oriented model would become subjects of historical investigation rather than plausible institutional alternatives to the market-oriented shareholder protecting corporate ownership. Concluding their reasoning on the fall of the state ownership model as losing its' normative appeal, they claim that:

> '(b)oth before and after the Second World War, there was widespread support for a corporate system in which the government would play a strong direct role in the affairs of large business firms to provide some assurance that private enterprise would serve the public interest. Technocratic governmental bureaucrats, the theory went, would help to avoid the deficiencies of the market through the direct exercise of influence in corporate affairs. This approach was most extensively realized in post-war France and Japan. (…) But the state-oriented model, too, has now lost most of its attraction. (…) Today, few would argue that giving the state a strong direct hand in corporate affairs has much normative appeal'[2].

Meanwhile, they observed that the standard shareholder-oriented model superseded other institutional alternatives. Two questions remain. Firstly, is the assessment and evaluation of the driving force behind the evolution of company law really correct? Is this true that the history has come to an end? Obviously, further development of corporate ownership in different parts of global economy does not confirm their predictions. It seems that the Hansmann and Kraakman's

---

1   H. Hansmann, R. Kraakman, *The End of History for Corporate Law*, 'Harvard Law School Discussion Paper' No. 280, 3/2000.
2   Ibidem, pp. 6–7.

narrative of the end of history may be usefully confronted with a more recent and challenging narrative of the end of the free market hypothesis put forward by Ian Bremmer, which refers to the growing phenomenon of state capitalism[3]. State capitalism seems to be a real threat not only to dispersed ownership and shareholder-oriented corporate governance, but to the existence of a free market economy. This jeopardy is strongly correlated with the curious phenomenon of state control of the economy, so interestingly described by Ronald Coase in his *Nature of the Firm*[4]. The rise of state capitalism is truly discernible as governments seem to control economies in some countries through the ownership of market-dominant companies and capital, under the assumption that either the market fails or a strategic consideration has to supersede typical shareholder-oriented myopia and short-termism, enabling states to invest in long-term projects and focus on social values. In fact, states are apt to use their economic power just transforming it into short-time oriented political gains. At least Ian Bremmer believes so and warns against this process as a real danger for the existence of the free market-based global economy. The process is marked by the rise of state-owned and state-controlled enterprises in countries such as emerging powers (Brazil, Russia, India, China and South Africa), authoritarian oil-based regimes (the Arab states, Iran, Venezuela), and other places, not excluding Europe. He demonstrates the growing challenge that state capitalism will pose for the entire global economy – a narrative strikingly different from the optimistic prophesies endorsed by Fukuyama, Hansmann and Kraakman[5].

As for them, the starting point for Bremmer's narrative seems to be located in 1990s and the alternative paths of development adopted by different states after the collapse of communism[6]. Almost all of them seemed to have adopted a market economy, but the structure of the market, the approach to privatization and relations between public and private seemed to be dramatically different. Whereas many South American and European states actually adopted a privatization strategy and attempted to create strong private ownership; some regimes, such as China, decided to create market-based capitalism with serious limitations and active control by the state, expecting to maximize control over wealth and

---

3   I. Bremmer, *The end of the free market: who wins the war between states and corporations?*, New York 2010.

4   R.H. Coase, *The Nature of the Firm*, 'Economica. New Series', Vol. 4, No. 16/1937, pp. 386–405.

5   F. Fukuyama, *The End of History and the Last Man*, New York 1992; H. Hansmann, R. Kraakman, *The End of History…*, passim.

6   I. Bremmer, *The end…*, pp. 10–24.

political assets alike. As I. Bremmer observes, in China, Russia, Saudi Arabia and other non-democratic authoritarian regimes, state-owned companies and privately owned national champions alike play a sufficiently important role in a political game dominating core sectors of national economy ranging from energy and military production to aviation and telecommunications. Those enterprises in fact became key players in various branches of the global market, especially in the energy sector. However, when participating in the active industrial economic policy, those states do not remain benevolent organizers and promoters of social development through wealth, but rather political decision-makers transferring economic gains into political assets. The ultimate goal of this strategy is not economic, but rather political, consisting in maximizing political dominance and influence alike. Hence the rise of state capitalism becomes appealing as an alternative model and sometimes leads to economic nationalism even in countries still maintaining free market and democratic institutions, where politicians remain under constant pressure. On the other hand, Bremer observes that in fact state capitalism is driven by the world's fastest growing emerging market powerhouse and many of the world's largest energy exporters. Moreover, global economy needs these countries to succeed. At the same time, the process of empowerment of those enterprises undermines free markets in several ways. Firstly, many state-owned companies and investment funds are in fact inefficient, since their decisions are driven by political motives rather than economic goals. Besides, companies and investors operating in China, Russia and other state capitalist countries discover that once they develop technical, management and marketing expertise and are ready to compete with outsiders, their governments can use a variety of legal and administrative tools supporting their position on the market. Finally, the doubt arises whether the driving forces shaping the institutional structure of contemporary corporate law are still limited to the factors indicated by Hansmann and Kraakman, namely the alleged failure of alternative models and the competitive pressures of global commerce. It seems that an alternative explanation potentially adds another dimension and brings political dynamics into picture. As Mark Roe observed, policy may well influence the structure of corporate law, in a direct or indirect way[7]. For example, strong support for social democracy leads to a wider gap between shareholders and management due to the influence of different stakeholders on the managerial strategies[8]. Moreover, the causality of the

---

7   M.J. Roe, *Political determinants of corporate governance: political context, corporate impact*, Oxford 2003, pp. 29–37.

8   M.J. Roe, *Political preconditions to separating Ownership from Corporate Control*, 'Stanford Law Review' Vol. 53, No. 2000, pp. 539–606.

process leading to the establishment of any model of corporate control has to be broader, encapsulating political, social and cultural conditions[9]. Thus it seems that both political structure and political governance play an important role in shaping the face of present state capitalism in general and the strategic enterprises supported by governments in particular. These companies are often referred to as national champions – a term which embraces different types of firms supported by states. In general, those state interventions may take different forms such as various institutional mechanisms by which states exercise control. We propose a conceptual framework based on a functional approach in order to understand state capitalism in a more nuanced and detailed way. The urgent need for an analytical and conceptual framework means that the concept of national champions should be analysed from the perspective of the state and market as institutional alternatives, albeit encapsulating some intermediary hybrid institutional forms, as well as a paradigmatic concept such as public vs. private ownership.

2. Towards conceptualization of the national champions

The question of what those firms are about and how they should be different seems to be the most pertinent. It has to be recalled that the theory of the firm is deeply rooted in this kind of considerations, since R. Coase pondered why not to have one firm only, rather than a multitude of different firms immersed into the ocean of transactions on different markets[10]. But the form of state capitalism prevailing in the twenty-first century seems to be slightly different from what could be observed in the second half of the twentieth century. Then state involvement in enterprises took the form of centrally managed command economies or mixed economies in which governments owned a large number of state-owned enterprises, directly controlling the allocation of strategic resources. It seems, however, that the privatization and liberalization wave of the 1980s and 1990s, mentioned by Hansmann and Kraakman, led to the creation of a new form of hybrid capitalism where the government influences the investment decisions of private companies largely through minority capital. In fact, we observe both models, with the dominating state majority ownership in countries such as China, Russia and certain Asian countries, and state minority ownership in Europe and South America. These observations are reflected in the growing interest in national champions and state capitalism in the contemporary world. Facts and figures suggest that

---

9   Cf. L.A. Bebchuk, M.J. Roe, *A Theory of Path Dependence in Corporate Ownership and Governance*, 'Stanford Law Review' Vol. 52, No. 1999, pp. 127–170.

10 R.H. Coase, *The Nature...*, pp. 386–390.

Haansman and Kraakman's conclusions on the malaise of state capitalism and corporate governance as the normative model are no longer true. However, it does not mean that the prosperity of the state capitalism may be safeguarded in the long run. Firstly, the policy aspect mentioned by Roe plays an important role, but not necessarily favours state-owned enterprises as a stable institutional equilibrium. A more interdisciplinary approach to the evolution of state-owned enterprises may well disclose some economic and policy based determinants which actually confine further expansion of state capitalism.

From theoretical perspective, there are three sets of constraints which should be taken into account.

Firstly, the limits of a long-term economic policy and economic limitations of a state-owned corporation as restricted to a relatively narrow scope of strategic sectors, where market failures generally justify at least tentatively the idea of regulatory means and industrial policy as some remedies against those market failures. In the first part of the paper we simply review such situations which *prima facie* call for a state intervention and justify it.

Secondly, the question arises if and under which conditions market failures may be cured by state intervention. Three potential institutional models could be analysed in this respect. Firstly – the majority state ownership, secondly – the minority state ownership and finally – an external regulatory interim solution.

Thirdly, the question arises which of those institutional frameworks is the most appropriate from the perspective of both corporate governance and policy governance. In particular, the question should be asked about the long term efficiency in the context of the agency problem, which seems to be the most significant issue from both corporate governance and political governance perspectives. The first one concentrates on three different institutional solutions to the agency problem, depending on how the problem could be solved in the case of majority state ownership, minority state ownership and external administrative interventionism. Secondly, the agency problem will also be analysed from the wider policy-oriented perspective, taking into account not only the divergence of incentives between private and public organizations, but also a specific difference between private agents acting on behalf of shareholders and public agents acting on behalf of multiple political principals: departments and the ruling party. The last comparison leads to the conclusion that patronage and the multiplication of principals may effectively block the extension of state ownership and result in the comparative advantage of the third model, namely the external administrative regulation supervised by court.

Following the debate on the state-owned model of enterprises, which for Hansmann and Kraakman lost its normative appeal whereas for I. Bremmer regained its significance especially in the form of national champions, we propose a functional approach to the state control of firms. It has to be observed that those enterprises primarily seem to be of vital importance not only for economic activity, but also for tsecurity and long-term development of states. It could be suggested that there are two potential sources of anxiety about the existence of companies performing certain special functions related to security and prosperity. It could rightly be claimed that in some sectors, market failures seem to loom large, especially if we take some potential problems of a free market-oriented model of dispersed ownership into account. The rise and growth of the so-called national champions may result from two potential sources, namely market imperfections and governance failure in the form of so-called missing ownership. From this perspective, it seems that the concept of the so called 'national champions' refers to the companies which are perceived as of vital importance for the national interest. Thus, we define national champions by the fact that they represent special assets rather than by the forms of state intervention, such as those in firms which are intentionally influenced by the government in the economy, either by owning majority or minority equity positions or through other means, such as protection against takeover (poisonous pills) or special rights vested in government (golden share). Generally, there are two sources of their particular importance. Firstly, the companies may have access to unique resources relevant to economic and security considerations. These resources are generally vaguely defined and protected in different ways by national regulations securing essential influence of the government upon the company's decisions and structure. However, the question remains whether state control through property rights in the form of either majority ownership or minority ownership with some special rights (e.g. golden share) is the most appropriate institutional response to the problem of strategic resources. It seems that the separation of ownership and control of those assets is possible through extensive administrative regulation which could potentially be superior to state ownership. This, however, requires considering two decisive institutional factors, namely the disadvantages of public vs. private ownership and the mode of separation between internal and external control of those assets. In order to analyse a whole repertoire of different strategies, we need to take a look at the European landscape, where state capitalism has also left its trace in the practices of governments and the responses of the EU institutions alike.

3. National champions in the EU context

The so-called 'national champions' doctrine is the bedrock of Polish state policy with respect to the supervision of the biggest companies in which the state holds a controlling interest. Pursuant to the doctrine, the experience of the financial crash of 2009 has proved that the state should keep its controlling stake in strategic economic industries (banks, insurance, oil and gas extraction and processing, power generation and transmission, ports, noble metal extraction). The mass privatization of state-owned businesses (not only in the energy, but also in banking and insurance sectors) has weakened the economies of a number of states and significantly hindered the process of solving financial problems. In extreme cases, the state had to intervene anyway to protect the entire economy against the adverse impact of the uncontrolled bankruptcy of large entities (e.g. the renationalization of a portion of *Citi* in the United States). As a result, a belief in the free market dogma assuming the superiority of private ownership over state ownership has been shaken. This shift has been reinforced by positive stories of companies which remained state-owned and continued to develop dynamically (e.g. the Norwegian showcase company, *Statoil*). What is more, in the Polish context the biggest state-supervised companies have also managed to significantly increase their share value (e.g. PKO BP S.A., PZU S.A., KGHM S.A.). However, the weakness of state-appointed management lay in its lack of stability when it comes to the composition of company authorities and in appointments[11] motivated by political reasons rather than merit. To eliminate these negative factors, the competence to appoint members of company authorities was to be delegated by the political authority (the Minister of State Treasury) to independent experts serving on a newly established Appointments Committee.

These assumptions were codified in the draft act laying down the rules for the exercising of certain State Treasury rights submitted by the government to the 6th Sejm[12]. The draft contained a new, comprehensive solution concerning proprietary oversight by the State Treasury, but most importantly it stipulated the establishment of the Appointments Committee referred to above (Art. 20–23 of the draft). The tasks of the Committee were to involve recommending candidates in the

---

11 The number of changes to the supervisory and management boards of PKN Orlen S.A. in the period 1998–2008 (105) as compared to its Hungarian – MOL (19) and Austrian – OMV (12) equivalent companies.

12 Sejm publication no. 3580, 6th Sejm, available at: http://orka.sejm.gov.pl/Druki6ka.nsf/0/029DA30B8BEAF88CC12577DD00479FC6/$file/3580.pdf [access on 20 February 2017].

supervisory boards of companies classified as enterprises of key importance to the State Treasury and evaluating motions for the dismissal of members serving on the supervisory boards of such companies (Art. 20(2)(1) and 20(2)(3) of the draft). The Committee was to be composed of ten members appointed by the President of the Council of Ministers for a five-year term, whose preterm dismissal would be substantially impossible. Art. 45(1) of the draft introduced a crucial provision that only a person holding the Committee's recommendation could be appointed by the Minister of State Treasury to serve on the supervisory board of a company classified as an enterprise of key importance. The draft act codified the 'national champions' political-economic policy, introducing – in Section II – a category of 'entities of key importance to the State Treasury'. Pursuant to the definition in Art. 44(1) of the draft, this category was to include companies with the State Treasury interest having special importance to the economic interests of the State Treasury or a special influence on the stability and security of the infrastructure necessary for the correct functioning of the national economy.

There is a lot of controversy when it comes to depriving political authorities of their influence on significant elements of state powers (e.g. prosecution). It has been argued that the political mandate of ministers stems from the intent of the majority of citizens expressed in democratic elections and in consequence such persons bear political (with respect to the representatives of such a majority) and in extreme cases also constitutional and criminal liability. Meanwhile, had the act come into force, ten persons would have been entrusted with full control of the assets regularly generating as much as two hundred and fifty billion Polish zloty in revenue per year, without any liability for their decisions (apart from potential damage to their reputation). These doubts have ultimately caused work on the draft to be abandoned. It is hard to assess the effects of a law which has never come into force. However, in my opinion, the arguments which could be considered reasonable when it comes to the prosecution do not necessarily apply to company management. The only way to develop an efficient model of managing state-owned assets is to ensure that it is based on competence and merit rather than on political criteria. To date, the draft of 2010 has been the boldest attempt at such a change.

Furthermore, a point has to be made with respect to the coherence of the above-mentioned doctrine with EU law, and especially with the case law of the ECJ with Treaty freedoms, notably the free movement of capital. According to the established judicial practice of the Court, the 'restrictions' in the meaning of Art. 63(1) TFEU include such provisions of domestic law which may pose a barrier to or limit the acquisition of shares in specific companies or which may discourage investors from other member states from investing in the capital of such companies. The proceedings pending before the European Commission in the context of Art. 258 TFEU and subsequent judgments of the Tribunal have covered various provisions granting privileges to a state. Examples included voting restrictions (the so-called voting caps), personally vested rights with respect to the appointment and dismissal of the members of a company's authorities, and various forms of shares carrying multiple voting rights or veto powers. In general, the ECJ has concluded that such privileges violate the TFEU. It is noteworthy that the ECJ has not differentiated between external influence of the state in the form of administrative actions and the internal exercise of state's power as one of the shareholders of the company. Instead, the ECJ has focused on the merits of the state's action and whether it discourages investors from other member states from investing in such companies. It has to be noted also that the term 'discouragement' was construed objectively, and the ECJ has repeatedly ignored empirical data with respect to changes to the volume of trade in shares following the introduction of specific restrictions that have clearly shown no measurable deterrence on the part of investors. Finally, one needs to ask whether the state can do less than a private investor. The European Commission has never quoted the use of company law instruments enhancing the corporate position of a private (in the sense: non-state) investor as a cause to institute infringement proceedings. Questions that require elaboration:

– do the experiences of the recent years force us to assume a different perspective on the dogma of the superiority of private ownership, and if so, what experiences are they?
– what is of higher value: the stabilisation and professionalization of company authorities or the democratic mandate to appoint such authorities? Are these values necessarily mutually conflicting? How about the political and constitutional liability of the government for the supervision of the property entrusted to it?
– are the specific, empirical examples underpinning the national champions doctrine indeed evidence backing up the argument in support of which they are used? Would PKO BP S.A. or PZU S.A. have a lower share value today if they were privately-owned? Doesn't the strength of the companies (and also, e.g. PKN Orlen S.A.) come from their dominant position within their respective markets?

4. National champions as a response to missing ownership problem

It has already been observed that the lack of control of a given company may result in the externality effect for the national economy. This refers particularly to some special added value for a particular economy, not reflected in the shareholder's value. Some countries could be sensitive to the takeover of a national champion by a foreign enterprise, regardless of whether this enterprise is privately or publicly owned. However, the situation in which investors in the sector are foreign public companies seems to be especially intriguing, leading to the illusive privatization and real impact of one government on the sensitive sector of the other. Thus privatization which consists in offering equities of formerly public enterprises for sale seems to lead to further empowerment of state-owned or controlled monopolies from other countries. As an effect, the rise of a potentially capable public investor in one state may well lead to protectionism in other states, protecting their markets against this kind of political dependence, and in the long run leading to the spill-over effect, spreading economic nationalism and justifications for interventionism. Additionally, the problem of externalities may also be taken into consideration. It should be pointed out that if a company is perceived as more valuable to the economy than to its shareholders because of the spinoff of the positive external effect not reflected in the value of its shares, such as human capital or goodwill, then the purchase through a foreign state-controlled entity may be regarded as internalizing these effects or appropriating them for the domestic state-owned enterprises in the domestic economy. It seems, however, that national champions and state interventionism are also perceived as a response to the failures and shortcomings of the market-oriented corporate control, especially in the form of dispersed ownership of strategic companies which require a long term strategy.

It is a real perspective of the corporate governance agenda swinging around consecutive financial scandals beginning with the Great Depression which resulted in the first analysis on corporate governance, namely *The Modern Corporation and Private Property* by A.A. Berle and G.C. Means (firstly published in 1932)[13]. In economic activity, as very often elsewhere, we don't see the problem until hitting the wall. But does it mean that corporate governance is just a precarious response to the financial scandals? To address the problem of the essence of corporate governance – whether it is only a matter of managers' accountability

---

13 A.A. Berle, G.C. Means, *The Modern Corporation and Private Property*, reprint, New Brunswick 2002.

to shareholders – it is useful to point out to the context of the above statement. (The above statement refers to the agency model – the economic and legal concept of agency is a principal rationale for Anglo-Saxon company law and the structure of corporations. What is the point of reference for the model of ideal corporate governance? The two criteria of corporate governance are dynamism, understood as the system which permits the management of an enterprise to drive it forward without undue fear of governmental interference, and accountability, which makes it possible to ensure that in exercising its freedom, the management is effectively accountable for its decisions and actions and that appropriate remedial actions can be taken by shareholders dissatisfied with the management. The relation between dynamism and accountability is thus essential for good corporate governance. However, the proposed standards and recommendations should not be limited only to the accountability of managers to directors. A broader scope of corporate governance does not necessarily indicate the paradigm shift from shareholder theory to stakeholder theory, but it is necessary – to discuss the issue of such a possibility from a broader methodological perspective. Nonetheless, even taking into account the so-called 'narrow approach' i.e. the relation between directors and shareholders focused on the economic theory of agency and minimising agency costs, the problem of accountability is not the crucial issue – the system of accountability seems to be a result of wider legal, economic, financial or just interpersonal relations. To some extent the impression that corporate governance is a contingent response to real market failures and financial scandals is justified. On the other hand, several styles of corporate governance should be mentioned; the German and Japanese approach concentrated on co-operation and long term thinking. The opposite strategy of conflict and competition is adopted in the British and American systems. This rough generalisation discloses the pluralistic nature of corporate governance. However, according to the authors of Hampel Report: 'Corporate structures and governance arrangements vary widely from country to country [but] the underlying issues of managerial accountability are the same everywhere'[14]. If it were the case, it would be perfectly feasible to provide universal recommendations for good corporate governance. The problem is that corporate governance is not only the matter of governance as a structure of the firm perceived as an economic institution. The economic theories of the firm are based on the model of agency. It is believed that managers as agents of shareholders are likely to act in their self-interest and not necessarily on

---

14 Hampel Committee, Final Report (January 1998), available at: http://www.ecgi.org/
    codes/documents/hampel_index.htm [access on 20 February 2017].

behalf of their principal – the shareholders. The problem of agency costs is addressed in 2 ways; by virtue of monitoring ensuring transparency and accountability and by the link between shareholder's risk and the risk of the agent. It is achieved by the implementation of a whole set of constrains, checks and balances as well as a system of incentives for manager's loyalty. The economic model of agency, however, does not solve many problems of corporate governance, such as the lack or weakness of ownership and the lack of managers' interest in developing a long-term strategy or the lack of management's pro-active approach to increasing shareholder value, despite their honesty and loyalty[15]. According to the Anglo-Saxon model of corporate governance, shareholders, as residual claimants and ultimate risk bearers, are regarded as real owners, since the capital delivered by them and the risk they bear give them priority, and the company law with its 'legal conferring' rules equips them with power. There are many justifications for this solution. According to the contractarian theory of the company, the company is just a nexus of contracts[16]. Because shareholders are residual claimants, they are principals. The theory does not, however, answer the question why the contract of agency between shareholders (as owners) and managers (as controllers) bestows power upon shareholders. Referring to this issue, Olivier Williamson claims that shareholders cannot recover their investment and 'have more at stake'[17]. However, it is not entirely convincing, since one may claim that certain stakeholders have also invested in the firm. This aspect is especially significant in a broad context of a transition from the central to market-oriented economy, where firms have been created as an output of a political process and industrial economy engaging whole groups rather than shareholders alone. Finally, according to Hansmann and Kraakman, the governance costs are the least for shareholders since their interest are more homogeneous[18]. It is believed that owners of the

---

15 Cf. R. Monks, N. Minow, *Corporate Governance*, New York 1995.

16 E.F. Fama, M.C. Jensen, *Separation of Ownership and Control*, 'Journal of Law and Economics', Vol. 26, No. 2/1983, pp. 301–325;

17 O. Williamson, *The Economic Institutions of Capitalism*, London 1985, p. 83.

18 'The problem, at root, seems to be one of governance. While direct employee participation in corporate decision-making may mitigate some of the inefficiencies that can beset labor contracting, the workforce in typical firms is too heterogeneous in its interests to make an effective governing body and the problems are magnified greatly when employees must share governance with investors, as in codetermined firms. In general, contractual devices, whatever their weaknesses, are (when supplemented by appropriate labor market regulation) evidently superior to voting and other collective choice mechanisms in resolving conflicts of interest among and between a corporation, investors and employees", H. Hansmann, R. Kraakman, *The End of History...*, p. 6.

company will be the best group in whose interest, which seems to be homogeneous, the company is to act. But this theory assumes that shareholders are active
and use their rights to control and to ensure efficiency in terms of earnings and
shareholders' value. The crucial issue here is whether shareholders are really capable of enforcing their right. It seems that in reality shareholders who possess
minor proportions of shares are likely to sell those shares rather than to enforce
their rights. Hence the problem of the dispersed ownership model consists in the
fact that there is no real long-term owner who is really interested in the long-term
prospect of the firm rather than in the short term value. As it has been observed
by Robert Monks and Allen Sykes, 'the missing ownership' becomes a real problem and results in a disproportion of power between ownership and control[19].
But this is not the problem of accountability only – this is a wider structural
problem of the Anglo-Saxon model of a company. There is another explanation
for the division of ownership and control in the arm – length system (UK model):
the evolutionary path-dependent origins of the UK company and UK company
law. A Ltd-type of a company is regarded as a firm where at least some shareholders are directors. The link between shareholders and directors used to be closer.
When companies began to grow, the link weakened and the whole system ended
up with the present model of dispersed ownership, and the diluted power of
shareholders was conferred to managers. The institution of the company remi-
niscent of a continental company based on the 'organic' legal fiction changed into
the overlapping sets of markets linked by power and hierarchy based on the
agency model with the central position of the board of directors. Thus the horizontal integration is focused on the agency relationship, whereas the firm seems
to be just a nexus of contracts made on different markets and on different terms;
the most flexible market (capital market) is at the same time the most 'short-term'
market. The market of control limited e.g. to 3 years etc. is a medium-term market, while the labour market is more long-term oriented. The market of creditors
is also more flexible. As a result, the flexibility of capital market reduces the risk
of shareholders and shifts the risk to other groups. The model of corporate governance focused solely on accountability does not take into account the other part
of the agency relation – the agent. The principal is of course exposed to the risk
of manager's misconduct. But managers have also a lot at stake – their human
capital. There are limits to the market of control and its relatively lower flexibility
as compared to the capital market. There seems to be inequality between the

19 R. Monks, A. Sykes, *Capitalism Without Owners Will Fail: A Policymaker's Guide to Reform*, London 2002, pp. 7–10.

position of the owner whose risks are flexible, as financial capital is relatively easier to recover, and the manager who loses human capital. The same applies to the other level of the agency relationship between directors, especially CEO as an employer, and employees[20]. The problem can be solved in different ways – using the system of incentives and by binding agents with the principal. It is nevertheless very difficult to implement if the principal is unstable and short-term oriented[21]. In this remark, the link between legal framework and economic theory is emphasised. It seems that a bare analysis of accountability is too narrow even if we take into account the shareholder theory only. The problem of agency refers to both the principal and the agent. Accountability alone is not capable of solving complex problems such as ensuring efficiency and productivity of the firm. The notion of corporate governance from economic perspective includes a whole variety of factors determining productivity and efficiency. This approach embraces a set of different factors; economic, legal, social, financial ones, etc. To some extent corporate governance is the function of the theory of the firm. The theory of the firm seems to detect the constituencies and groups between which the 'bargaining over quasi-rents' takes place – the economic theory of the firm as an internal organisational power[22] (Williamson) or just as a unit of production being a result of what may be called just as a nexus of contracts[23] (Demsetz). Both approaches refer to the economic activity of the firm and have to respect basic axioms of welfare economics, such as the necessity of enhancing efficiency, competitiveness, productivity, and so on. It is perhaps just a kind of microeconomics implemented to analyse an economic institution from an internal point of view. As an example, one may mention the notion of 'X efficiency' purported by Lebenstein and referring to the ability to adapt to a changing environment (market) – a kind of flexibility and productivity of the firm at the same time. On the other hand, some principles of good governance may be just characterised as business practices or customs. The economic theory depends on an institutional and legal framework which is path-dependent. Realistic corporate governance is interdisciplinary and takes into account the differences between states and economies -- hence its different models. Finally, corporate governance depends on the recognition and evaluation of diverse groups, different interests and incentives to co-operate. I would call this approach a 'dynamic' one – different groups and different forms of ownership seem to determine the institutional environment of

20 O. Williamson, *The Economic Institutions...*, pp. 240–273.

21 R. Monks, A. Sykes, *Capitalism Without Owners...*, pp. 22–23.

22 O. Williamson, *The Economic Institutions...*, p. 206.

23 Ibidem, pp. 324–326.

the system of corporate governance. The claim that 'Good Corporate Governance is about ensuring that managers are accountable to shareholders' seems to be just an oversimplification based on the fixed UK/US model of agency and the 'static' approach disregarding the evolution and dynamism of both the company and its market environment. Corporate governance solves the problem of information asymmetry by differentiating the code into the 'default' and 'mandatory' rules. As the name itself suggests, the courts and regulatory agencies interpret transactions according to default rules unless otherwise declared. Opting-out from the default rules is often cheap; parties have incentives to reveal their preferences and relevant information in order to reach a modified agreement[24] Unlike in the case of mandatory rules, enforcement and monitoring costs of default rules are rather small. Furthermore, default rules as a whole act as a public good, providing the starting point and guideline for negotiations and thereby creating positive externalities. When the gains from concealing information are still greater than the benefits from opting-out under the default system, mandatory rules are imposed. Dynamic efficiency, however, does not necessarily illustrate efficient allocation of costs and risks. Especially when multiple players engage in the chain of transactions, principal-agent problems occur. In the area of corporate governance, Kraakman et al. (2001) identify three fundamental principal-agent problems: shareholders v. managers, non-controlling shareholders v. controlling shareholders, and stakeholders (e.g. employees and creditors) v. the firm itself[25]. As managers still hold autonomy in a variety of policy areas, the opportunism of agents[26] may lead to inefficiencies in both private and public firms. However, the structure of the incentive is different. In private companies, including the companies with minority state ownership, the agency problems refer to monitoring and control of the Board by the shareholders.

5. National champions and the illusive power of the state capitalism

Public companies are different in this respect. Representatives of the state are not just agents of the state, but they have many different principals, such as senior government officials, junior officials directly supervising firms, and policy leaders on different level of governance within the ruling party. Jean Blondel convincingly puts forward a claim that patronage of political parties is one of the key

---

24 H. Hansmann, R. Kraakman, *The End of History...*, pp. 9–11.
25 H. Hansmann, R. Kraakman, *The End of History...*, pp. 7–9.
26 O. Williamson, *The Economic Institutions...*, passim.

factors shaping the structure of incentives and the influence of party leaders[27]. He defined party patronage as an exchange relationship in which a variety of political assets may be traded between the two parties to the political transaction, namely the patron and the client. The nature of patronage as a basic unit of political transaction is more or less the same, notwithstanding the differences between particular types of assets, which generally may be identified with some goods and services such as expertise, legislation, jobs, contributions, information and, last but not least, appointments in both administrative agencies and state-owned enterprises. The most important aspect of patronage as confronted with national champions and state-owned enterprises is the right to appoint certain managers as representatives of a state agency or department. These appointments range from public tenders (public management) to the appointments of party loyalists to managerial boards in state-owned corporations (cronyism). Thus the relationship between management and shareholders in the case of state-owned enterprises seems to be simply transformed into the relation between the patron (party official) and the client or between state and its representatives in a given board of management, constituting a typical agency problem. However, there is a significant difference between the shareholder model of corporate governance and the state-oriented model applied in national champions. Whereas in the case of corporate control of a private company the principal is unified albeit probably weak when confronted with management acting as its agent, patronage seems to reflect a much more complex network of dependencies involving different principals located in different places and institutions, such as party representatives in government (usually ministers), but also junior ministers and department directors in the case of a party coalition, party representatives in parliament and local party institutional structures such as circuits, municipalities or regions. Political scientists underline the fact that patronage is shaped by four different elements, namely the characteristics of the two actors involved (patron and client) and the nature of the two goods to be exchanged (from patron to client and vice versa). In the context of national champions managements, the patrons are political parties, and the clients are party loyalists and sometimes also hired experts. Parties in fact award their clients positions on managerial boards in state-owned enterprises on the basis of their loyalty and commitment rather than expertise. This obviously looms large on the quality of management in state-owned companies. However,

---

27 J. Blondel, *Party Government, Patronage, and Party Decline in Western Europe*, in: R. Gunther, J.R. Montero, J.J. Linz (eds.), *Political Parties: Old Concepts and New Challenges*, Oxford 2002, pp. 233–256.

the lack of knowledge and professional experience is not the most pernicious effect of state-controlled firms[28]. The other side of the coin, namely the service or asset received by the party in exchange, seems to be even more problematic, since in fact what parties actually receive from their clients in return is entirely dependent on the purpose of the appointment itself. I. Bremmer suggests that parties simply intend to transform economic assets into political assets exerting control over management, whereas a more precise characteristic presented by other authors includes reward and control[29] or influence over some area of public policy[30]. These observations on the more general aspect of loyalty lead to the problem of multi-principality, as there are typically many different, sometimes competing centres of power within a political party or within its different segments, such as party in government, parliament and local structure[31]. Mediating between different competing expectations of different political actors seems to be, at least in Europe, much more common than the alleged interdependence between the state and managers pictured by I. Bremmer, when he attempted to characterise rising state capitalism in such countries as China, Russia or Arab authoritarian regimes form Persian Gulf[32]. Moreover, this distinction provides an important insight into the different characteristic of patronage and state capitalism in democratic and authoritarian states. Although in general it could be stated that the reward for the control-transactional paradigm is clearly related to the notions of office seeking and policy seeking that drive the theories of rational party behaviour, it must be admitted that party patronage also involves the distribution of appointments, it is even more apt to equate reward and control with the concepts of intrinsic and instrumental office seeking under the conditions of government coalition[33] or at

28 A. Shleifer, R.W. Vishny, *Politicians and firms*, 'The Quarterly Journal of Economics' Vol. 109, No. 1994, pp. 995–1025.

29 P. Kopecký, P. Mair, M. Spirova, *Party Patronage and Party Government in European Democracies*, Oxford 2012, pp. 10–15.

30 L. Ennser-Jedenastik, *The Politics of Patronage and Coalition: How Parties Allocate Managerial Positions in State-Owned Enterprises*, 'Political Studies' Vol. 62, No. 2014, pp. 398–417.

31 J. Blondel, *Party Government…*, in: R. Gunther, J.R. Montero, J.J. Linz (eds.), *Political Parties…*, pp. 233–256.

32 W.C. Müller, *Patronage by National Governments*, in: J. Blondel, M. Cotta (eds.), *The Nature of Party Government*, Houndmills 2002, pp. 141–160.

33 Ibidem.

least the so-called multifaceted party which plays different functions in different segments of administration or branches[34].

Additionally, some party leaders may use patronage as a means to safeguard support from the other party activists, especially regional or local leaders, so as to prevent a potential intra-party rebellion in case of an electoral defeat or unpopular decisions taken by the government.

In general, however, patronage could be regarded as a price paid for relative political stability and control. Thus Blondel puts forward the claim about the intrinsic nature of patronage as a tool for obtaining a smoothly functioning party-based political system. Moreover, as Blondel suggested, patronage as a kind of shock absorber is arguably even more significant and indispensable in democracy, where political cycles create an additional source of instability and short-termism[35]. Party patronage is thus one of the most important links between the party in government, the party in parliament and the party in its' regional and local structures, reflecting the need for delegation between voters, parties and the political party apparatus[36]. The concept of patronage as a medium between parties and different segments of government has become an important heuristic device which could also be useful in the context of institutional and transaction cost analysis applied to political exchanges on a political market. Multi-actor games and dispersed political power remain the subjects of transaction economics. As Olivier Williamson suggested, transaction cost may explain economic and political institutional structures alike[37]. It seems though that treating R. Coase seriously, one can no longer believe in a centralized political decision-making system, since if the political cost of administration exists, decentralization of the decision-making process seems to be inevitable[38]. However, the scope of this process seems to be conditioned and depends on particular contingences. A simple comparison of corporate governance deficiencies and political governance weakness leads to a suggestion that both structures seem to be seriously challenged by the agency problem. However, whereas corporate control in a free market-oriented model of dispersed ownership suffers from the problem of missing ownership and indeed a

34 J. Blondel, *Party Government…*, in: R. Gunther, J.R. Montero, J.J. Linz (eds.), *Political Parties…*, pp. 233–256.
35 Ibidem.
36 Ibidem, p. 240–245.
37 O. Williamson, *Public and Private Bureaucracies: a Transaction Cost Economics Perspective*, 'Journal of Law, Economics and Organization' Vol. 15, No. 1/1999, pp. 306–342.
38 A. Dixit, *The Making of Economic Policy: A Transaction-Cost Politics Perspective*, Cambridge 1996, pp. 45–61.

missing principal, as suggested by Monks and Sykes[39], the state-oriented model seems to be affected by the problem of multiplicity of principals representing different segments of the ruling party[40]. Thus going back to the theory of agency as an analytical tool enabling a proper institutional analysis of different forms of corporate control, it should be emphasized that in the standard models of agency the agent's incentives link the agent's compensation to his or her performance. Thus, as Holmström and Milgrom observe, the reward schemes are linear functions of performance, where the output is at least discernible and the value of the output serves as a benchmark for the evaluation of the agent's effort. However, it has also been suggested that if the agent's performance depends on some random conditions or contingencies, the principal is no longer able to evaluate the agent's effort precisely and eventually, in cases where the agent is risk-averse, the optimal scheme involves smooth incentives rather than progressive ones[41]. Applying the standard agency model to politicians and their clients means that one has to depart from many of the core assumptions behind this theory.

Firstly, the incentive scheme for public institutions and politically motivated agents appointed and monitored by party officials is strikingly different from the regular incentive schemes for managers, who are able to diversify risk of under-performance in a much more efficient way. Analysing the difference between public and private incentives, Avinash Dixit observed that in fact step functions encapsulating the minimum standard and different degrees of extra performance may be preferred by politicians to linear contracts suggested by Holmström and Milgrom, because politicians seem to be very risk-averse. Moreover, their risk aversion results from the fact that they simply cannot diversify the risk of bad outcomes of public policies, not to mention lost electoral campaigns. Therefore, in public agencies and state-controlled agencies, the remuneration including both the minimum standard of performance and a bonus for extraordinary performance are much more common. However, at the same time, such incentive schemes are more sensitive to manipulation by agents[42].

Secondly, one of the key features of the public sector is that agents have to serve many principals. As it has been suggested by many authors, delivering incentives in these circumstances is more complex if not almost impossible, because those

---

39   R. Monks, A. Sykes, *Capitalism Without Owners...*, pp. 9–13.

40   O. Williamson, *Public and Private...*, pp. 306–342.

41   B. Holmström, P. Milgrom, *Aggregation and Linearity in Provision of Intertemporal Incentives*, 'Econometrica' 55(2) 1987, pp. 303–328.

42   A. Dixit, *Incentives and organizations in the public sector: an interpretative Review*, 'The Journal of Human Resources' Vol. 37, No. 4/2002, pp. 696–727.

principals are usually interested only in some very narrow dimensions of outputs, and varying interests of many different political actors are not perfectly aligned. As an example we can think of the representatives of the party in government such as ministers who are focused on strategic parameters in some sectors of national economy, junior or deputy ministers who are more interested in medium-term goals and local party leaders who rely on short-term effects translated into political support for local party leaders. As it has been demonstrated by Dixit[43], who extends his analysis to a multi-principals setting, in these settings each principal generally offers a positive coefficient on the element he or she is interested in and negative coefficients on the other dimensions, which in the end creates a negative externality on the other principals who have to face lower efforts in those dimensions. Eventually, this process of bifurcation and splitting strategic goals lead to a situation in which the aggregate marginal incentive coefficient is decreasing for each outcome with regard to the number of principals. Assuming that the agent's efforts for different principals are substitutes, obviously each agent is more willing to offer his or her efforts to those principals who pay higher coefficients. This situation will result in the reinforcement of the effect of the negative externality and hence will further weaken the aggregate marginal incentives eventually causing the race to the bottom and spiral effects. However, as Dixit demonstrated, even in the context of public incentive schemes the negative externality created by the interaction among the different principals may be at least to some extent internalised by separating the information regarding each outcome or by grouping together those principals whose interests are aligned[44]. The question remains how to apply this solution to the specific context of national champions. It seems that such a separation of principals seems to be highly unrealistic and contradictory to the double nature of party officials who at the same time work in government[45]. There are some natural limits of both strategies when it comes to the ability to overcome the multi-agency problem. It has to be pointed out that in some political context such as the legislature or the executive it seems to be impractical and unrealistic

---

43 A. Dixit, *The Making…*, pp. 1–31; idem, *Power of Incentives in Private vs Public Organisations*, 'American Economic Review Papers and Proceedings' Vol. 87, No. 1997, pp. 378–382.

44 A. Dixit, *Power of Incentives…*, pp. 378–382.

45 J. Blondel, J. Nouisiainen, *Governments, Supporting Parties and Policy Making*, in: J. Blondel, M. Cotta (eds.), *The nature of party government: a comparative European perspective*, New York 2000, pp. 161–195; L. Hurwicz, *But who will guard the guardians?*, 'American Economic Review', Vol. 98, No. 3/2008, pp. 577–58.

to restrain the actions of the involved political principals from the outside[46]. This unfortunately seems to apply to the principals who monitor the economic performance and exert control over managers in national champions either in the form of majority or minority state-owned companies, which, however, are still supposed to be influenced by different political actors.

Hence, it has to be concluded that the multi-agency problem looms large and leads to inevitable underperformance of state-owned enterprises or the enterprises over which the government exerts its control. The patronage inevitably leads to the multi-agency problem and, finally, to underperformance. Thus it seems that the cure in the form of state intervention through ownership rights and quasi political appointments of managements does not seem to be much better than the illness in the form of missing shareholder's ownership. Against this background yet another solution could be tested, namely the private ordering through the market-oriented corporate governance model of relatively dispersed ownership over strategic firms, based on the separation of strategic control and day to day management. It has already been stated that the EU Council Directive 2008/114/EC of 8 December 2008 on the identification and designation of European critical infrastructures and the assessment of the need to improve their protection[47] aims at constituting the framework in which governments may exert some power in order to protect critical infrastructures by virtue of external regulatory means rather than by the ownership control. Such a critical infrastructure coincides with the concept of strategic assets which generally refers to unique resources relevant to economic and security considerations, or the lack of control of a given company may result in the externality effect for national economy. Typically, the situation results from the so called spin-off effect in terms of specific assets such as infrastructure. The directive specifies that 'critical infrastructure means an asset, system or part thereof located in Member States which is essential for the maintenance of vital societal functions, health, safety, security, economic or social well-being of people, and the disruption or destruction of which would have a significant impact on a Member State as a result of the failure to maintain those functions'. In other words, the specific externality or spin-off effects resulting in market failure have been addressed in a purely functional manner, where the regulation concentrates on assets rather than on companies. Then the assets themselves have become subject to special administrative legal rules. The concentration on asset specificity seems to be interesting from the perspective of

---

46 A. Dixit, *Power of Incentives…*, pp. 378–382.
47 Official Journal of the European Communities L 345 of 23 December 2008, p. 75.

the neoinstitutional economic analysis. In particular, asset specificity has been identified by Olivier Williamson as a key factor determining the institutional structure of a market and the level of transaction cost[48].

Fig. 1. Institutional alternatives reflecting types of asset specificity and frequency of interaction.

	Non-Specific	Mixed Specificity	Idiosyncratic
Low Frequency	Market (No-Integration)	Market with Trilateral private law system (company law based judicial arbitration)	Trilateral public law based (administrative decisions with judicial control)
High Frequency		Bilateral (State minority ownership with additional powers)	Unified (State majority ownership)

From this perspective, it seems that the governance structure may be comparatively evaluated through the lens of institutional analysis and policies taking three factors into account: (1) incentive-giving mechanisms to solve information asymmetry, (2) cost-benefit analyses on both static transaction and dynamic transition, and (3) governance strategies to solve multi-layer principal-agent problems. It aims to establish the 'best practices' for EU governance, and international organisations management at large. In addition, based on the 'critical dimensions' – i.e. frequency, specificity and costs of transaction – Williamson identifies efficient mechanisms for (corporate) governance among market-oriented external governance, trilateral governance with third party arbitration, bilateral governance with mutual arbitration, and unified hierarchical governance[49]. Translated into the governance of National Champions, market governance refers to the absence of integration (i.e. national authorization), trilateral governance refers to contracts (company law) with a third-party arbitrator (e.g. external regulation on strategic infrastructure or assets, supervised by the administrative courts), bilateral governance refers to minority-majority ownership relations within a publicly held (listed) company, unified governance refers to majority state ownership. The 'best practices' apply the 'critical dimensions' to address some of the aforementioned principal-agent problems. From the dynamic efficiency point of view, the

---

48 O. Williamson, *The Economic...*, pp. 68–85.

49 O. Williamson, *Transaction-Cost Economics: The Governance of Contractual Relations*, 'Journal of Law and Economics' Vol. 22, No. 2/1979, pp. 233–261.

combination of these governance mechanisms preserves the competitiveness of national economies, particularly in the area where market governance is preferred.

Literature

Bebchuk L.A., Roe M.J., *A Theory of Path Dependence in Corporate Ownership and Governance*, 'Stanford Law Review' Vol. 52, No. 1999;

Berle A.A., Means G.C., *The Modern Corporation and Private Property*, reprint, New Brunswick 2002;

Blondel J., Nouisiainen J., *Governments, Supporting Parties and Policy Making*, in: Blondel J., Cotta M. (eds.), *The nature of party government: a comparative European perspective*, New York 2000;

Blondel J., *Party Government, Patronage, and Party Decline in Western Europe*, in: Gunther R., Montero J.R., Linz J.J. (eds.), *Political Parties: Old Concepts and New Challenges*, Oxford 2002;

Bremmer I., *The end of the free market: who wins the war between states and corporations?*, New York 2010;

Coase R.H., *The Nature of the Firm*, 'Economica. New Series', Vol. 4, No. 16/1937;

Dixit A., *Incentives and organizations in the public sector: an interpretative Review*, 'The Journal of Human Resources' Vol. 37, No. 4/2002;

Dixit A., *Power of Incentives in Private vs Public Organisations*, 'American Economic Review Papers and Proceedings' Vol. 87, No. 1997;

Dixit A., *The Making of Economic Policy: A Transaction-Cost Politics Perspective*, Cambridge 1996;

Ennser-Jedenastik L., *The Politics of Patronage and Coalition: How Parties Allocate Managerial Positions in State-Owned Enterprises*, 'Political Studies' Vol. 62, No. 2014;

Fama E.F., Jensen M.C., *Separation of Ownership and Control*, 'Journal of Law and Economics', Vol. 26, No. 2/1983, pp. 301–325;

Fukuyama F., *The End of History and the Last Man*, New York 1992;

Hansmann H., Kraakman R., *The End of History for Corporate Law*, 'Harvard Law School Discussion Paper' No. 280, 3/2000;

Holmström B, Milgrom P., *Aggregation and Linearity in Provision of Intertemporal Incentives*, 'Econometrica' Vol. 55, No. 2/1987.

Hurwicz L., *But who will guard the guardians?*, 'American Economic Review', Vol. 98, No. 3/2008;

Kopecký P., Mair P., Spirova M., *Party Patronage and Party Government in European Democracies*, Oxford 2012;

Monks R., Minow N., *Corporate Governance*, New York 1995;

Monks R., Sykes A., *Capitalism Without Owners Will Fail: A Policymaker's Guide to Reform*, London 2002;

Müller W.C., *Patronage by National Governments*, in: J. Blondel, M. Cotta (eds.), *The Nature of Party Government*, Houndmills 2002;

Roe M.J., *Political determinants of corporate governance: political context, corporate impact*, Oxford 2003;

Roe M.J., *Political preconditions to separating Ownership from Corporate Control*, 'Stanford Law Review' Vol. 53, No. 2000;

Shleifer A., Vishny R.W., *Politicians and firms*, 'The Quarterly Journal of Economics' Vol. 109, No. 1994;

Williamson O., *Public and Private Bureaucracies: a Transaction Cost Economics Perspective*, 'Journal of Law, Economics and Organization' Vol. 15, No. 1/1999;

Williamson O., *The Economic Institutions of Capitalism*, London 1985.

Abbreviations

ECJ – European Court of Justice, Court of Justice of the European Union

EU – European Union

Ltd – limited company (in English law)

S.A. – spółka akcyjna (Polish joint-stock company)

TFEU – Treaty on the Functioning of the European Union (consolidated version Official Journal of the European Union C 326 of 26 October 2012, p. 47);

UK – United Kingdom;

US – United States of America.

Lex et Res Publica
Polish Legal and Political Studies

Edited by
Anna Jarón

www.peterlang.com